THE POETRY OF EDWARD THOMAS

ANDREW MOTION

THE POETRY OF EDWARD THOMAS

ROUTLEDGE & KEGAN PAUL
LONDON, BOSTON AND HENLEY

First published in 1980
by Routledge & Kegan Paul Ltd
39 Store Street, London WC1E 7DD,
9 Park Street, Boston, Mass. 02108, USA, and
Broadway House, Newtown Road,
Henley-on-Thames, Oxon RG9 1EN
Set in 9 on 12 Baskerville by
Columns of Reading
and printed in Great Britain by
Page Brothers Ltd, Norwich, Norfolk
© Andrew Motion 1980

British Library Cataloguing in Publication Data

Motion, Andrew

The poetry of Edward Thomas.
1. Thomas, Edward, b.1878 — Criticism and
interpretation
I. Title
821'.9'12   PR6039.H55Z/   80-41118

ISBN 0 7100 0471 0

For Joanna Jane

CONTENTS

ACKNOWLEDGMENTS

A large number of people gave me their help, advice and encouragement while I was writing this book. I am particularly indebted to John Fuller, under whose supervision it began life at the University of Oxford in 1975. I should also like to thank Dr Philip Larkin and Joanna Jane Motion for reading it at a later stage, and Margaret Bowen for typing the manuscript.

Throughout the transition from thesis to book — and before — Myfanwy Thomas was enormously generous with her time and good counsel. I am very grateful to her, and to Dr William Cooke, Edna Longley and Professor George Thomas for their kindness in answering questions. Their own work on Edward Thomas has been invaluable to me.

My warm thanks are also due to Dr Stephen Gill, Alan Hollinghurst, Sir Geoffrey Keynes, Michael Launchbury, Annick Léty, Sandy Nairne, Marion Shaw and Anne Stevenson.

I wish to thank the following libraries for their assistance, and for permission to quote from material in their collections: The Berg Collection of the New York Public Library; The Bodleian Library, Oxford; Dartmouth College Library, Hanover, New Hampshire; The Library of University College, Cardiff; The Poetry/Rare Books Collection of the University Libraries, State University of New York at Buffalo.

Except where otherwise stated, all quotations from Edward Thomas's poetry are taken from *The Collected Poems of Edward Thomas*, edited by R. George Thomas (The Clarendon Press, Oxford, 1978). The text and titles of the poems in this edition differ in some cases from the more familiar version. I am grateful to R. George Thomas for permission to quote from his edition.

I should like to thank Myfanwy Thomas and R. George Thomas for permission to reproduce published and unpublished works and letters of Edward Thomas. Extracts from Helen Thomas's *As It Was*, *World Without End*, and *Time & Again* are reprinted by permission of Myfanwy Thomas. Material from Edward Thomas, *Poems and Last Poems*, edited by Edna Longley, is reprinted by permission of Edna Longley and of Macdonald & Evans (Publications) Ltd. Material from *Edward Thomas: A Critical Biography* by William Cooke is reprinted by permission of the author. Lines from 'The Waste Land' in *Collected Poems 1909-1962* by T. S. Eliot (copyright 1936 by Harcourt Brace Jovanovich, Inc.; copyright © 1963, 1964 by T. S. Eliot), are reprinted by permission of the publishers, Faber and Faber Ltd and Harcourt Brace Jovanovich, Inc. Acknowledgments are made to the Estate of Robert Frost and to the publishers, Jonathan Cape Ltd and Holt, Rinehart and Winston, for permission to reprint the following material: lines from 'Home Burial' and 'Mending Wall' from *The Poetry of Robert Frost*, edited by Edward Connery Lathem (Copyright 1930, 1939, © 1969 by Holt, Rinehart and Winston. Copyright © 1958 by Robert Frost. Copyright © 1967 by Lesley Frost Ballantine); extracts from *Robert Frost: The Early Years* by Lawrance Thompson (Copyright © 1966 by Lawrance Thompson. Copyright © 1966 by The Estate of Robert Frost); and extracts from *Selected Letters of Robert Frost*, edited by Lawrance Thompson (Copyright © 1964 by Lawrance Thompson and Holt, Rinehart and Winston). Acknowledgments are made to The Society of Authors as the literary representative of the Estate of A. E. Housman, and to the publishers, Jonathan Cape Ltd and Holt, Rinehart and Winston, for permission to reprint lines from 'Reveille' from 'A Shropshire Lad' — Authorised Edition — from *The Collected Poems of A. E. Housman* (Copyright 1939, 1940, © 1965 by Holt, Rinehart and Winston. Copyright © 1967, 1968 by Robert E. Symons). Material from W. B. Yeats's Introduction to *The Oxford Book of Modern Verse*, edited by W. B. Yeats (1936), is reprinted by permission of Oxford University Press. Lines from 'A Dead Mole' from *Complete Poems* by Andrew Young (1950), edited by Leonard Clark, are reprinted by permission of Martin Secker and Warburg Ltd.

INTRODUCTION

Edward Thomas's first collection of poems appeared shortly after his death in 1917 and was given half a page of praise in the *Times Literary Supplement*. A few months earlier the same journal had reviewed the first publication in England of T. S. Eliot's *Prufrock and Other Observations*: 'Among other things which pass through the rhapsodist's mind are "dust in crevices, smells of chestnuts in the streets, and female smells in shuttered rooms, and cigarettes in corridors and cocktail smells in bars". The fact that these things occurred to the mind of Mr Eliot is surely of the very smallest importance to anyone — even to himself. They certainly have no relation to "poetry", and we only give an example because some of the pieces, he states, have appeared in a periodical which claims that word as its title.'[1] These antithetical reactions neatly summarise the quarrel which dominated English poetry during the first quarter of this century. On one hand imperialists like Alfred Austin and Sir Henry Newbolt fought a rearguard action on behalf of Victorian values, and on the other experimenters like Ezra Pound and Eliot himself accused them of producing 'a horrible agglomerate compost, not minted, most of it not even baked'.[2] In the middle, and criticised by both sides, but enormously popular with the public at large, stood the Georgians.

Subsequent years have seen this latter group treated with increasing hostility. Instead of being praised for reconciling the best old and new attitudes they have been mocked as 'gently unambitious'[3] or dismissed as reactionary. They have, in fact, commonly been denied any important role whatsoever in the formation of distinctively 'modern' poetry.

The credit for this, and the term 'Modernist' itself, has been given to Pound and Eliot. Reasons for the shift in opinion are easily adduced. Many Georgian attempts to escape the constraints of the nineteenth century appear at best half-hearted and at worst futile. But such criticism has had unfortunate side effects. While accurately identifying weaknesses in the Georgians themselves, it has risked misrepresenting those who were only loosely connected with them. And among the casualties of this general condemnation, Thomas is pre-eminent. Either he is found guilty by association or — more usually — separated from them altogether on the grounds that no one who sympathised with their aims could write with his distinction. As a result, the proper context of his work has been denied, and its various debts and allegiances overlooked. The following evaluation finds him writing, as it were, slightly to the left of centre — drawing much from the Georgians but also anticipating the Modernists in several important respects. It is a position which allowed him, like Thomas Hardy and Robert Frost, to effect 'a "quiet" and unaggressive poetic revolution as important as the more publicised *coup d'état* of Pound and Eliot'.[4]

Although Thomas never knew the Modernists by that name, his reviewing acquainted him with the conception, if not the fulfilment, of their purpose. The various groups which prepared the way for their achievement were active in London from at least 1912, when the Futurist Marinetti gave a series of lectures expounding a broadly symbolist aesthetic that led, in due course, to 'The Love Song of J. Alfred Prufrock' and *The Waste Land* (1922). Of all these blows to orthodoxy the most forceful were struck by the Vorticists and the Imagists, and Thomas, who had already (in 1911) published a study of Maurice Maeterlinck, was well equipped to interpret their effect. This did not, on the face of it, lead him to admire them. He had described Maeterlinck's symbolism as 'nothing but wind',[5] and was similarly scornful of the anthology *Des Imagistes* (1914): 'The majority fall into two categories. Either they are translations or paraphrases, or they are written in the manner of translations.'[6] Privately, in a letter to his Georgian friend Gordon Bottomley, he had been even more damning: 'What imbeciles the Imagists are.'[7] A more celebrated and extended attack had previously been directed against Pound, whose early book *Personae* (June 1909) Thomas had approved because it contained 'no golden words shot with meaning; a temperate use of images and none far fetched; no flattering of modern fashions; ... no apostrophe, no rhetoric'.[8] This praise outraged many of Thomas's friends, but it was not

2

their advice which moved him, five months later, to criticise 'the turbulent opacity of [Pound's] peculiarities'[9] in *Exultations*. His change of heart conformed in every respect to his poetic credo, and by repudiating Pound's more adventurous subversions he defined the boundaries of his tolerance:

> a poem of the old kind has a simple fundamental meaning which every sane reader can agree upon; above and beyond this each one builds as he can or must. In the new there is no basis of this kind; a poem means nothing unless its whole meaning has been grasped.[10]

These reservations about Imagism were less constricting in practice than they seem in theory. When Amy Lowell listed six attributes in her anthology *Some Imagist Poets* (1915) she identified qualities which could equally well characterise his own poetry:

1. To use the language of common speech . . .
2. To create new rhythms . . .
3. To allow absolute freedom in the choice of subject . . .
4. To present an image . . .
5. To produce poetry that is hard and clear, never blurred nor indefinite.
6. Finally, most of us believe that concentration is of the very essence of poetry.[11]

The fact that these aims are sufficiently indeterminate to describe not only Thomas but a wide variety of authors suggests that strict Imagists were not espousing entirely new principles, but isolating a number of old ones and thereby making them seem unfamiliar. Imagism, in other words, is a matter of selection and amplification. The same can also be said of fully-fledged Modernism, which shares many of its strategies; but because the point to which Eliot and Pound developed them is so advanced, it is easy to overlook any equivalents in Thomas. Yet the Imagists' juxtaposition of miniature fragments, and the Modernists' generous use of collage and montage, both find their discreet counterpart in his poems. 'The long small room' is typical of the way in which he refers to a variety of objects with such quick clarity that orthodox pictorial and narrative techniques are replaced by what one of his earliest reviewers called 'disconnected impressions':[12]

> The long small room that showed willows in the west
> Narrowed up to the end the fireplace filled,

3

Although not wide. I liked it. No one guessed
What need or accident made them so build.

Only the moon, the mouse and the sparrow peeped
In from the ivy round the casement thick.
Of all they saw and heard there they shall keep
The tale for the old ivy and older brick.

When I look back I am like moon, sparrow and mouse
That witnessed what they could never understand
Or alter or prevent in the dark house.
One thing remains the same — this my right hand

Crawling crab-like over the clean white page,
Resting awhile each morning on the pillow,
Then once more starting to crawl on towards age.
The hundred last leaves stream upon the willow.

The sense of insecurity and isolation conveyed here in visual terms appears elsewhere in linguistic ones. But Thomas's 'intolerable wrestle / With words and meanings' is more reticent than Eliot's. Instead of toying with incoherence in order to reflect a bafflingly complex and fragmented society, he prefers to record individual moods and intuitions hovering at the limit of articulation. 'Old Man' shows him doing so at length, and in a number of other poems his fascination with what is evasive takes a more local form. As he struggles to bring himself as close as is possible in language to the very grain and texture of experience, he is aware that the words he employs establish a difference between themselves and their object. The opening of 'Adlestrop' is a neglected instance:

Yes, I remember Adlestrop —
The name, because one afternoon
Of heat the express-train drew up there
Unwontedly. It was late June.

Thomas wrings from the name 'Adlestrop', by suspending it at the line-end, a series of unspoken associations with ideal rural communities. But when he returns half way through the poem to repeat that 'What I saw / Was Adlestrop — only the name', it is a signal for those associations to accelerate away from his reach. They satisfy him for no more than the 'minute' he stops there:

And for that minute a blackbird sang
Close by, and round him, mistier,
Farther and farther, all the birds
Of Oxfordshire and Gloucestershire.

These various kinds of disruption affect the form as well as the content of Thomas's poems. In Chapter 3 his rhythms and syntax will be discussed at length, but in the present context it is worth stressing that his persistent modifications of the regular iambic pentameter anticipate Eliot's bolder experiments. (Seventy-six of his 142 poems show this in operation.) Both poets arouse traditional expectations only to disappoint them, with the result that attention is drawn to the autonomy of the artefact at the same time as its subject becomes apparent. One consequence of this is that 'reality' is denied an absolute identity, and is seen instead to be conditioned by the temperament, mood and circumstances of the person observing it. Prufrock, for example, acknowledges that his view of the universe is highly individual, and thereby insists on the plurality of experience. And when Eliot introduces phrases from foreign languages and other poets — as he frequently does in *The Waste Land* — this emphasis is still more strongly felt. Every inclusion shows the concern with relativism which stands at the heart of the Modernist movement:

I sat upon the shore
Fishing, with the arid plain behind me
Shall I at least set my lands in order?
London Bridge is falling down falling down falling down
Poi s'ascose nel foco che gli affina
Quando fiam uti chelidon — O swallow swallow
Le Prince d'Aquitaine à la tour abolie
These fragments I have shored against my ruins
Why then Ile fit you. Hieronymo's mad againe.
Datta. Dayadhvam. Damyata.
Shantih shantih shantih

Thomas's borrowings are nothing like as persistent as this, and they always create a specifically English rather than an international context. References to folk-songs and ballads are particularly common, and although they have gone almost unnoticed, Bottomley's observations that 'his memory for them was extraordinary, his repertoire unfathomable'[13] is amply justified by numerous outbursts of enthusiasm in the prose. 'Of all music,' Thomas wrote in *The Heart of England* (1906),

> the old ballads and folk songs and their airs are richest in the plain immortal symbols. The best of them seem to be written in a language that should be universal, if only simplicity were truly simple to mankind. . . . They are in themselves epitomes of whole generations, of a whole countryside.[14]

Almost exactly a hundred years before, Wordsworth had justified the *Lyrical Ballads* with similar protestations, and more recently several other poets had taken up the cause. W. B. Yeats was chief among them, and introduced his *Oxford Book of Modern Verse* in the knowledge that 'if any one will turn these pages attending to poets born in the 'fifties, 'sixties, and 'seventies he will find how successful are their folk songs and their imitations'.[15] It is important, too, for Thomas's admiration to be seen against the background of research done by such folk-song collectors as F. J. Child and Cecil Sharp, and to realise that the war emphasised what he called ballads' 'national'[16] character. But he no more needed these influences to form his taste than he needed the war to shape his patriotism. His profound admiration for White, Cobbett and Jefferies had already created it. Throughout the decade before the first Georgian anthology appeared, he founded his belief in a poetic revival on the conviction that recovery of folk material would give 'a vigorous impulse'.[17] Whenever he found signs of its good effect — as he did in John Masefield's *The Tragedy of Nan* (1909) — he praised it as evidence of a healthy correspondence between past and present: '[This book] has been able to preserve the simplicity of the ballad while enriching it with the beauty of a grave and sensitive modern spirit that has brooded long upon it.'[18]

The same quality is evident in Thomas's own work, as one of the two poems called 'An Old Song' illustrates. The original ('The Lincolnshire Poacher') is simultaneously relished and adopted as a discipline:[19]

I was not apprenticed nor ever dwelt in famous Lincolnshire;
I've served one master well and ill much more than seven year;
And never took up to poaching as you shall quickly find;
    But 'tis my delight of a shiny night in the season of the year.

Elsewhere such precise parallels shrink to the diminutive scale of inversions and archaisms like ''tis,' 'o'er' and ''neath'. These, which have usually been interpreted as a sign of arrested development in Thomas's diction, are strategically placed throughout his poetry to hint at its 'pedigree of dimmest antiquity'.[20] The same purpose is filled by more extensive references: they are the literary equivalent of stable, ideal landscapes where 'every swelling of the grass, every wavering line of hedge or path or road [is] an inscription brief as an epitaph'.[21] Among many other examples, the re-use of the Elizabethan lyric 'There is a Ladie sweet and kind' in 'Song'; the weather-rhyme which begins 'November Sky' ('November's days are thirty: / November's earth is dirty'); and the reference to traditional poems in the titles and bodies of 'The Ash Grove', 'Song' ('Early one morning') and 'Over the Hills' — all provide him with the touchstone he seeks. A similar debt occurs in 'Lights Out': the lines 'all must lose / Their way, however straight / Or winding, soon or late' glance at the literally time-honoured phrases of an early English poem called 'The Ploughman', which Thomas had included in his anthology *This England*:

> The plowe gothe mony a gate,
> Botherly and eke late,
> In winter in the clay.

The same principles govern his choice of quotations from more recent poems. The function of his selection is to convey a sense of responsibility and indebtedness to the native English past, and to bring its admirable qualities forward into the present. As he says in the fruitful paradox of 'Words', they are 'Worn new / Again and again'. The line 'Moments of everlastingness', from 'The Other' is conspicuous as an adaptation of Vaughan's 'Bright shootes of everlastingness'; the description of thrushes singing in 'March' is closely modelled on Coleridge's 'The Nightingale'; and the opening of 'Lob' almost reproduces the first line of Swinburne's 'Tale of Balen'.

All these borrowings, and the characteristics they summarise, testify to a number of important distinctions between Thomas's aims and those of his avant-garde contemporaries. Where he gives only 'disconnected impressions', they provide a series of fragments; where he subtly upsets conventional forms and modes of depiction, they radically reshape them; and where he establishes a national context for his work, they create a cosmopolitan one. No matter how much one insists on the similarity in intent, the differences in degree are significant. But while they make it impossible to call him a covert Modernist, they are not absolute enough to brand him as a pure and simple Georgian either. He built his poems in the same wide gap between the two camps that he had occupied in a theoretical sense during his years as a reviewer. From 1900 to 1912 he chronicled the rise of Georgian poetry and commended many of its aspects — particularly its appearance of being 'English yet not aggressively imperialist.'[22] But he also criticised its defects with such vigour that he may be said to have taken the role of mentor to an entire poetic generation. Close friendship with many of its members — notably Bottomley, W. H. Davies and Walter de la Mare — strengthened his association: it did not prevent him from asserting his independence.

Edward Marsh introduced the first *Georgian Poetry* anthology[23] 'in the belief that English poetry is once again putting on a new strength and beauty'.[24] But Thomas's reviews were quick to point out that work by several of those included had 'taken an unmistakable direction before the accession of George V'.[25] He had praised the virtues they claimed for themselves as early as 1903, when he had said, 'I know of no other age that has abounded in lesser writers of verse with so much originality. We have to look back as far as Tottel's *Miscellany* or *England's Helicon* for an assembly of contemporaneous writers anything like this.'[26] His objection to Georgian poetry, in other words, was more often made with regard to its name than its intentions, which were strikingly like his own:

> To be Georgian in 1912-1915 . . . connoted several things. It meant
> to be 'modern', in the sense that Georgians shared with most pre-war
> poets the prevailing spiritual euphoria and the confidence that
> poetry was being infused with a new, vital release of creative energy.
> It meant also to be anti-Victorian, to write poetry which, in tone,
> form and diction, was free from both *fin de siècle* weariness and
> Victorian 'painted adjectives'.[27]

As this suggests, the term describes 'primarily a certain temper, or a set of mind, and not (strictly speaking) a poetic school',[28] and it is from this imprecise context that Thomas's poems grew. The Georgians' colloquial diction, their pastoralism, and their experiments with drama-tic verse complement his own practice. To say, with Philip Hobsbaum and others, that 'only a superficial classification would relate [him] to the Georgians'[29] risks allowing scorn of their shortcomings to obscure the fact of their influence.

But while sharing many of their aims, Thomas was quick to chastise their failures. It is difficult now to consider the poets as 'revolutionary' at all, but Abercrombie's insistence that 'the whole of language must be left open to the poet',[30] and the crude attempts at realism typified by Brooke's sonnet 'Channel Passage', shocked contemporary sensibilities. It was only as the war advanced, and the original Georgians were dispersed or replaced by less gifted successors, that polemicism gave way to complacency. Thomas had been alert to these dangers from the first, and when he reviewed Gibson's *The Nets of Love* in 1905, he commented on them:

> Just as, in thinking about life, we cry out for a return to nature and her beneficent simplicity, so we are apt to cry out for a return to simplicity in literature. . . . [Gibson is] trying to write as if there were no such thing as a Tube, Grape Nuts, love of Nature, a Fabian Society, a bill for the reform of the marriage laws.[31]

The same distinction was made with regard to Gibson's book *Fires*, in which the lack of 'false poetical writing' was approved, but the plainness 'rather drearily galvanised into movement'[32] was condemned. Thomas realised that even the pioneer Georgians sometimes replaced natural simplicity with coy naïveté, and never made the same mistake in his own poems. Indeed, his objectivity as a reviewer, and his integrity as a poet, allowed him to distil their aims so successfully that many of them were unable to recognise him as a kindred spirit. Marsh was 'largely ignorant of him',[33] Munro refused to publish his poems or argue for their inclusion in the anthologies, and he admitted himself that they were 'sufficiently new in their way to be unacceptable if the reader . . . doesn't get any effect before he begins to consider and see their "unfinish" '.[34]

As well as defining his poetic theories in relation to the Georgians and early Modernists, Thomas also acknowledged the influence of two other contemporaries who resist categorisation: Robert Frost and Thomas Hardy. He called Frost's *North of Boston* (1914) 'one of the most revolutionary books of modern times'[35] and, in his reviews, outlined his own aesthetic:

> These poems are revolutionary because they lack the exaggeration of rhetoric, and even at first sight appear to lack the poetic intensity of which rhetoric is an imitation. Their language is free from the poetical words and forms that are the chief material of secondary poets. . . . Many, if not most, of the separate lines and separate

sentences are plain and, in themselves, nothing. But they are bound together and made elements of beauty by a calm eagerness of emotion. . . .[36]

Hardy's example was equally supportive. Like Frost, he encouraged Thomas to cultivate an understating and colloquial diction, and shared his dislike of the bardic and mythological modes used by the avant-garde. Hardy's folk-songs, and his presentations of rural scenes and characters also show strong resemblances to Thomas's, and there are a number of moments at which these become specific. In 'Lob', for instance, Thomas uses the blackbird's song ('Pretty dear') from Hardy's poem 'The Spring Call' as an expression of stable Englishness. But such similarities should not conceal the fact that, in at least two respects, the poetic temperaments which inform them are substantially different. Where Hardy's irony is cosmic, Thomas's is provisional; and where Hardy usually trusts the past as a means of illuminating the present, Thomas is less sanguine about the chance and value of recall. As 'Over the Hills' indicates, he has no difficulty in relating 'now' to 'then', but habitually does so only to find the connections imperfect and the comfort unreliable:

> Often and often it came back again
> To mind, the day I passed the horizon ridge
> To a new country, the path I had to find
> By half-gaps that were stiles once in the hedge,
> The pack of scarlet clouds running across
> The harvest evening that seemed endless then
> And after, and the inn where all were kind,
> All were strangers. I did not know my loss
> Till one day twelve months later suddenly
> I leaned upon my spade and saw it all,
> Though far beyond the sky-line. It became
> Almost a habit through the year for me
> To lean and see it and think to do the same
> Again for two days and a night. Recall
> Was vain: no more could the restless brook
> Ever turn back and climb the waterfall
> To the lake that rests and stirs not in its nook,
> As in the hollow of the collar-bone
> Under the mountain's head of rush and stone.

For all its singularity, Thomas's 'distinctively modern sensibility'[37] was formed by profound familiarity with writers who were, to use his own words in 'Lob', 'English as this gate, these flowers, this mire'. It is this quality which he believed that Hardy and (in theory more than practice) a few Georgians exemplified. By manifesting it himself he came to occupy a crucial place in the development of twentieth-century poetry. Although frequently passed over by critics — Donald Davie, for instance, does not mention him once in *Thomas Hardy and British Poetry* — he was one of the first, and most subtle, colonisers of the fruitful middle ground on which many subsequent poets have established themselves. W. H. Auden, R. S. Thomas, Philip Larkin and Ted Hughes have all recorded their debts to him. In doing so, they have made clear the good effect of his originality, and justified his evolutionary rather than revolutionary aims. Throughout the following chapters these are analysed in detail, with the intention that their remarkably successful execution should be appreciated, and in the belief that they are of the utmost importance for understanding our contemporaries.

CHAPTER ONE
BIOGRAPHICAL

Edward Thomas's poetry has been victimised by his life. Hardships delayed its appearance until his final two years, and since his death at Arras in 1917 biographies have outnumbered critical appreciations. The following narrative does not, therefore, provide more than a survey of his career.[1] Subsequent chapters discuss four of its dominant features — his melancholy, his friendship with Robert Frost, his patriotism, and his social isolation — but their main concern is his poetry.

Philip Edward Thomas was born in Lambeth on 3 March 1878, the eldest son of Philip Henry and Mary Elizabeth Thomas (née Townsend). His mother, whom Edward resembled in looks and temperament, was twenty-five years old, and like his father had been born and brought up in Wales. But her 'very retiring and shy and sad' character[2] was dominated by her husband's more stern and ambitious personality. Mr Thomas had trained as a teacher, and while other members of his family went to work in the railway workshops at Swindon, he joined the Board of Trade in London as a staff clerk for light railways and tramways. His real interests, however, were politics — he was a Lloyd-George Liberal — and religion. Although instinctively a free-thinker, he had not entirely abandoned formal religious practice, and after sampling various orthodoxies, eventually renounced Unitarianism for Positivism in 1910. Nine years later he became a minister in the Holborn 'Church of Humanity'. While this allegiance led him to claim that 'The master I follow is one who sets me free to make the most and best of whatever is within me',[3] his wish for self-improvement led him to tyrannise Edward. Four junior schools were tried and rejected, evening classes were encouraged, and weekly attendance at the local Unitarian chapel was made compulsory. Not surprisingly, the result of these good intentions was a serious and painful difference between the two, as the unforgiving poem 'P.H.T.' later made plain:

> I may come near loving you
> When you are dead
> And there is nothing to do
> And much to be said.
>
> To repent that day will be
> Impossible
> For you, and vain for me
> The truth to tell.
>
> I shall be sorry for
> Your impotence:
> You can do and undo no more
> When you go hence,
>
> Cannot even forgive
> The funeral.
> But not so long as you live
> Can I love you at all.

When Edward was nearly two the family moved to Wakehurst Road, Wandsworth, and subsequently to 61 Shelgate Road, Clapham. It was here that he began to find a replacement for his father's material aspirations. Exploration of the nearby common, and visits to relatives in Swindon, bred a love for the English countryside which was to shape his mature life. At this stage, too, he started to read the rural writers whose interests were to influence his own. Richard Jefferies, in particular, served as a model for his prose style, and he gave the last words of *The Amateur Poacher* (1879) the status of a creed:

> Let us get out of these narrow modern days, where twelve hours have somehow become shortened, into the sunlight and the pure wind. A something that the ancients thought divine can be found, and felt there still.[4]

His identification with Jefferies did not simply loosen the ties of his 'accidentally Cockney nativity',[5] it sapped his inherited sense of belonging to Wales as well. In spite of other holidays spent with his parents' families in Newport, Caerleon and Swansea, he came to see himself as being only 'flimsily connected [with it] by birth, a few acquaintances, love of the country and a useless sentiment'.[6] The reformed poacher David ('Dad') Uzzell, whom Thomas frequently met in Wiltshire, captured his imagination more completely than any ancestral loyalties. On their walks together through the woods between Wooton Bassett and Swindon he began to note down details of the scenery in a manner 'as near as possible to the style of Jefferies',[7] and thereby to map the course his life would take.

His father, however, had different ideas, and when Thomas was sent to Saint Paul's, Hammersmith, it was with the express wish that he should be educated for the Civil Service. But his resistance increased with age, and the social inferiority he felt at school confirmed his independent resolve. Although he was placed in a lively History VIII which included E. C. Bentley and G. K. Chesterton, his greatest pleasures were not provided by formal lessons, but by expanding his nature notes into essays. Several of these were shown to the minister of his chapel who, feeling them to be of more than average competence, showed them to a distinguished member of his congregation, James Ashcroft Noble. Noble — retired from the editorship of the *Manchester Examiner* and now working as a literary critic for the *Spectator*, the *Academy* and the *Daily Chronicle* — had in fact only recently moved to London from Liverpool. After reading the essays he invited their author round to his new home at 6 Patten Road, in Wandsworth. His interest was strengthened by the coincidence of his having had a son called Philip, who had died young; and the admiring company of his wife and three daughters helped to make the house a congenial refuge for Thomas. The girls quickly nicknamed him 'the genius', and the second of them, Helen Berenice, slowly wore down his reserve with her open and friendly manner.

Thomas's experience of female society at this age — he was seventeen — was negligible, and his natural shyness made any sort of close friendship difficult. But as his visits to Patten Road continued into 1895, Noble encouraged him to court Helen. Their walks and conversations are charmingly recounted by Helen herself in *As It Was* and *World Without End*, and, as she says, their mutual sympathy soon became 'unconscious love'[8] in spite of some opposition. Although Noble had helped Thomas by placing some of his essays in the *Speaker* and the *New Age*, and had recommended him to keep the diary which was included in his first book, *The Woodland Life* (1897), Mrs Noble resented his intrusion into the family. Moreover, the advice she gave her daughters directly contradicted their instincts. Helen, especially, was intensely aware of natural beauty, and throughout her life she tended to see herself as a kind of earth mother: 'I took a pride in my health and strength. [Edward] and I read Richard Jefferies, and with delight I found the joy in one's body spoken of there as if it were right and good.'[9] When she impulsively introduced herself to Mrs Thomas, Mrs Noble was shocked by her forwardness, and forbade further meetings with Thomas. When Helen's father died early in April 1896, the affair seemed hopeless. For Thomas, too, all was not well. His own father interpreted his rural wanderings as listlessness, saw Helen as a hindrance to his career prospects, and frowned on his wish to go to university. But such interference only increased their affection: correspondence became secret, and before he went to Oxford in 1897 they had become lovers.

Their refusal to marry was a deliberate rebellion against the conventional morality of their parents. 'We hated the thought of a legal contract', Helen said. 'We felt our love was all the bond that there ought to be, and if that failed it was immoral to be bound together. We wanted our union to be free and spontaneous.'[10] For Thomas's first few months at Oxford their freedom was unconstrained. Before and after their 'honeymoon' with the Uzzells they had no thought of marriage until, in May 1899, Helen realised she was pregnant. On being told the news, the family for which she was working as a nursery governess in London sacked her, and her mother refused to see her. Alarmed by this intolerance, she turned to some friends in Hammersmith, the Potburys, whom she admired for their Bohemianism. But to her dismay, Mrs Potbury counselled marriage and, more importantly, so did Thomas. It was their first serious disagreement and when, on 20 June 1899, the despised 'legal contract' was signed in Fulham Registry Office, she was aware that her husband felt burdened with responsibilities he could not adequately support.

In the year he had spent as a non-collegiate student, living at 113 Cowley Road, Oxford, Thomas had worked for and won a history scholarship to Lincoln College. Here, when his reticence and social naïveté had started to disappear, he found a community in which he could realise his potential. His tutor, whom he liked, was Owen Edwards, and in addition to his set work he found time to row in torpids, collect rare books and begin a novel, *Olivia Patterson*, with one of his several friends, E. S. P. Haynes. This, like the pastoral essays he continued to write, was strongly influenced by the presiding genius of Oxford letters, Walter Pater. For many years after, in fact, Thomas struggled to free himself from this debt, and the shadow it cast was not finally dispelled until 1913, when he published a full-length, hostile study of his erstwhile hero. Other, more pragmatic debts were also making themselves felt. Although his father generously agreed to pay for his final year as an undergraduate, Thomas could see no means of increasing the income of £80 a year that he made by writing, and the anxiety this provoked was enough to threaten his happiness. 'I love Helen', he wrote to a friend, 'and that is enough; though I wish the affair had not such a bad outlook on the face of it.'[11] His fears quickly appeared well-founded. No sooner had their son, Merfyn, been born, in January 1900, than poverty forced Helen to move in with the Thomases, and her husband to ask Haynes for money to pay the nurse. Their original carefree optimism was dashed still further when, six months later, Thomas managed to get only a second-class degree. The disappointment finally exhausted his father's patience: believing that Edward had not done himself or others justice, and angry with him for refusing advice to enter the Civil Service, he told him to leave home.

The first flat which the young family took was in a notoriously depressed part of London — Atheldene Road, Earlsfield. They were charged 7s. 6d. a week for three ugly rooms. Early the next year they escaped its squalor by moving to Nightingale Road, Balham, but the relatively high rent made another move inevitable. A legacy of £250 which Helen had inherited from her father was nearly spent, and Thomas, who still owed money at Oxford, was forced to canvass for work as a reviewer. His shyness made appealing to editors a hateful ordeal, and although H. W. Nevinson employed him for the *Daily Chronicle*, the damage these requests did to his pride was immense, as Helen realised:

> How anxiously I waited for [his] homecoming on these days, and
> how with the first glance at his face I knew what the day had been.
> If it had been a bad one there was no need of words, and none were
> uttered. I could do nothing, for if I said one word which would
> betray that I knew what he endured and was enduring, his anger
> and despair and weariness would break out in angry bitter words
> which would freeze my heart and afterwards freeze his for having
> uttered them.[12]

But Thomas's unhappiness was not simply the result of financial anxiety.

Since he often had to review as many as fifteen books a week in order to realise the £52 he earned in the year following his move to Balham, the time available to write essays was severely limited. And this frustration was exacerbated by the distance between himself and his favourite subject — the countryside.

Late in 1901 the Thomases moved to Rose Acre Cottage, in Bearsted, Kent, hoping to recover their obscured ideal. It was as if they had at last persuaded themselves to take an active, rather than a merely theoretical, part in the 'Back to the Land' movement which had been so forcefully advocated by Edward Carpenter and Havelock Ellis. The latter's 'Fellowship of the Good Life', founded in 1883, had espoused values similar to those that Thomas admired in Jefferies, though any possibility of his developing a facile faith in the simple life was out of the question. He was too nearly poverty-stricken to become a noble savage, and Rose Acre was too ugly to become a pastoral Utopia. The house was one of a series in which he tried, and failed, to make a clean break with the past. Shortly after moving there, Helen became pregnant again, the weight of reviewing increased, and he declined from relative content to despair. The birth of his daughter Bronwen in October 1902, the publication of his collection of essays *Horae Solitariae* (for which Haynes guaranteed part of the printing costs), and Helen's tireless efforts to make a happy home mocked him by recalling his vanished hopes. Natural self-doubt was transformed into self-pity, and his love for Helen was corrupted into bitterness with her patience.

Although her faith in him sometimes seemed a reproach it was, before they left Rose Acre, rewarded. A. & C. Black offered him £100 to write a book on Oxford. As was to happen so often later, this payment replaced monetary cares with professional ones. The subject was one he welcomed, but the speed with which he had to tackle it — 60,000 words in four months — sickened him. When the task was finished, and the family had moved the short distance to Ivy Cottage, in Bearsted, on its proceeds, he wrote to his friend Gordon Bottomley, '*Oxford* hasn't done me any service. I am not in the least in demand, except in quarters where moderate work is wanted for worse pay.'[13] His disappointment was increased by the realisation that his new home was hopelessly insanitary; first Bronwen then Helen fell ill, and he began looking round for somewhere to make yet another fresh beginning.

The place chosen, Elses Farm on the Weald near Sevenoaks, all but exhausted their funds. When they arrived in May 1904, Thomas had 5s. in his pocket and the prospect of £1 due in the summer to come. But they were saved, once again, by a commission — on this occasion to write *Beautiful Wales*. No sooner was it finished than he was busy with another, *The Heart of England*, and the account he gave Bottomley illustrates how apt the description of himself as 'a writing animal' was becoming:

I work continuously in the cottage[14] from 9.30 to 4.30 every day and squeeze from 1000 to 15000 words out of myself and the result is my worst book. There are plenty of landscapes and 'spurred lyric' — in fact ¾ of the book will be of this kind, and far inferior to *Wales* because I have less impulse and less material. The rest is pseudo-genial or purely rustic — Borrow and Jefferies sans testicles and guts.[15]

His 'impulse' was slackened still further by the reviewing he undertook simultaneously. It was not so much vanity that prevented him from treating it lightly, as a refusal to abandon his original high standards. He had, he said, 'no easy and genial command of nonsense, flowing as from an overfilled pen',[16] and the constant stream of work which soon began to pour into the farm replaced his fear of having too little to do with anxiety about having too much. His only compensations were money and, sometimes, the chance to praise a good new book. One such was W. H. Davies's *The Soul's Destroyer*, which appeared in 1905. Thomas reviewed it in the *Daily Chronicle*, met Davies, and in February the following year rented a cottage for him in nearby Egg Pie Lane. Since moving to Elses Farm, Thomas's income had been relatively healthy, but the 8*s.* a week he paid for Davies, in addition to his own rent for the farm and a *pied-à-terre* in London, stretched it to the limit. He furnished the cottage, provided food, arranged the purchase of a new wooden leg for Davies, and eventually, in 1911, got him a Civil List pension of £50 a year. Had someone shown him the same kindness, he might have had sufficient tranquillity to write poems earlier. As it was, he remained trapped in the double bind of self-criticism and self-denial.

The comparative security of Elses Farm was abruptly shattered in October 1906, when the Thomases were given notice to leave. Their son, Merfyn, was now of school age, and it was this fact which determined the choice of Berryfield Cottage, near Steep in Hampshire, as their new home. Bedales School was in the same village, and its curriculum, which was based on the teachings of William Morris, attracted them. Helen even joined the staff for a while, and although she gradually came to share Thomas's suspicion that the school had 'no bigness, no unevenness, no spontaneity, no savour of the earth',[17] the disappointment was off-set by pleasure in the surrounding country. Thomas's improved earnings assured them relative comfort, too, but the price he paid for their servant and attractive house was high. He became a regular reviewer for the *Morning Post*, as well as continuing his work for the *Daily Chronicle*, and accepted what should in theory have delighted him: an invitation to write a life of Richard Jefferies. Q. D. Leavis was to call the result 'a classic in critical biography, to stand with Lockhart's *Scott* and Mrs Gaskell's *Brontë*',[18] but the speed with which he had to produce it made the book seem a burden. Renewed unhappiness between himself and Helen led him to visit a specialist about his 'melancholia', and in order to finish his task without distractions he took a cottage at Mins-mere in Suffolk. But instead of solitude he found a young girl there, Hope, for whose family Helen had once worked, and on their walks together he flattered her into an infatuation with him. The friendship ended in embarrassment, when the girl's father reprimanded him, but it had been little more than a flirtation with the fantasy world which recurs throughout his early prose. In *Beautiful Wales* he had idealised 'the vague persons of poetry, which are but as large eyes or eloquent lips discerned in fleeting darkness',[19] and in Hope he thought he had found one. As soon as *Richard Jefferies* was finished, he realised just how evanescent her comfort was.

A request to write *The South Country* followed hard on the heels of *Richard Jefferies*, but Thomas's financial security was suddenly dis-turbed by a reduction in his review work. Helen was forced to take in some Bedales pupils who were unable to go home for the holidays, and he despaired so absolutely of his prospects that he allowed his father to recommend him for the post of Assistant Secretary to a Royal Commis-sion on Welsh Monuments, in London. But the job did not provide him with the travelling he anticipated, and after five months, in December 1908, he resigned. In addition, it failed to give what he most wanted — time to produce original work. When he returned to Steep he had the pleasure of finding a little of that. In the early months of 1909 he finished the two volumes of essays *Rest and Unrest* and *Light and Twilight*, and they were enough to strengthen his resolve to remain a writer. 'Life for him', Helen realised, 'would always be painful, but at least he had the country which meant so much to him, and the freedom within the limits his poverty imposed.'[20] His new sense of purpose did not, however, improve his lot, and for all the support his family gave, he was distressed by the selfishness of his choice. 'The bed is mainly of my own making', he told a friend; 'I wish I could lie on it without making so much noise.'[21] In one respect he was to blame for this insecurity: previously, when times had been good, he had sometimes spent money quite recklessly. Helen recalled that one day when a cheque was bigger than expected they bought 'a beautiful and costly brass lamp made in the William Morris workshops';[22] and even while helping to pay Davies's way Thomas told Bottomley he was 'buying a dinner gong with my last sovereign'.[23] What was, on the face of it, reasonable and commendable became, in the shadow of his poorly paid work, extravagance. And when the two collections of essays were finished he had no funds with which to help himself.

A crisis was obviously imminent, but its arrival was delayed by an offer from Geoffrey Lupton, a master at Bedales, to build Thomas a house at Wick Green, overlooking Steep. Lupton, who was a disciple of William Morris, worked to the best principles of the Arts and Crafts Movement, and the family moved there late in 1909. The spectacular setting and attractive design at first seemed all they could wish, but as Thomas began to attempt commissioned work again their happiness faded. Helen, finding that she was pregnant, had to give up teaching at Bedales, and was therefore no longer able to help pay the children's school fees. In order to do so, and to provide for Myfanwy when she was born in August 1910, Thomas worked harder than ever. Twelve books were written between 1910 and 1912, including *Feminine Influence on the Poets*, *Maurice Maeterlinck*, *George Borrow* and *Algernon Charles Swinburne*. The need to produce yet more is evident from his having asked his agent C. F. Casenove, 'Is a book on Dryden possible? Or on Evelyn the diarist? Or on England . . . as seen in literature, both native and foreign? Or on Lord Jeffrey? . . . I should like Cowper better than any of the above.'[24] As the work increased, so did his exhaustion, and when he came to describe Wick Green in the poem 'Wind and Mist' (written on 1 April 1915), he made the house seem a prison in which he struggled to support his family:

> 'In that room at the gable a child
> Was born while the wind chilled a summer dawn:
> Never looked grey mind on a greyer one
> Than when the child's cry broke above the groans.'
> 'I hope they were both spared.' 'They were. Oh yes.
> But flint and clay and childbirth were too real
> For this cloud castle. I had forgot the wind.

Pray do not let me get on to the wind.
You would not understand about the wind.
It is my subject, and compared with me
Those who have always lived on the firm ground
Are quite unreal in this matter of the wind.'

Not even Thomas, who had proved his powers of endurance innum-
erable times already, could resist the simultaneous pressures of work
and an oppressive home, and in September 1911 his health broke. 'I
have got too low', he told Haynes, 'and have been down too long to
think much about getting up again.'[25] As before, but much more
grievously, illness made him reject the one stable element in his life,
Helen, while at the same time forcing him to rely on her faithfulness.
Her tolerance and patience only made him detest himself for disappoint-
ing her hopes. 'Tired is not what I am', he explained. 'I'm sick of the
whole of life — of myself chiefly, of you and the children. You must
hate me and despise me, but you can't hate me as much as I hate the
whole business, and as I despise myself for not putting an end to it.'[26]
Faced with threats of suicide, Helen's sense of her own inadequacy
grew: 'He is my whole life, my love in whose existence I exist and yet I
can do so little, so very little for him. I know that a lot of the spirit in
me is gone, and I had been a far better, wiser, more helpful wife if I had
not let him mould me as he liked. One can love too well.'[27] His doctor
did little more than diagnose 'neurasthenia' and recommend a vegetarian
diet, but when Helen turned to friends, more practical help was forth-
coming. Norman Douglas offered to buy a village shop and put Thomas
in charge; Harold Munro wanted to lend his house in Locarno; and
some publishers suggested that he should write a book on the Black Sea
and visit Constantinople to collect material. 'If every difficulty was
smoothed over at the start', he answered, 'I should go, but I dread the
new faces and new ways. I was born to be a ghost.'[28] His own proposals
included schoolteaching and librarianship, but any sudden decision was
postponed by the intervention of Haynes. He encouraged Thomas to
holiday in Wales while working on a new commission — 80,000 words
on Borrow — and when he returned to Steep in time for Christmas he
was in slightly better spirits. But his 'habit of introspection'[29] was not
easily altered. Lack of money, and the strong sense of responsibility
he felt towards his family, undoubtedly increased the bitterness which
derived from neglecting his original work. And faults lay, as he was
painfully aware, in himself as well as his circumstances. When he was

treated the following year by Godwin Baynes — a young nerve specialist and follower of Freud — he was forced to identify them clearly, but knew all he had to fight them with was 'the knowledge that in truth I am not the isolated selfconsidering brain which I have come to seem — the *knowledge* that I am something more, but not the belief that I can reopen the connection between the brain and the rest.'[30]

In spite of continuing frustrations Thomas applied himself to his work with a new sense of purpose once this crisis in his health had passed, although from this time until his death he was frequently ill with nervous and digestive problems. Precisely what the new purpose was, he would have been hard-pressed to say: with hindsight it is obvious that he was clearing the ground for his poems. The critical studies of Swinburne and Pater written between 1911 and 1913 consistently reject the rhetoric of his former idols, and his autobiographical novel *The Happy-Go-Lucky Morgans* indicates the growth of his self-reliance. Progress towards this end was accelerated late in 1912 when his friend Clifford Bax introduced him to Eleanor Farjeon. Her cheerful company, and the undemanding love which she was to give, contributed enormously to the composure which made his poetry possible. Moreover, their relationship was approved by Helen; as she said herself, 'Edward was aware of Eleanor's devotion, but with the most sensitive tact kept it at a light-hearted level which she happily accepted.'[31] This improvement in his social relations was matched by the relief he felt when leaving the hostile, creaking newness of Wick Green for another home. Yew Tree Cottage, in the village of Steep itself, was a cheap semi-detached worker's house, and to overcome the disadvantages of its relatively small size he retained the separate study at Wick Green. It was here that he finished *In Pursuit of Spring*, *Keats* and *Four-and-Twenty Blackbirds*, began his autobiography, and continued his reviewing. But in due course the strain of work took its toll, and rather than submit Helen to his melancholy and irritation he went to London and looked for temporary lodgings. Not for the first time, his marriage seemed on the point of collapse, but in the autumn an event occurred which was to save it by saving his talent. It was Thomas's custom, every Tuesday, to join other writers — among them Ralph Hodgson, Walter de la Mare and W. H. Davies — for tea in St George's Restaurant, St Martin's Lane. He attended these meetings so regularly that he was known as 'The Iambic' by his friends (he normally stayed in London a day one week and overnight the second), and on 4 October 1913 Hodgson introduced him to Robert Frost.

The story of Frost's effect on Thomas's personality and work is well known. The instinctive understanding they were to show for each other's poetry had its origins in similarities between their backgrounds and temperaments. After Thomas's death Frost called him 'the only brother I ever had'.[32] Both had been disappointed by some aspects of marriage, both had threatened suicide, and both resented the public's neglect of their work. But Frost was more combative, and during the winter of 1913, when Thomas became 'obsessed with the notion that he should divorce his wife',[33] he advised against such a move. In addition he encouraged Thomas to find ways of realising his true potential, and recommended that he use passages in his prose books as the framework on which to build poems. In return for this kindness, Thomas exerted his influence as a reviewer to boost Frost's reputation. Even so, when *North of Boston* was published in May 1914 the notices that he gave it in the *Daily News*, the *New Weekly* and the *English Review* were more than charity. They were the final stage in the evolution of a poetic theory he had explored throughout his own work:

> Mr Frost has, in fact, gone back, as Whitman and as Wordsworth
> went back, through the paraphernalia of poetry into poetry again.
> With a confidence like genius, he has trusted his conviction that a
> man will not easily write better than he speaks when some matter
> has touched him deeply, and he has turned it over until he has no
> doubt what it means to him, when he has no purpose to serve
> beyond expressing it, when he has no audience to be bullied or
> flattered, when he is free, and speech takes one form and no other.
> Whatever discipline further was necessary, he has got from the use of
> the good old English medium of blank verse.[34]

The transformation of these theories into practice was quickened when, in August, the Thomases went to stay with the Frosts in their rented cottage near Ledbury in Gloucestershire. Lascelles Abercrombie and John Drinkwater were neighbours, and Rupert Brooke occasionally visited to assist with the distribution of the Georgian anthology *New Numbers* from Drinkwater's house. But it was Frost's society that Thomas found most congenial. On their walks together he heard, questioned and corroborated Frost's ideas about 'the sound of sense', and was confirmed in his slowly acquired belief that idealisation of landscape and ornamentation of language were largely responsible for his artistic frustration. He was later to tell Eleanor Farjeon 'If I am consciously trying to do anything I am trying to get rid of the last rags of rhetoric and formality which left my prose so often with a dead rhythm.'[35] Left to his own devices, it seems likely that Thomas would have started 'trying to do something' in verse before long, but the need to begin was made more urgent by a coincidence which overshadowed his stay in Gloucestershire. On the day that Helen came up from Steep to join him, war was declared. It was as if his remark of two years earlier had been prophetic: 'I am certain in my own mind that nothing can seriously affect me for good except some incalculable change that *may* come with time or by some spiritual accident or by no possible deliberate means.'[36]

At first, as he recalled in 'The sun used to shine', the war seemed 'remote', but it nevertheless made time, and England, doubly valuable. And the sense it gave of 'growing into a conscious Englishman'[37] was intensified when, on his return home, he was commissioned to write essays on public reaction to its declaration. In all of them he praised the mixture of resolution and fundamentalism which made up his own patriotic ideal:

> Two things in early English history suggest England more vividly to me than bigger things. One is the very stunted hawthorn round which the Battle of Ashdown mainly clashed. . . . The other little thing is the hoar apple tree where Harold's host met the Conquerer near Hastings. Here I have a foretaste of the England of Chaucer and of Langland.[38]

A request to compile the anthology *This England* (1915) offered him the chance to look for the same attitude in other writers, and as he found them he identified the spirit of war poetry he was soon to produce himself. He wanted, he told Bottomley, 'to give as various an impression as possible of English life, landscape, thought, ambition & glory. The thing is to arrange it so that it will be as simple & rich as a plum pudding.'[39]

Even doing such sympathetic commissioned work as this increased Thomas's desire to please himself. As the war advanced, the demand for commissioned work and reviews fell away, and for the first time in years he found time on his hands. After wryly asking Eleanor Farjeon, 'Did anyone ever begin at 36 in the shade?'[40] he started to write poetry. Between 3 and 7 December, in his study at Wick Green, he finished 'Up in the Wind', 'November Sky', 'March', 'Old Man' and 'The Signpost'. Five more poems followed the same month, and over the next two years, with occasional breaks, he wrote steadily — sometimes at the rate of three poems a day. His fluency alarmed him, but from the very first he showed a remarkable and consistent maturity. His rapid output during the early part of 1915 is partly explained by the fact that on New Year's Day Thomas made himself bedbound with a sprained ankle. As well as giving time to write, this accident gave him the opportunity to send some of his work to friends. When — with one or two exceptions, Frost among them — they failed to share his sense of self-discovery he was not downcast so much as forced to recognise his individuality. The most serious blow was Harold Munro's refusal to publish from his Poetry Bookshop. Had he done so, Thomas would have lived long enough to see his own first collection. But this disappointment did not deter him, as Helen later explained: 'years after Edward's death [Munro] wrote to me a rather grovelling sort of letter saying in effect that now when others saw their merit his eyes had been opened too etc. etc. I felt bitter towards him for what a little praise would have meant to Edward. Except that as for the poems, of these he was sure, in a way he'd never been before about his work and was not put off by the repeated refusal of them.'[41]

Nor was he put off by another consideration: whether to enlist or take up Frost's invitation to visit America. In the same month that he began writing poems, he welcomed the idea of the army as a 'release from the mess of journalism'[42] but feared that he was too old, at thirty-six, and too uncertain of his motives, to join up. The attractions of America were more obvious: sympathetic company, a final break with the past, and the chance to find 'a market out there for what I really want to do'.[43] With no call-up, his fastidious cast of mind made the problem seem endless, and when Frost returned to America in February 1915 (taking Merfyn to stay with a former headmaster of Bedales in New Hampshire), he had still not reached a conclusion. Immediate departure was ruled out by his accepting a commission to write a 75,000-word life of the Duke of Marlborough. When this was completed in June, after twenty-six days' writing, he took himself off on a long bicycle ride through Gloucestershire and Warwickshire, hoping to clear his mind. En route he was interviewed for — and turned down — the post of assistant headmaster at Bablake School, and shortly after returning to Steep he travelled to London and enlisted in the Artists' Rifles. He was accepted on 13 July.

Thomas's motives, which were as complex as they were considered, are best explained by an incident Eleanor Farjeon recalled in her auto-biography. When she asked him, 'Do you know what you are fighting for?' he bent down, picked up a handful of earth and, crumbling it between his fingers, replied, 'Literally, for this.'[44] More than the expense of visiting America, or his fears of continuing self-consciousness when he arrived, acute and refined love for his country determined his decision. In so far as it could be rationalised, it was in the essay 'This England':

> All I can tell is, it seemed to me that either I had never loved
> England, or I had loved it foolishly, aesthetically, like a slave, not
> having realised that it was not mine unless I were willing and
> prepared to die rather than leave it as Belgian women and old men
> and children had left their country. Something I had omitted. Something, I felt, had to be done before I could look again composedly at
> English landscape.[45]

Once Thomas was committed to the army he applied himself to his new life unstintingly. Having first been billeted with his parents in Balham he was moved to Hare Hall Camp in Essex, during November, as a map-reading instructor. Now a lance-corporal, he was able to perform duties for which his past as a rural writer had equipped him admirably, but they also frustrated him by proving 'first too comfortable, & then too uncomfortable a job'.[46] To say, as many have done, that the army cured him of his melancholy is to oversimplify the facts considerably. He appreciated the time it gave to write (twenty-eight poems in the first five months of 1916), was grateful for the small income it provided,[47] and liked the undemanding company: 'we fix things up somehow', he told a friend, 'by getting down to our lowest common denominator.'[48] Another advantage derived from the fact that necessary routines prevented him worrying about the future. He wrote to Eleanor Farjeon:

> Part of me envies you getting about and envies me of twelve months
> ago at Ledington [in Gloucestershire], without a pang though. I
> have to learn to keep my buttons bright. . . . I have conspired with
> God (I suppose) not to think about walks and walking sticks for 6
> months or 6 years hence. I just think about when I shall first go on
> guard etc.[49]

For Helen it was not so easy. After being told by her landlady to shift all Thomas's belongings from the study at Wick Green, she decided to move nearer his camp. The house she found at High Beech, in Epping Forest, was ugly and inhospitable, but it appeared to offer her the chance of seeing him more often. It brought her closer to her son, as well, who had returned from America and was working in Walthamstow. But in November, the month after she arrived, Thomas was posted to Trowbridge. Having received his second stripe earlier that year, he had applied for a commission in the Royal Artillery and had trained in London. And while Helen made what she could of her makeshift home, Thomas scraped through his final exams, was appointed second lieutenant with 244 Siege Battery, RGA and stationed at Lydd in Kent. In December he volunteered for service in France. Why he should have hastened his own destruction in this way is explained by recalling his reasons for enlisting. Joining the Artillery — which was notoriously dangerous — was not simply 'to get a better pension'[50] for Helen, but to defend in practice the same England that he was celebrating in poetry. His promotion from the post of map-reader had not been delayed by attempts to save himself, but because he had offended his superiors by failing to report absent a man in his charge. Once the oversight had been forgiven he did everything he could to quicken his progress down the road to France.

As soon as active service was certain, Thomas began a long round of farewells. It left all his friends with the impression that his departure was not a suicidal flight from failure but an understandable conclusion to his original choice. James Guthrie, Joseph Conrad, Bottomley and Abercrombie were all visited, and so too, of course, was Helen — on a final, unexpected Christmas leave at Steep. Here he sorted out his papers, telling a friend, 'I thought I should be accused of making a beacon for Zeppelins I had such a huge bonfire',[51] and also reassured her of his love. During his years as a prose writer she had borne a steadily increasing burden of criticism and bitterness, and for much of his life as a poet she had suffered his absence in the army. But her faith in him had never broken and neither, in spite of many waverings, had his in her. Throughout the years to come this was her consolation: 'Our life together was a restless sea, tide in tide out, calm and storm, despair and ecstasy; never still, never easy, but always vivid and moving wave upon wave a wide deep glorious sea, our life was terrible and glorious but always life.'[52]

Thomas arrived at Le Havre on 30 January 1917 and was quickly commandeered as an adjutant to the HQ of his group of batteries. But a similar sense of discomfort to that which made him end his days as a map-reading instructor led him to request for duty in the front line. He did not, he said, want to be 'a sort of lackey to the colonel, or someone who answers telephones'.[53] By 11 February he was at Arras, assisting in the preparations for the Easter offensive, and recording impressions in his diary which, had he lived, would have provided the genesis for more poems. On the 23rd, for instance:

Flooded fields by stream between the 2 sides of Achicourt. Ruined churches, churchyard and railway. Sordid ruin of Estaminet with carpenter's shop over it in Rue Jeanne d'Arc — wet, mortar, litter, almanacs, bottles, broken glass, damp beds, dirty paper, knife, crucifix, statuette, old chairs. Our cat moves with the Group wherever it goes, but inspects new house inside and out, windows, fireplace etc. Paid the Pool gunners (scrapings from several batteries doing odd jobs here). 2 owls in garden at 6. The shelling must have slaughtered many jackdaws but has made home for many more.[54]

While his duties at Arras left no time in which to finish new poems, Thomas received encouraging news of those he had written in England from friends. Before leaving he had arranged with Roger Ingpen of Selwyn & Blount to publish a collection dedicated 'To Robert Frost', and in March Frost himself wrote to say that *Poetry* (Chicago) had accepted 'The Word' and 'The Unknown'. 'I should like to be a poet', he replied, 'just as I should like to live, but I know as much about my chances in either case.'[55] The same month, soon after his thirty-ninth birthday, he saw that his chances of surviving as a poet, at least, were improving. Bottomley had argued successfully for him to be represented in *An Annual of New Poetry* which included work by most of the leading Georgians — Abercrombie, Davies and Drinkwater among them. Like the two poems he had slipped almost unnoticed into *This England*, the four that Guthrie had published in *Form* and *Root and Branch*, and the six he had privately printed, these poems appeared under the pseudonym 'Edward Eastaway'. His purpose in using this — a name from his mother's family — was to prevent readers being 'confined by what they know or think of me already'.[56] In the event he need hardly have worried: although he read a favourable review of the *Annual* in the *Times Literary Supplement*, he never saw the book itself.

As April began, preparations for the forthcoming battle intensified, and Thomas realised that his time was short. He wrote to Helen:

I am just, as it were, tunnelling underground and something sensible in my subconsciousness directs me not to think of the sun, at the end of the tunnel there is the sun. . . . If I could respond as you would like me to your feelings I should be unable to go on with this job in ignorance whether it is to last weeks or months or years. I never even think will it be weeks or months or years.[57]

But not even concentrating on the present, which had comforted him during training, could save him. On Easter Monday, 9 April, the battle of Arras began with an Allied bombardment over forty-five miles of the northern German line. At 7.36 a.m. Thomas, who was directing the fire of his battery from an observation post, was killed by the blast of a shell.[58] That same evening his unmarked body was recovered, and he is buried now at Agny, south of Arras. The small, attractive military cemetery is approached down a lane called 'La Route Verte' — a phrase which translates the title of one of his last poems. There is no mention on the gravestone of his having written a line.

CHAPTER TWO
DOUBLE VISION

I

Between 3 December 1914 and his death two years and four months later, Edward Thomas wrote 142 poems. In the previous sixteen years he had published thirty volumes of topography, biography and *belles-lettres*, compiled sixteen editions and anthologies, and produced over a million and a half words of review. The poetry came in a burst of creative activity during which he found 'when it came to beginning I slipped into it naturally';[1] the prose was soul-destroying. It kept him, he said, 'so confoundedly busy I feel as if the back of my head would come out'.[2] The result was not simply a wasteful sacrifice of his time and talent but — as his remark on *Oxford* (1903) testifies — a failure to express himself satisfactorily: 'It is neither good hack work nor good Edward Thomas. It will hurt me very much to see it in print.'[3] The 'good Edward Thomas' of the poems had been pre-empted by a 'doomed hack'[4] who was simultaneously everything he described and nothing at all. Because he was unable to discharge his commissions lightly, and had 'no genial command of nonsense',[5] their burden grew in proportion to his fastidiousness. In 1906 he complained that he was 'destined to reflect many characters and to be none',[6] and throughout the following years the sense of isolation from his identity increased. By 1913 it had reached almost schizoid proportions: 'My head ... is almost always wrong now — a sort of conspiracy going on in it which leaves me only a joint tenancy and a perpetual scare of the other tenant and wonder what he will do.'[7]

As this indicates, the discrepancy between Thomas's achievements and his ideal led to fears about the division of personality itself. And in their most extreme form these prompted him to describe encounters with his double. Elsewhere in Europe and America pioneering studies of schizophrenia were being made at the same time, and their findings illuminate the effect of his early enslavement on his eventual poetic flowering. Psychoanalysts such as Israel Levine, Morton Prince and Freud shared a belief that dual personality may be interpreted by 'the concept of repression'.[8] In normal, healthy life Levine identified this as the means by which an individual becomes fit to share in the life of a civilised community, but he realised that in extreme forms it was likely to produce an alternative identity. The same division into primary and secondary selves was made by Prince, who noted that under the weight of rigorous self-denial, 'the synthesis of the original consciousness known as the personal ego is broken up and shorn of its memories, perceptions, acquisitions or modes of reaction to the environment'.[9] The terms that Thomas used to analyse his condition are not, of course, the same as these. Where Prince noticed that 'particular emotional states, like fear or anxiety or general mental stress, have the tendency to disintegrate the mental organisation in such a way that the normal associations become severed or loosened',[10] Thomas described his experience as a sense of acute and divisive self-consciousness. His letters abound with references to it. 'I have attained a degree of self-consciousness', he told Bottomley in 1906, 'beyond the dreams of avarice',[11] and again, later, 'Oh my self-consciousness, it grows & grows, & is almost constant now, & I fear perhaps it will reach the point of excess without my knowing it.'[12] It was a theme to which he returned early in his correspondence with Eleanor Farjeon: 'You see the central evil is self-consciousness carried as far beyond selfishness as selfishness is beyond self-denial . . . and [it is] now amounting to a disease.'[13] These admissions provide a private account of the alienation which is conveyed in more general terms elsewhere in his writing. In a short story called 'Hawthornden', which includes a lengthy self-portrait, he admits that 'he was becoming more and more incapable of being passionate himself and of meeting the passion of another'.[14] This conforms exactly to R. D. Laing's observation that, under repression likely to cause schizophrenia, 'the self avoids being related directly to real persons but relates itself to itself'.[15] Such implosive self-awareness eventually prompted him to create an ideal image of himself which he fearfully pursued, but which, being always at one remove, was also a visible reminder of his frustration.

Thomas's most celebrated meeting with his double occurs in only the sixth poem he wrote, 'The Other' (December 1914). It represents such an extraordinary departure from his usually orthodox pastoral mode that it has always been regarded as something of an odd man out in his work. But it does, however, have a large number of precedents in his earlier prose, and a summary of these helps to clarify his eventual poetic purpose. It is also revealing to distinguish his use of the figure — throughout his career — from the German tradition of *Doppelgänger* literature with which it is obviously associated. The most striking difference is that instead of appearing as the prime mover in what is principally an adventure or horror story, the main function of Thomas's double is to make intimate psychological revelations. Although his medical condition was never severe enough to become certifiably schizophrenic, his sense of an 'other tenant' forced him to create a shadowy middle ground between allegorical artefact and private trauma. He made more clear-cut, structural innovations as well. In its Middle European originals and later descendants, the *Doppelgänger* appears after the separation of the benevolent and malevolent forces inherent in a single character. E. T. A. Hoffmann's *Die Eliziere des Teufels*, James Hogg's *Confessions of a Justified Sinner*, Dostoevsky's *The Double* and R. L. Stevenson's *Dr Jekyll and Mr Hyde* are conspicuous examples. In all of them the image is produced by someone 'whose conflicting inclinations have become almost incompatible, and at last announce their presence to his consciousness as distinct, and alternate, entities'.[16] Further illustration of this can be found in Oscar Wilde's *The Picture of Dorian Gray*, during which the hero grows 'more and more enamoured of his own beauty, more and more interested in the corruption of his own soul'.[17] Dorian Gray's cry that 'each of us has Heaven and Hell in him'[18] echoes Jekyll's confession that 'though so profound a double dealer, I was in no sense a hypocrite; both sides of me were in deadly earnest'.[19]

The division of character in all these fictions is made along what Prince calls 'ethical lines of cleavage'. In Thomas's poem 'the splitting of personality is along intellectual and temperamental lines'.[20] It is not that one part of him is siphoned off to indulge in vicious and hedonistic pursuits, but that he is engaged in a search for integration with his better self. This is the central difference between his encounters and those described by his precursors or contemporaries. Instances like 'The Other', in which the double appears liberated and desirable, are very rare, and may be said to reverse the normal role of the figure. Even the well-meaning *alter ego* of Edgar Allan Poe's *William Wilson* seems to be motivated by 'a whimsical desire to thwart, astonish or mortify'.[21] It is, in fact, oppression and rivalry which form the usual motivation in *Doppelgänger* literature — either because evil seeks to overcome virtue, or because it strives to resist the correctives of conscience. In this respect, and because of its candidly autobiographical element, Thomas's poem represents a departure from the received tradition. It also constitutes a modification of the doubles which appear in his own prose.

'The Other's' earliest original is Philip, his constant but imaginary boyhood friend. Philip (his own first name) was not simply the externalisation of his entire character but 'a part of himself, a higher part, a spiritual self ... [which] disappeared "after a process of envanishment" '.[22] Amplification of one aspect of personality to fulfil a role of companion and confidant is common among children, but when Robert P. Eckert, Thomas's first biographer, described Philip as 'a sort of Peter Pan who could not grow up'[23] he underestimated his importance. Philip grows into the *Doppelgängers* of *The South Country* (1909), *The Happy-Go-Lucky Morgans* (1913), *The Icknield Way* (1913), and *In Pursuit of Spring* (1914). In all these books the image is frequently a magnification of one aspect of Thomas's personality, but it is not 'a higher part of himself' so much as a means to ruthless self-analysis.

The 'tall, spare, shock-headed man'[24] of *The South Country* is an early example. He has escaped from London during the summer months to help with the harvest, invites Thomas to camp with him for the night, and is recognisably Thomas in appearance and in the autobiographical details that he gives. Thomas, however, retains his own identity as the first-person narrator, describing himself as 'a hack writer',[25] and uses the double to articulate his sense of isolation from the natural world. Instead of having a mystic's visions of felicity by 'feeling out with infinite soul to earth and stars and sea and remote time and recognising his oneness with them',[26] the double experiences 'a terror that enrolled me as one of the helpless, superfluous ones of the earth'.[27] Thomas responds to these complaints by recording his own sense of isolation — of similar intensity, but from a different goal: 'The hack writer is asked to give everything that can be turned into words at short notice, and so the collar round his neck is never taken off as yours was between six in the afternoon and nine in the morning.'[28] In this exchange the two speakers dramatise and contrast two of the most common themes in his prose: isolation from nature and people which leads to a perception of only 'the outside of things',[29] and the grim task of translating anything and everything into words. These are actually two faces of the same coin: they both amount to frustration and compromise of wholeness. Although the double insists that his condition is the more pernicious, because to the prose writer, at least, it is open 'to do good or bad',[30] Thomas is so scornful of his own ability that that potential to 'do good' remains beyond his reach, and the distinction theoretical rather than actual.

In his novel *The Happy-Go-Lucky Morgans* Thomas again draws a self-portrait whose alienation from his genuine artistic personality is emphasised by his sense of isolation from the world about him. But as was the case in *The South Country*, the double's function at this early stage in its development is a melancholy convenience, rather than a psychological necessity. Once again Thomas retains his own personality in the character of a narrator (Arthur Froxfield), while simultaneously describing himself in the person of another — Mr Torrance, who 'wrote what he was both reluctant and incompetent to write, at the request of a firm of publishers whose ambition was to have a bad, but nice-looking, book on everything and everybody'.[31] But where he had previously debated the relative demerits of prose writing and social or natural isolation, he now suggests that the compromise of personality is inextricably linked with the loss of traditional geographical origins. Mr Torrance's books are criticised because they 'contain not one mention of the house under the hill where he was born'.[32] The double of *The South Country* had mourned the same lack of natural origins when he admitted, 'I belong to no class, or race, and have no traditions. We of the suburbs are a muddy, confused, hesitating mass.'[33] And during yet another meeting with his double, in his short story 'The Pilgrim', Thomas repeats his belief that wholeness depends on contact with tradition. Here the figure is discovered on the Pilgrims' Way making a cross on a piece of rock, and when questioned about his motives he explains, 'I had a feeling that while I was doing as the pilgrims did I might become like one of them.'[34] As their conversation develops, the double's need for correspondence between himself and a source of revered stability is explained by the hiatus which exists within his personality. He is, in Thomas's own words, 'a poet of a kind, who made a living out of prose',[35] and he wishes, with a desperate humour, for the memory of his thwarted personal past to be replaced by communion with the secure past of his country:

I must be born again: that is certain. So far as it is in my power, I have tried hard. For example, there is no ordinary food or drink or article of clothing I have not given up at some time, and no extra-ordinary one that I have not adopted. There remains only to wear a silk hat and to drink beer for breakfast.[36]

In this scene, as in its two predecessors, the source of potential good is recognised, but seen to be beyond Thomas's earnest grasping. Imprisoned and divided by prose, he continues to pursue his goal in the knowledge that it grows more distant as he advances.

The intensity of his search increases in proportion to its duration. By *In Pursuit of Spring* his original use of the double as a convenient means of objective self-analysis has been transformed into a sinister portrait of 'the other tenant' who haunted his mind. A glimpse had been given in *The Icknield Way* the previous year, during a fine introspective passage that was to be reused in his poem 'Rain'. But where Thomas himself speaks in the poem, in the prose it is 'a ghostly double'[37] that addresses him from his bedside, and provokes his despair:

He was muttering: The all-night rain puts out summer like a torch. In the heavy, black rain falling straight from invisible, dark sky to invisible, dark earth the heat of summer is annihilated, the splendour is dead, the summer is gone. The midnight rain buries it away where it has buried all sound but its own. I am alone in the dark still night, and my ear listens to the rain piping in the gutters and roaring softly in the trees of the world. Even so will the rain fall darkly upon the grass over the grave when my ears can hear it no more. I have been glad of the sound of rain, and wildly sad of it in the past; but that is all over as if it had never been; my eye is dull and my heart beating evenly and quietly; I stir neither foot nor hand; I shall not be quieter when I lie under the wet grass and the rain falls, and I of less account than the grass. The summer is gone, and never can it return. There will never be any summer any more, and I am weary of everything. I stay because I am too weak to go. I crawl on because it is easier than to stop. I put my face to the window. There is nothing out there but the blackness and sound of rain. Neither when I shut my eyes can I see anything. I am alone. Once I heard through the rain a bird's questioning water cry — once only and suddenly. It seemed content, and the solitary note brought up against me the order of nature, all its beauty, exuberance, and everlastingness like an accusation. I am alone. There is nothing else in my world but my dead heart and brain within me and the rain without.[38]

The macabre setting, the suicidal promptings, and the ruthless nihilism of this figure distinguish it from its more moderate predecessors, and recall instead the malevolent image seen by Jekyll's bedside in *Dr Jekyll and Mr Hyde*, 'to whom power was given, and even at that dead hour he must rise and do its bidding'.[39] The encounters are connected by more than the fact that both occur in a bedroom: they share a similar atmosphere of menace and bafflement.

In Pursuit of Spring was written immediately before Thomas began to write poetry, and the double which appears in it bears the closest resemblance to 'the other'. Theirs is no chance encounter, but a series of meetings on a journey from London to the Quantocks which become increasingly mysterious, sinister and disconcerting. 'The other man', as Thomas calls him, is slow to open conversation, although not to recognise his replica, who eventually provokes in him an appearance of fearful surprise: 'His expression changed ... from a melancholy and too yielding smile to a pale and thin-lipped rigidity.'[40] Their talk, when it has begun, turns on clay pipes, inn names and weathercocks — all subjects which Thomas associates throughout his work with an old order of Englishness, but which in this spectacularly odd context assume a threatened, obsessive quality. The stability they usually embody is challenged by his divided apprehension of them. This gulf between recognition and attainment, which parallels that described in 'The Pilgrim', is confirmed during their meeting at Bemerton. Here Thomas comes close to experiencing a moment of communion engendered by the place itself and by his recital of George Herbert's poem 'Sunday', 'with a not wholly sham unction'.[41] But he is ridiculed by his image: 'From Parents, Schoolmasters, and Parsons, from Sundays, and Bibles, from the Sound of Glory ringing in our ears, from Shame and Conscience, from Angels, Grace, and Eternal Hopes, and Fears, Good Lord or whatever Gods there be, deliver us.'[42] This dismissive, sour and iconoclastic tone is explained to Thomas's satisfaction when he discovers that 'the other man' is a writer who did not like writing:

He had been attempting the impossible task of reducing undigested notes about all sorts of details to a grammatical, continuous narrative. He abused notebooks violently ... if he had taken none, then only the important, what he truly cared for, would have survived in his memory, arranged not perhaps as they were in nature, but at least according to the tendencies of his own spirit.[43]

The double is visible proof of the harm done by this self-denial. One part of Thomas suspects and cannot admit the ideal, the other hankers after it, recognises it to be possible, but cannot attain it at all, unless too late. In their final meeting at Kilve (famous because of its connections with Wordsworth's 'Anecdote for Fathers'), his desire to reconcile both aspects of himself is touched with fear, just as in 'The Other' he 'felt fear' too. The double 'laughs nervously at the encounter',[44] and in doing so recalls an incident in a walking race which Thomas himself had experienced as a child: 'I hated being pursued ... and when I was within a hundred yards of the tape I began to believe that the running boy was gaining on me. I could not stand it. Turning off the track I threw myself down on the grass on the pretext that I had a stitch.'[45] It is a fear justified by the fact that the sceptical, disillusioned aspect of his personality, represented by the double, persistently destroys his attempts to reflect 'on the spirit's readiness to grasp at all kinds of unearthly perfection'.[46] The conflict between ideal and real, potential and circumstantial, imagined and actual, does not even afford the temporary wholeness of 'The Other'.

In the poem itself, Thomas includes the image of his former frustration without any loss of urgency, but in the knowledge that, with regard to form at least, he has reached the end of his long quest. But his exchange of one medium for another does not disguise his retention of themes and images from the prose, or his characteristic self-doubt. His remark to John Freeman is instructive: 'What I have done so far have been like quintessences of the best parts of my prose books.'[47] This acknowledgment of continuity between the two forms is substantiated by Garnett: '[He] had always been a poet in grain, if not in form.'[48] The double of 'The Other' is, as these remarks indicate, not simply 'first sketched ... in *In Pursuit of Spring*'[49] but is the apogee of all such figures in the prose. During his encounters with them, Thomas gradually revealed his sense of angry compromise, and converted an artefact of convenience into a dramatic expression of alienation from himself, his fellow human beings, and the natural world.

Thomas begins 'The Other' by seeming to escape alienation:

> The forest ended. Glad I was
> To feel the light, and hear the hum
> Of bees, and smell the drying grass
> And the sweet mint, because I had come
> To an end of forest, and because

> Here was both road and inn, the sum
> Of what's not forest.

The development of natural description to overt symbol here is quickly accelerated. His use of an indefinite article in the phrase 'an end of forest' generalises the statement away from its specific, organic meaning into one of clear-sighted purposefulness. Yet although four of the senses are brought at once into full, sensuous play — the light is felt in line 2 and 'tasted' in line 15, the bees are 'heard', and both grass and mint are 'smelt' — clear sight is crucially absent. Such an omission would seem insignificant were it not emphasised by this systematic enrolment of its companions, and by Thomas's insistence that the 'moving goal' he pursues is 'unseen'. These two facts amount to a sub-merged confession that vestiges of his former isolation linger even when he has evaded its worst restrictions. This qualification is supported by the triple mention of the word 'forest' within the poem's first seven lines. 'What's not forest' is certainly an improvement on what is, but its repeated mention suggests that Thomas cannot empty his mind of its shadowy misdirections. His residual uncertainty contradicts the 'gladness' that he feels at his escape and provides a suitably ambivalent context for the first mention of his double:

> But 'twas here
> They asked me if I did not pass
> Yesterday this way. 'Not you? Queer.'
> 'Who then? And slept here?' I felt fear.

The staccato questions, with their final huddled rhyme 'here'/'fear' confirm the anxiety so deftly introduced in the opening lines. Whatever compromised chance he had foreseen of enjoying the daylit world with its potential for travel (roads) as well as stability (inns), is now changed to dread. It is, moreover, a fear which compels him to identify its source, even though this will mean forgoing the opportunity of personal or social harmony.

The sacrifice is, in fact, mellowed by Thomas's understanding that his hopes of associating with the vagabond solitaries of the road, or the small attractive communities of the inn, are limited. In 'The Attempt' he had described how, after failing to emulate the appearance and life-style of 'wayfaring men', 'his wife flattered him by saying that anyone could see what he really was, whatever his disguise'.[50] But while this self-knowledge affords some consolation, its comforts are quickly obliterated by his departure:

> I learnt his road and, ere they were
> Sure I was I, left the dark wood
> Behind, kestrel and woodpecker,
> The inn in the sun, the happy mood
> When first I tasted sunlight there.

The rapidity of his leave-taking has the additional advantage of allowing him to escape without an awkward disclosure of his distinct identity. But it also sows the first seed of concern that what he conceals from others is also concealed from his own knowledge: himself. Flight from the social world becomes, in other words, pursuit of his identity, and illuminates the foundations upon which his original 'fear' was founded. His anxiety is not prompted by the malevolence of his double (as is the case, for example, in *The Confessions of a Justified Sinner* and *Dr Jekyll and Mr Hyde*) but by its very presence, which confirms his suspicion that the triumphant exodus from the forest was not complete and thoroughgoing.

By thus becoming the pursuer rather than the pursued, Thomas reverses the roles usually allotted to self and image.[51] And this innovation is compounded by another: it is a characteristic of *Doppelgänger* fictions for the double to be invisible to all but the character of whom it is the image. Poe's *William Wilson* and Dostoevsky's *The Double* are typical; so too is Wilde's *The Picture of Dorian Gray*, in which the debauched roué of the painting and the eternally youthful hero exchange their visible characteristics on the latter's death, so as to preserve his secret. But in 'The Other' Thomas's double is pointed out, and his own route determined, by people he meets. Their advice does not, however, produce quick results. Frustration is still mingled with indecision:

> I travelled fast, in hopes I should
> Outrun that other. What to do
> When caught, I planned not. I pursued
> To prove the likeness, and, if true,
> To watch until myself I knew.

The implication here that 'the likeness' might *not* be 'true' renews the temptation to evade self-discovery. But even as he suggests this to himself, the syntax of the passage forces him to define and confront his goal: the phrase 'When caught' applies to both the narrator and 'the other'. Although the two aspects of his personality are unreconciled, they are locked in pursuit of one another by language itself. Uncertainty and confusion might hinder fulfilment, but the very fabric of Thomas's future career, as it is prophesied by the poem, forbids him to abandon the attempt to secure it.

In the third stanza the consequence of this becomes apparent:

> I tried the inns that evening
> Of a long gabled high-street grey,
> Of courts and outskirts, travelling
> An eager but a weary way,
> In vain. He was not there. Nothing
> Told me that ever till that day
> Had one like me entered those doors,
> Save once. That time I dared: 'You may
> Recall' — but never-foamless shores
> Make better friends than those dull boors.

Whatever 'overlapping and mingling of one self with the other'[52] was suggested by the grammatical complexities of the previous stanza, the two are now no longer within one another's sight or reach. This contrast is strengthened by differences between the social world Thomas has left and the one which he now enters. The former, rural context, in spite of his muted reservations, offered him a prospect of relative harmony and content. Birds of prey (the kestrel), other potentially vulnerable birds (the woodpecker), the inhabitants of the inn, and Thomas himself coexisted in a single 'happy mood' which was broken by news of the double. But in the latter, urban context to which he now turns, 'The inn in the sun' has been exchanged for 'the inns .../ Of a long gabled high-street grey', and social harmony has been replaced by isolation. So complete has his alienation become, that even the alarming information of his original inquisitors has given way to silence. But the eager weariness of his search — the paradox of which is poignantly unravelled by the disappointed 'In vain' being placed after the hopeful suspension of a line-ending — leads him to another phrase of rewarding syntactical complexity. By saying of his attempts to jog the memories of those that he is interviewing about his double's appearance 'That time I dared', he suggests that he should appear as his own image.

In other words, he offers to risk merging himself with what he fears. This is, of course, the conclusion towards which the entire poem tends, but until now Thomas's (understandable) nervousness has prevented him from postulating anything more intimate than watching 'until myself I knew'. And the 'dull boors' who provide him with no active assistance spur him to define his intention more cogently by their wooden ignorance.

But their inarticulate and unintended reward is not sufficiently clear to sustain him during his disappointed pursuit. He has already expressed his preference for the hostile wildness of 'never-foamless shores' — never-foamless because their antagonism is perpetually renewed — to the unyielding indifference of human society, and during the fourth stanza his despair deepens until it actually becomes suicidal:

> Many and many a day like this
> Aimed at the unseen moving goal
> And nothing found but remedies
> For all desire. These made not whole;
> They sowed a new desire, to kiss
> Desire's self beyond control,
> Desire of desire.

The hero of *The Confessions of a Justified Sinner*, in a harrowing bid for escape from his double, also felt himself to be 'the child of misery and despair'.[53] Thomas's own developing wish for escape from his trial is conveyed both by the exhausted rhyme of 'this'/'remedies' and by its clipped, telegraphic syntax. The absence of personal pronouns indicates a premature effacement of self. And what is suggested by the manner of the stanza is confirmed by its matter. In the same breath as he anatomises his 'goal' (it is only susceptible to the vaguest analysis, being both 'unseen' and 'moving'), he confesses that its elusiveness tempts him to avoid the pursuit altogether, by making use of the self-induced unconsciousness offered by the 'remedies / For all desire'. This instinct is recurrent in other *Doppelgänger* stories, but there it erupts into a wish to destroy the pursuer rather than the self. As Otto Rank says, 'the impulse to rid oneself of the uncanny opponent in a violent manner belongs . . . to the essential features of the motif'.[54] It is a testament to Thomas's personal courage, and to the influence of those augurs of fulfilment mentioned above, that he puts these temptations behind him by choosing to seek integration rather than escape. Death is, in fact, rejected because it is seen to embody a destructive paradox: the apparent offer of oblivion is really a means by which his exasperation is provoked. Once this has been appreciated, the road to recovery is open:

> And yet
> Life stayed on within my soul.
> One night in sheltering from the wet
> I quite forgot I could forget.

The resolution to continue his search has survived its trial, and now, like Bunyan's Christian overcoming one difficulty only to confront another, Thomas continues his interrogation of the social world, strengthened by his conviction that the very capacity to imagine a means by which he might enter oblivion has itself been forgotten.

The search immediately returns to that epitome of social life, an inn:

> A customer, then the landlady
> Stared at me. With a kind of smile
> They hesitated awkwardly:
> Their silence gave me time for guile.
> Had anyone called there like me,
> I asked. It was quite plain the wile
> Succeeded. For they poured out all.
> And that was naught. Less than a mile
> Beyond the inn, I could recall
> He was like me in general.

During the course of this fifth stanza, however, his new-won determination suffers an articulate disappointment which is as wearying as the ignorance that he had received previously: both inns are places where, in the words of 'Over the Hills', 'all were kind, / All were strangers'. Although his self-knowledge enables him to interpret his companions' silence, to translate it into speech, and to organise the conversation so as to glean the information he needs, the fact that he sees this unsurprising use of previously established material as 'guile', and later, with emphasis by means of the rhyme, as a 'wile', undermines the confidence that he appears to have found. It implies a furtiveness which rests as awkwardly with his bland questioning as his own appearance does with the customers' memories, and nourishes a suspicion that his lack of complete frankness with them will provoke duplicity in their treatment of him. Revealingly, the hero of Conrad's 'The Secret Sharer', confronted by his double, similarly but frankly admitted that 'the mental feeling of being in two places at once affected me physically as if the mood of secrecy had penetrated my very soul'.[55] While Thomas's own behaviour conforms exactly to this experience throughout his interview, it develops more oppressive attributes after his departure from the inn. Not only does the 'all' given in good faith by his informants prove to be 'naught' when it is examined later, but his own memory seems to conspire against his remembering their assessment of the double. Their advice dwindles to the recollection of a 'general' likeness — a fact which was established in the poem's opening stanza and therefore represents no progress towards a solution.

In spite of the degree to which both self-secrecy and secrecy in others preserve the double as a blurred, indefinite figure, Thomas's reflections lead him to recognise a crucial distinction between himself and his image:

> He had pleased them, but I less.
> I was more eager than before
> To find him out and to confess,
> To bore him and to let him bore.

For the first time it is stated openly that he is not simply pursuing his replica, but an improved version of himself. Where he has confronted or provoked his own isolation, his double has 'pleased' the communities that he has entered. This confirms the poem's earlier suggestion that, of all the evils consequent upon sixteen years of prose writing, social alienation was the worst. And the possibility that reconciliation with his image could dissolve the barriers between himself and others, as well as erasing artistic frustration, quickens the journey towards his goal. The eagerness with which he seeks to realise it is emphasised by his desire 'to bore him and to let him bore'. Such an instinct implies disconcerting extravagance: why not simply 'talk'? The desire is illuminated by a passage in *In Pursuit of Spring* during which Thomas, after successfully joining his image, talked to him at inordinate length until 'the other man' 'awoke from the stupor to which he had been reduced by listening'.[56] The latter then replies so fully that Thomas admits 'not long after this I was asleep'.[57] The effect of the boredom that they induce, in both prose and verse, is twofold: it testifies to their wish to make their whole selves freely available, and to the profound ambivalence of their relationship. Thomas recognises that the instinct to reconcile the distinct aspects of his personality is exhausting and precarious:

> I could not wait: children might guess
> I had a purpose, something more
> That made an answer indiscreet.
> One girl's caution made me sore,
> Too indignant even to greet
> That other had we chanced to meet.

In these six lines, as so often before, personal diagnosis obtrudes on the sustained allegorical function of the poem to render its meaning complex. Children are consistently envisaged by Thomas as possessing a store of instinctive wisdom and sensitivity which is denied to adults,[58] and as he continues his inquiries in the social world it is to them that he now turns. For no apparent reason other than that they are children, he credits them with the ability to see through the 'guile' of his seemingly innocent questions, and discover the frustration which had been concealed during his recent visit to the inn. It is this intuitive perception which would make their answer to his questions 'indiscreet', because in answering him at all they would publicise the divisive extent of his malaise. Moreover, in the case of one particular child, reluctance to answer his demands actually makes him 'sore' (as if the irritation were physical as well as mental), because the degree of her hesitancy stands in direct relation to the amount of information about his condition that she has surmised. He had originally undertaken this second search in the social world believing that he could conceal his real motives, and the girl's unspoken discovery of them not only forces him to leave society for solitude in order that he should keep his secret, but temporarily provokes him into disowning the existence of the double altogether. Because his condition has been recognised, he is made to feel 'Too indignant even to greet / That other had we chanced to meet'.

But what appears to be harmful to his pursuit proves once again to be beneficial and leads him to the poem's one moment of stability:

> I sought then in solitude.
> The wind had fallen with the night; as still
> The roads lay as the ploughland rude,
> Dark and naked, on the hill.

Had there been ever any feud
'Twixt earth and sky, a mighty will
Closed it: the crocketed dark trees,
A dark house, dark impossible
Cloud-towers, one star, one lamp, one peace
Held on an everlasting lease:

The solitude which impregnates this scene is 'accepted as organic to
the process of self-discovery',[59] but the ecstasy for which it provides the
context is not achieved by abandoning his pursuit. Until now, in spite
of his desire for reconciliation, his divided self has taken the form of
two distinct physical entities who evade, embarrass and contradict one
another. Now their diverse elements are transformed into organic terms
and held in perfect equipoise. The scene's stillness is both the catalyst
and the manifestation of this: wind and darkness mingle by falling
together, and darkness and light cancel each other's alarms by setting
themselves in balance. This breathless equanimity is repeated in the
larger elements of earth' and sky. Where in 'November Sky' the 'dirty
earth' stands in stark contrast to the sky's 'cloudless heavenly light', in
'The Other' 'No difference endured between / The two.' Unearthly aspi-
ration and pedestrian realities are blended. Thomas himself takes part in
this pervasive union of opposites, but its effect on him is not a 'loss of
identity involved in ... [the] fusion of his self with the natural world'.[60]
It is, rather, a grateful *discovery* of personality — a realisation that
wholeness is not achieved by ignorance or concealment of division, but
by a fully conscious acknowledgment of its presence even when it
seems least apparent. Sealed in the benevolent embrace of earth and
sky, and cherished by both light and 'crocketed dark trees' (the archi-
tectural term for ornamental buds and leaves carries with it an appro-
priate impression of stasis, and a half-echo of 'locked'), Thomas is able
to relish his moment of integrated completeness in full recognition of
the frustration upon which such moments are founded.

Thomas enlarges upon his discovery of melancholy 'in the very
temple of delight' throughout the stanza. The 'mighty will' which
closed earth and sky attracts an alternative meaning to itself in the light
of his statement that the moment of stability is held 'on an everlasting
lease'. The primary sense of 'will' as 'omnipotent power' shifts to
accommodate the secondary meaning of 'binding legal document', and
it is this which authorises his 'lease' of stability: it draws up, as it were,
a contract in which diverse elements combine. But the agreement is

founded on a paradox. The exhaustible tenure suggested by the word 'lease' is directly opposed by its own adjective 'everlasting', and in this startling contradiction lies the essence of successful self-pursuit. At precisely the same time as he rejoices in union with his thwarted desires, he acknowledges that their fulfilment must be transitory:

> And all was earth's, or all was sky's;
> No difference endured between
> The two. A dog barked on a hidden rise;
> A marshbird whistled high unseen;
> The latest waking blackbird's cries
> Perished upon the silence keen.
> The last light filled a narrow firth
> Among the clouds. I stood serene,
> And with a solemn quiet mirth,
> An old inhabitant of earth.

Thomas's sense of integration is stimulated by signs of its disappearance. Dog and marshbird are concealed rather than visibly entering into communion with him, and the 'latest' blackbird and the 'last light' complement each other in a suggestion that dusk's transitional balance of opposites must soon end. Even the silence is transformed from an expression of security into a potential agent of destruction. It is now 'keen' where it had been conciliatory, and on its sharpness the blackbird's cries 'perish' as if the bird itself was struck down. But these warnings of termination, while they overshadow the triumphant lack of 'difference' between earth and sky, intensify it with pleasing, incipient nostalgia. They provide a context of realistic brevity, and revere and conclude, but do not compromise, his ecstatic 'moment of everlastingness'.

Throughout all his prose writing, Thomas had searched for 'an ideal country, belonging to itself and beyond the power of the world to destroy',[61] which exemplified traditional, ancient aspects of England. These qualities, which suggest a wholeness that his divided self can imitate, are found in 'The Manor Farm', where he describes a 'season of bliss unchangeable' which has been preserved as a Golden Age:

> Safe under tile and thatch for ages since
> This England, Old already, was called Merry.

This necessary correspondence between himself and 'the old, roomy

England'[62] recurs in 'The Other' when he refers to himself as 'An old inhabitant of earth' — an identical phrase to that used of a similar moment in his story 'The First Cuckoo'. In 'The Stile', too, he had employed a phrase which echoes and glosses this — 'a strong citizen of infinity and eternity'[63] — and again in *The Icknield Way* he had spoken of himself as 'a better citizen not of the world but eternity'.[64] A further illustration may be found in 'February Afternoon', during which 'Time swims before me, making as a day / A thousand years'. It is communion with such stable aspects of English landscape that provides the foundation upon which his experience of wholeness is based in 'The Other'. And even as it dissolves, he struggles to convey rationally the satisfying harmony that he has previously described in organic terms:

> Once the name I gave to hours
> Like this was melancholy, when
> It was not happiness and powers
> Coming like exiles home again,
> And weaknesses quitting their bowers,
> Smiled and enjoyed, far off from men,
> Moments of everlastingness.
> And fortunate my search was then
> While what I sought, nevertheless,
> That I was seeking, I did not guess.

Here too, opposing instincts are held in equipoise. While the poem reaches its solitary culmination, its emphasis swings back, via mention of the 'search', to pursuit in the social world. *In Pursuit of Spring* provides a commentary on this lingering euphoria when Thomas, immediately before joining 'the other man', experiences a similar moment of stability in which 'no people or thoughts embarrassed me. I fed through the senses directly but very temperately.'[65] And another poem, actually called 'Melancholy', emphasises that his recognition of such calm is achieved by admission, rather than forgetfulness, of both the tenuous control that he has over it, and of the inevitable presence of contradictory elements:

> What I desired I knew not, but whate'er my choice
> Vain it must be, I knew. Yet naught did my despair
> But sweeten the strange sweetness, while through the wild air
> All day long I heard a distant cuckoo calling

And, soft as dulcimers, sounds of near water falling,
And, softer, and remote as if in history,
Rumours of what had touched my friends, my foes, or me.

In 'The Other' itself the union of earth and sky (or, as he calls it in *In Pursuit of Spring*, 'the marriage of heaven and earth'[66]) results simultaneously in self-knowledge, and recovery of the past. The 'powers / Coming like exiles home again' are those abilities which were suffocated by the years of prose writing, and their recovery is accompanied by the removal of his social alienation. Although his rapture is experienced 'far off from men', it is safe in the belief that the community of which he has become a member is not confined to the present, but includes 'the days of Wordsworth, of Elizabeth, of Richard Plantagenet, of Harold, of the earliest bards'.[67] In these three central stanzas 'The Other' has already, in a sense, 'reached its climax and solution',[68] but the integration they describe — which is oblique in itself — is challenged still further by the two stanzas which remain. If Thomas's return to the social world simply entailed a repeat performance of trials described in the first third of the poem, narrator and reader could be confident that he would eventually, briefly, recover the goal that he achieved there. But although the tribulations that he suffers are similar in kind to their original counterparts, and although the setting of road and inn recur, their threats and menaces are intensified:

That time was brief: once more at inn
And upon road I sought my man
Till once amid a tap-room's din
Loudly he asked for me, began
To speak, as if it had been a sin,
Of how I thought and dreamed and ran
After him thus, day after day:
He lived as one under a ban
For this: what had I got to say?
I said nothing. I slipped away.

The shifts of emphasis recorded here are not merely from solitude to society, and from wholeness to division. They also involve a return to the tradition of *Doppelgänger* literature. But just as his early association with it was coloured by private demands, so too is the genre adapted to his own ends now. In the precursors of Thomas's 'other' it is usual for the narrator's initial, anxious meetings with his image to develop into horrified repulsion. Jekyll's alarmed confusion is typical: 'I became, in my own person, a creature eaten up and emptied by fever, . . . languidly weak both in body and mind and solely occupied by one thought: the horror of my other self.'[69] In 'The Other', Thomas's original 'eager weariness' is converted to 'dread' in the closing stanzas, and while this conforms to tradition, the change in his attitude is effected by novel means. Where earlier doubles – notably those of *The Confessions of a Justified Sinner*, *Dr Jekyll and Mr Hyde* and *The Double* – had pursued their better selves from the outset, addressing them malevolently or provocatively, it is only in the final moments of his poem that Thomas and his image speak at all. And instead of threatening, 'the other' simply accuses him (correctly) of being the irritating follower. Thomas's fear, in other words, is stimulated by a reversal of the traditional roles (instead of being the pursued he is the pursuer), and by the eventual confounding of those expectations that he had cherished (instead of achieving a welcome reunion he is angrily rebuffed). This confusion of both traditional and personal expectations is deepened by the stanza's intrinsic complexity. Why is Thomas's longed-for meeting so unheralded and precipitate, and why does he have nothing to say, when he has – directly or indirectly – rehearsed a conversation for the previous ninety lines? In *In Pursuit of Spring* a moment of stability had similarly preceded a meeting with 'the other man', and there the sense of well-being spilled over into the encounter itself. In 'The Other', each of the two selves is unremittingly hostile. And it is precisely this antagonism which provides an explanation of the apparently arbitrary meeting. What confronts Thomas is not so much the anger of a distinct entity as the disappointment he feels at failing to prolong the wholeness described in previous stanzas. He realises that he must continue to pursue it despite the difficulties which will beset his journey. In other words, Thomas 'bans' himself from rejecting his quest, and thereby commits himself to a long search for contentment which will only be intermittently rewarded. The self-inflicted rigours of his pursuit jeopardise a conventional, peaceful, social existence, as a more extreme, but none the less related, moment in another account of a double confirms. Frankenstein, on his return from an interview with his horrendous creation, admits to feeling 'as if I were placed under a ban – as if I had no right to claim [my family's] sympathies'.[70] The similarity of phrasing burns through more general differences of situation to illuminate

Thomas's dilemma. Just as the 'home' to which his 'powers' returned during his moment of ecstasy was not a material building but an internal condition, so too will happiness only be possible in the future if he continues his pursuit and distinguishes the perils of forgetful ease from the rewards of unselfconsciousness.

Where Thomas's 'Moments of everlastingness' succeeded in reconciling opposing forces into a harmonious whole, the encounter with his other self arranges them into positions of hostility. Enthusiasm, friendliness, and the prospect of artistic fulfilment are subdued by — rather than poised against — despair, fear and the prospect of compromise. Although apparently unforeseen by the narrator himself, this conclusion has been anticipated by preceding stanzas. The self-consciousness of which he had complained, and which had featured prominently both as a cause and as a symptom of his self-division, is represented in its most marked form by this final point-blank confrontation with his own image. The intensity of his experience is stressed by the fact that although he remained eloquent during his earlier moment of integration — despite its elements of unworldliness — he is now struck silent. Union with his elusive goal cannot be achieved without the removal of self-consciousness, and it is the pervasive presence of this difficulty which is emphasised in the final stanza of the poem:

> And now I dare not follow after
> Too close. I try to keep in sight,
> Dreading his frown and worse his laughter.
> I steal out of the wood to light;
> I see the swift shoot from the rafter
> By the inn door: ere I alight
> I wait and hear the starlings wheeze
> And nibble like ducks: I wait his flight.
> He goes: I follow: no release
> Until he ceases. Then I also shall cease.

The nervous concluding phrases embody a last acknowledgement of, and deviation from, the received characteristics of *Doppelgänger* literature. Traditionally it is not, as Edna Longley says, 'death to meet one's *Doppelgänger* face to face',[71] but death to destroy one's image, as William Wilson, Jekyll, and Dorian Gray discover to their cost. 'The Other', however, does not rise to a murderous finale, but describes a continuous, fearful obedience in which all promise of 'release' both depends upon and is cancelled by its rhyme word 'cease'. The exodus that Thomas makes from 'The Other', still engaged in pursuit but now unhampered by illusions, may be enlightened, but it is also hazardous. The very fact that it echoes so much of the opening stanza suggests that the conclusion only returns him to the beginning of his search. And although this is moderated by the increase of self-knowledge, it is also emphasised by the intensification of his original statements. 'I felt fear' is multiplied into 'I dare not', 'dreading', and 'I steal out', and the initial relaxing harmony of bees, grass, mint and inn is replaced by isolation: instead of entering the inn, Thomas waits outside for his double to emerge. The posture that he adopts towards his image is one of respectful caution. Even the hint that his experience of integration will be repeated is overshadowed. The starlings which 'wheeze / And nibble like ducks' parody his search for fulfilment, and introduce a grotesque element which suggests that his attainment of it will be neither easy nor permanent.

II

Although 'The Other' ends by admitting the difficulties of complete fulfilment, it nevertheless celebrates Thomas's emergence from the forest of prose. Moreover, the unillusioned discovery of a medium which at least has the potential to express the full range of his personality is enriched by the use of a symbol which was to structure and characterise many of his subsequent poems: the journey. As 'The Other' itself illustrates, the journey and not the arrival provides him with the wholeness he seeks, because it is there that self-consciousness is at a minimum. In addition to this, the fact that his relationship with himself and his medium remains one of diligent searching rather than static intimacy, ensures that his imaginative and formal inventiveness stay undiminished. But it is not only as a prophecy that 'The Other' earns its crucial position in Thomas's work. It stands as a hinge between the frustrating years of prose writing and the 'new freedom' of poems. In those which follow, his position is frequently still one of compromise, but the haunting presence of the *Doppelgänger* is mellowed into a more reticent form of double vision. The 'enemy at his side and in his brain', and the 'self-consciousness . . . amounting to a disease' which led him to conceive of the ideal and the actual as two distinct entities, are modulated into an ability to detect within any given mood, situation or event an opposite or alternative to whatever perception immediately suggests itself. The pursuit of artistic, social and organic stability is undertaken in the certainty that its discovery will include knowledge of hardship, frustration and disappointment.

'The Glory' is an interesting example. Like so many of Thomas's poems, it offers a chance of ecstatic communion similar to that described in 'The Other', only to record the difficulty he finds in enjoying it:

> The glory of the beauty of the morning, —
> The cuckoo crying over the untouched dew;
> The blackbird that has found it, and the dove
> That tempts me on to something sweeter than love;
> White clouds ranged even and fair as new-mown hay;
> The heat, the stir, the sublime vacancy
> Of sky and meadow and forest and my own heart: —
> The glory invites me, yet it leaves me scorning
> All I can ever do, all I can be,
> Beside the lovely of motion, shape, and hue,
> The happiness I fancy fit to dwell
> In beauty's presence.

Faced thus with his shortcomings, Thomas debates whether to imitate the harmony experienced by unselfaware 'happy-seeming things / . . . in the hazel copse', or to resign himself to frustration and 'be content with discontent / As larks and swallows are perhaps with wings'. But the limitations to his happiness contain reticently hopeful and regenerative elements. 'Larks and swallows' are not only 'perhaps' discontent, but the comparison of his own condition with their obvious and energetic freedom makes his sense of confinement ironic. This recognition of potential escape from the 'dreary-swift' progress of time (itself a consoling paradox) is confirmed in the final lines:

> . . . shall I perhaps know
> That I was happy oft and oft before,
> Awhile forgetting how I am fast pent,
> How dreary-swift, with naught to travel to,
> Is Time? I cannot bite the day to the core.

Statement and language here pull in opposite directions. The former is despairing, but the latter — because its crisp diction suggests that 'he knows fully what "biting" means and involves'[72] — is affirmative. It provides an instance of Thomas's double vision operating to reveal the whole range of his feelings, with scrupulous honesty.

This truthfulness extends to his descriptions of isolation from people as well as nature. Social alienation was a problem with which he was preoccupied from his earliest years ('social intercourse is only an intense form of solitude'[73] — 1904), throughout his middle years ('Friends, Nature, books are like London pavements when an east wind has made them dry, harsh & pitiless. There is no joy in them'[74] — 1908), to the end ('Please forgive me and try not to give any thought to this flat grey shore which surprises the tide by being inaccessible to it'[75] — 1913). It frequently led him to believe that death would be a preferable alternative. 'Lights Out' and 'Rain' provide the most extreme poetic statements of this kind, but even their moments of extreme despair — like those in 'The Other' — contain the confession that he would be loath to resign his participation in the conscious, active world. In 'Rain', for instance, his longing for death is qualified by a doubt that it is possible to love 'what is perfect and / Cannot, the tempest tells me, disappoint'. And in 'The Attempt' he actually ridicules his own suicidal instincts by admitting their 'gloss of heroism and the kind of superficial ceremoniousness which was unconsciously much to his taste'.[76] A letter to Bottomley makes clear this ambivalence:

> How nice it would be to be dead if only we could know we were dead. That is what I hate, the not being able to turn round in the grave and to say 'It is over'. With me I suppose it is vanity: I don't want to do so difficult a thing as dying without any chance of applause after having done it.[77]

Although these temperamental problems threaten the traditional aspects of landscape upon which Thomas depends for wholeness, the tradition itself is seen as adaptable and permanent. In over twenty poems birds articulate the communion that he seeks: in 'The Glory', for instance, he celebrates

> The blackbird that has found it, and the dove
> That tempts me on to something sweeter than love.

And in 'Thaw' it is rooks that see 'What we below could not see, Winter pass'. The harmony birds express is often denied more than fleeting recognition but, as 'The Word' illustrates, is nevertheless a dependable source of comfort:

> While perhaps I am thinking of the elder scent
> That is like food, or while I am content
> With the wild rose scent that is like memory,
> This name suddenly is cried out to me
> From somewhere in the bushes by a bird
> Over and over again, a pure thrush word.

There are an equally large number of poems in which solitary, rural vagabonds suggest the same stability.[78] Jack Noman of 'May 23', 'shovel-bearded Bob' of 'Bob's Lane', and the interlocutors of such poems as 'Man and Dog' and 'House and Man' are, like the Leech Gatherer of Wordsworth's 'Resolution and Independence', so closely identified with their landscapes as to be almost indistinguishable from them. Culminating in 'Lob', their uninterrupted appearance over the centuries represents a tireless integration with the natural world which Thomas admires and wishes to emulate. But as is so often the case with the birdsong mentioned above, he is unable to share their communion for long. Their involvement with the natural world frequently amounts to a vanishing, as the conclusion of 'Man and Dog' illustrates:

> Stiffly he plodded;
> And at his heels the crisp leaves scurried fast,
> And the leaf-coloured robin watched. They passed,
> The robin till next day, the man for good,
> Together in the twilight of the wood.

This slow-moving solitary seems to be losing the race against crisp, scurrying leaves which will bury him. Yet his identification with the robin contains the muted possibility of survival. The fact that the robin is itself 'leaf-coloured' implies that it has been buried by leaves in the past as surely as the man will be in the future. But the process has not eliminated it so much as blurred its transition from one generation to another. Similarly, Jack Noman's disappearing 'for good' carries with it the prospect of benefit as well as perpetual loss: the ambiguity suggests exactly that blend of oppression and adaptability which 'Lob' explores.

This harmonious balance is struck throughout the poems, and often shows alternative worlds actually melting together. The song of 'The

Unknown Bird' is *'sad* only with *joy'*; in the 'Elysium' of 'Ambition' 'all
the folk astir / Made only plumes of *pearly* smoke to tower / Over *dark*
trees and *white* meadows'; the rain in 'Sowing' is 'half a *kiss*, half a
tear'; the *'bright* clouds of May / *Shade* half the pond' in 'The Pond'
and the birds of 'Two Pewits' are

> More *white* than is the moon on high
> Riding the *dark* surge silently;
> More *black* than earth.

This simultaneous recognition and acceptance of opposite elements in a
single moment is frequently complemented by a twilight setting — the
time, in Frost's words, of 'opposing light'[79] — in which the suggestive
worlds of dark and light merge. 'The Bridge', a poem concerned with a
moment of release from the oppression of memory as well as the threat
of the future, is typical:

> I have come a long way today:
> On a strange bridge alone,
> Remembering friends, old friends,
> I rest, without smile or moan,
> As they remember me without smile or moan.

Standing on a literal bridge, which is also a withdrawal from both day
and night and future and past, Thomas experiences a 'moment brief
between / Two lives'. But the falling night which embraces him, and
stimulates his release, does not only reconcile opposites by containing
'first lights / And shades'. At the same time as it presents him with the
chance of perceiving his ideal, it denies it:

> No traveller has rest more blest
> Than this moment brief between
> Two lives, when the Night's first lights
> And shades hide what has never been,
> Things goodlier, lovelier, dearer, than will be or have been.

Benefit and losses are contained in a single identical event to create a
balance which is clarified by the structure of the stanzas. His rhyming,
as Edna Longley says, 'appropriately suggests both progress and a state
of suspension. The internal rhymes in the first and third lines of each

stanza maintain a forward impetus which is retarded by the similar endings of the last two lines. The latter creates a curious effect of stasis or hiatus, as if the poem refuses to move on to a full rhyme or any kind of further conclusion but remains itself a "bridge" '.[80]

An equivalent moment of breathless, suspended integration is suggested by Thomas's intertwining of distinct seasons. Like the twilight setting, it is a means of recording a transition which is, paradoxically, stable. Such moments occur frequently in the prose books — the orchard in *Beautiful Wales*, for instance, where the blossom of all the trees 'was the same, so that they seemed to be Winter with the frail Spring in his arms'[81] — and in 'The Manor Farm', the ecstatic 'season of bliss unchangeable' is similarly withdrawn from the diurnal round by being an amalgam of all seasons:

> The Winter's cheek flushed as if he had drained
> Spring, Summer, and Autumn at a draught.

Again, in the fertile stasis of 'Haymaking', he notices that 'The smooth white empty road was lightly strewn / With leaves — the holly's Autumn falls in June —', and in 'The Thrush' he admits that 'April I love for what / It was born of, and November / For what it will die in'. The harmonious fusion described in these and all such passages stands as a witness to the benefits so slowly acquired in 'The Other'. Originally the oppression of prose writing had caused a hiatus between the articulacy he envisaged and that which he produced, and in doing so it had permanently threatened his apprehension of wholeness. In the congenial freedom of poetry, however, the acute sense of division represented by the *Doppelgänger* quickly developed into a capacity to see the potential for gain in the certainty of loss. This double vision constitutes a refusal by Thomas to settle for easy and firm conclusions, and leaves him in a position of anxious honesty with neither 'the benefit of the intellectual certainty of universal let-down, nor the enfolding comfort (a paradoxical consolation) of the settled romantic melancholy'.[82] It allows him to comprehend failure and fulfilment simultaneously, and, in every poem, justifies the statement of his poetic philosophy given at the end of 'Liberty' with an appropriate echo of Keats:

> And yet I still am half in love with pain,
> With what is imperfect, with both tears and mirth,
> With things that have an end, with life and earth,
> And this moon that leaves me dark within the door.

CHAPTER THREE
THE SOUND OF SENSE

I

On 5 October 1913 Thomas wrote to Eleanor Farjeon: 'My dear Eleanor, Will you forgive me if I do not turn up tomorrow? I have an appointment of uncertain time with an American . . . and may not be able to come.'[1] The American was Robert Frost, who in the years since this first meeting has become accepted as the man who found Thomas's tongue for him,[2] 'helped to thrust him out of the old nest of prose',[3] and who 'at once knew that he could and would write poetry and accepted him as a poet on equal terms'.[4] Until Frost's return to America on 13 February 1915, he and Thomas met regularly — first in London, and then in Gloucestershire after Frost had moved to Ledington to be near the homes of Wilfred Gibson and Lascelles Abercrombie. During this time the caution of Thomas's first reference ripened into a friendship which was as important for both men as it is for their literary heirs. Yet those appreciations of it which exist are frequently content to rehearse circumstantial details, and ignore the fact that Thomas evolved independently many of the verse theories he is thought to have learnt from Frost.

Frost's own verdict that 'Thomas frequently and generously admitted that he was my debtor not only in verse theory but in inspiration'[5] has done as much to obscure the real character of their literary relationship as early reviews. These often seemed motivated more by patriotism than by critical acumen. On the English front, Edward Garnett mentioned Frost's name so casually that no actual connection need be made: 'some of [the] poems are as new a departure in English verse as was

Mr. Robert Frost's *North of Boston* in American verse';[6] and de la Mare, when his foreword to the *Collected Poems* was reset sixteen years after he had written it, chose to retain his original statement that 'late in life there came to [Thomas] this sudden creative impulse, the incentive of a new form'.[7] Across the Atlantic, Conrad Aiken thought the poems 'not, perhaps, the work of a born poet ... the sense of rhythm is imperfect';[8] and Louis Untermeyer found 'the genius, the influence, the inflection, even the idiom of Robert Frost ... in almost all these English pages'.[9] Eleanor Farjeon, however — who frequently saw the two men together — described the effect of Frost's encouragement in terms which properly suggest that Thomas's poetry was not an imposed alien medium but a natural buried one:

> In the autumn of 1914 Edward's own living stream was undammed. The undamming was Robert's doing when, after reading his friend's prose, he told him he had been a poet all his life. . . . and produced . . . the enharmonic change that made him not a different man, but the same man in another key.[10]

Frost's ability to release Thomas's poems was at least partly the result of close resemblances between their histories and characters. At the time of their meeting Frost was thirty-eight, for the previous twenty years he had failed to interest the American public and publishers in his poems, and he had recently come to England in a (successful) attempt to sell his poems. Thomas was four years younger, for the previous sixteen years he had become increasingly entangled in journalism and commissioned prose work, and he had abandoned hope of ever writing anything which accurately expressed his full personality. In *The Happy-Go-Lucky Morgans* he had described himself as the prisoner of his profession:

> [His books] are known only to students at the British Museum who get them out once and no more, for they discover hasty compilations, ill-arranged, inaccurate, and incomplete, and swollen to a ridiculous size for the sake of gain.[11]

It was a wilderness of a different kind from Frost's, but a wilderness none the less. Both men had threatened suicide, both had absented themselves from their wives for days, and both had repeatedly hurt themselves in attempts to unfetter themselves. As Frost's biographer says, 'When their identically light-blue eyes met, each may have felt that he saw himself mirrored. Obviously they had more in common than a love of literature.'[12] It is, indeed, revealing to express their sympathy in (even) more dramatic terms — ones that Thomas would have relished: 'one senses that Thomas, but for his voice, was almost Frost's double in some aspects of personality'.[13]

Thomas's escape from prose is the more remarkable for occurring at a time when his hopes had reached their nadir. Frost himself said, 'I met [him] at his unhappiest',[14] and a letter from Thomas to his aunt early in 1914 confirms this:

> I am lacking in a sense of the whole of human life outside my own.
> . . . Even ambition would be a help, but I do not possess it. . . .
> Stronger than [my failure to express myself adequately] is my self
> obsession, and its consequence, the indulgence in . . . simple, ever-
> unsatisfactory pleasures.[15]

His sense of imprisonment was so complete that it denied him any sense of potential escape except by death. He asked Frost: 'why worry about a process that may terminate a kind of life which I keep saying couldn't be worse?'[16] In answering this, and in providing Thomas with the confidence to begin writing, Frost showed his own indebtedness to the philosopher William James — whom he described as 'A teacher who influenced me most I never had'.[17] Much of Frost's career up to this point had been 'a struggle against excessive fear of anything, real or imagined, if it seemed dangerous or difficult or painful',[18] and he had taken comfort from James's comment in *The Will to Believe* that 'so far as man stands for anything, and is productive or originative at all, his entire vital function may be said to have to deal with maybes. . . . It is only by risking our persons from one hour to another that we live at all.'[19] This acceptance of imponderables, and its accompanying awareness that 'All a man's art is a bursting unity of opposites',[20] paralleled and confirmed Thomas's growing belief that moments of happiness must be enjoyed by inclusion, rather than ignorance, of the realities of hardship. But the importance of James for Frost, and through him for Thomas, was not merely that he strengthened their resolve to hold life's opposing forces in a fruitful balance. He also stimulated self-confidence by insisting that 'a certain kind of selfishness . . . had to be asserted by the artist, in particular, for his fulfillment'.[21] In his *Psychology: Briefer Course* James had argued that 'each mind . . . must have a certain minimum of selfishness . . . in order to exist',[22] and in 1912 Thomas himself had similarly recorded the need for 'egotistical intensity'[23] in a writer, while mourning his own lack of it. This quality formed the essential ingredient of Frost's encouragement. His frequent demonstration that he possessed it in full measure animated the exemplary function that he was able to perform, and less than six months after the first meeting, Thomas began to feel its force: 'I wonder whether you can imagine me taking to verse? If you can I might get over the feeling that it is impossible – which at once obliges your good nature to say "I can".'[24] Paradoxically, the acute degree of Thomas's unhappiness made success more likely. During Frost's own disappointments, 'self-abasement and guilt [had] accumulated in him until it became a despairing kind of self-hatred'[25] exactly as it had in Thomas. The insights that this gave brought poetry perceptibly closer by cementing their friendship. Just as Frost called Thomas 'the only brother I ever had',[26] so Thomas called Frost 'the only person I can be idle with',[27] and said that 'the next best thing to having you here is having the space (not a void) that nobody else can fill'.[28]

Although the burden of reviewing did much to create the delay in Thomas's approach to poetry, it brought rewards as well. It gave him a profound knowledge of contemporary literature, offered him the opportunity to define his beliefs, and provided him with a platform from which he could publicise his preferences. His reaction to the Georgians, and his sympathy with many of their aims, has already been discussed in the Introduction, but his poetic theories began to form long before the publication of their first anthology. From the outset, his reviews had argued that the language of poetry should be colloquial. As early as 1901 he said that 'the best lyrics seem to be in poets' natural speech',[29] and throughout his regular and enthusiastic reviews of W. H. Davies, he championed his friend's 'ordinary diction, which never fails to convince us that we are listening to the honest voice of one who has met life simply and passionately'.[30] The same conviction was restated when, in a notice of W. B. Yeats's *Poems* (1908), Thomas admitted to being 'more than ever struck by the beauty of the ordinary speeches which, in their naturalness and real poetry, prove as much as Wordsworth's *Preface* that the speech of poetry can be that of life'.[31]

But his insistence did not confine itself to matters of vocabulary. A natural idiom without the animation of a voice ran the risk of dullness, and it was to avoid this that he evolved more intricate poetic arguments. In blank verse that he admired, he repeatedly pointed out how closely the form corresponded to the rhythms and pauses of talk, and praised any dramatisation of this sympathy which was achieved by adding or omitting feet. His judgment of Bottomley's *The Crier by Night*

(1902) is characteristic: 'The dialogue is remarkably monosyllabic, and modulated with such infinite legitimate variations as make the blank verse perhaps the most delicate of our time.'[32] Two years later, reviewing Yeats's *The King's Threshold*, he made clear the fruitful similarities between varied blank verse and the natural tones of voice:

> 'Speech delighted with its own music' is the best definition of
> Mr. Yeats' verse. He can do everything with it. He is incapable of
> using blank verse, as so many have done, as a mould with a few
> variations, into which anything can be poured. The thoughts and
> emotions of his characters may be seen to mould the verse. . . . Verse
> is the natural speech of men, as singing is of birds.[33]

This enthusiasm for what he called elsewhere 'the beautiful, but apparently irregular, varieties of blank verse'[34] constituted the foundation of his receptivity to Frost's theories. Thomas's ideas are based on the certainty that a speaking voice is best reproduced by using the phrase, rather than the foot, as the metrical unit. It is this ordering principle which allows natural speech to dominate metre, as he makes plain in one of his earliest articles on prosody. Reviewing Mark H. Liddell's *An Introduction to the Scientific Study of English Poetry* (1902) he approvingly quotes the author's opinion that 'the aesthetic arrangement of the thought moments is as vital an element of [English poetry] as are the aesthetic arrangements of stressed and unstressed syllables which mark these moments off for us'. When amplifying this, Thomas provides an abstract of the techniques that he was to employ himself, twelve years later:

> He speaks of 'thought moments' instead of 'phrases' because 'it is
> important here to dissociate them from words and to think of them
> as groups of notions'. . . . It is not a new system of prosody, though
> it makes the old one ridiculous. It affords no basis for a classification
> of metres; it leaves blank verse, as before, an infinitely varied line
> usually of ten syllables.[35]

In addition to prophesying his own practice, this extract summarises an essential feature of Frost's verse theory — namely, the necessary tension between the regular pre-established measure of metre, and the irregular measure of speech, in a line of blank verse. Another review of Liddell's book returns to the same theme, maintaining that 'stress in Shakespeare and in all good poetry is so exquisitely varied that the question of accents is impertinent'.[36] Throughout the following years, Thomas continued to argue that verse consists of 'such sounds and silences as can be co-ordinated by the ear . . . and exists by virtue of the simple time-relations between the units of sound'.[37] When Frost arrived in England, as his biographer says, 'he knew very well that he was not accurate in claiming that his was a one-man battle against "the assumption that the music of words was a matter of harmonised vowels and consonants" '.[38] Thomas had not only already established himself as the champion of close correspondence between poetry and familiar speech, he had also clarified the means by which blank verse might be made to imply the vocal inflexions, accents and gestures of its author.

The steady development of Thomas's beliefs is defined in the abstract by his reviews, but in practical terms by his attempts to find a more suitable form in which to demonstrate them. His complaint to Bottomley in 1904 that 'There is no form that suits me & I doubt if I can make a new form'[39] misrepresents the scale of his search. Even at this stage he was 'experimenting with pure observation and description, more rounded evocation of the countryside, the largely meditative or fanciful essay, "episodes", portraits and thinly disguised self-portraits, fantasies, [and] even eventually the novel'.[40] Later remarks substantiate this impression of thorough inquiry. In 1909 he told Bottomley: 'I am casting about for subjects which will compel me to depend simply on what I am — memory included but in a due subsidiary place.'[41] It was the same criterion which eventually led him to his only attempt at novel-writing, *The Happy-Go-Lucky Morgans*, which he described as 'a loose affair held together if at all by an oldish suburban home, half memory, half fancy. . . . The scheme allows me to use all memories up to the age of 20, and so far I have indulged myself freely. I feel however that it will be better than isolated essays & sketches . . . & more honest than the other pseudo-continuous books I have written.'[42] By the time he met Frost, he realised that the search for a form which would be true to himself had led to self-portraiture, and accordingly, in 1913, he wrote part of a straightforward autobiography, *The Childhood of Edward Thomas*. Because he considered the piece 'too dull or intimate for publication',[43] it allowed him to continue his self-discovery without any danger of alienating the public he relied on for income. In addition, and equally significant for the poems which were to follow, the style of *The Childhood* is plainer than anything that preceded it. As he suggests himself, it practises the 'thought moments' of which he had preached the benefits ten years before: 'I had feelings which I could not have explained as to forms of expression; I had at the back of my mind sometimes what seemed to me a right phrase and I groped for it.'[44]

This gradual exorcism of youthful rhetoric is also charted in Thomas's critical studies of other writers. In the retrospective account of his prose career, 'How I Began' (1913), he says:

> I ravaged the language (to the best of my ability) at least as much for ostentation as for use. . . . This must always happen where a man has collected all the colours of the rainbow, 'of earthquake and eclipse', on his palette, and has a cottage or a gasometer to paint. A continual negotiation was going on between thought, speech and writing, thought having as a rule the worst of it. Speech was humble and creeping, but wanted too many fine shades and could never come to a satisfactory end. Writing was lordly and regardless. Thought went on in the twilight, and wished the other two might come to terms for ever.[45]

The (by now familiar) insistence on speech owes nothing to Frost's example, although a celebrated letter to him in 1914 has obscured this fact:

> You really should start doing a book on speech and literature, or you will find me mistaking your ideas for mine and doing it myself. You can't prevent me from making use of them: I do so daily, and want to begin over again with them and wring all the necks of my rhetoric — the geese. However, my *Pater* would show you I had got onto the scent already.[46]

Frost, with characteristic egotism, wrote to a friend that 'Thomas thinks he will write a book on what my definition of the sentence means for literary criticism'.[47] But as the above evidence indicates, Thomas had been wringing necks even before his critical appraisal of Pater appeared. His complaint of 1898, 'What a small man Pater is! He is always talking about style',[48] and his irritation in 1904 that modern poetry 'had left the praise of rain to hop farmers and mud to boot blacks',[49] culminate in his studies of Lafcadio Hearn (1912), Swinburne (1912), and Pater himself (1913).

In 1907 Thomas had told Bottomley: 'I get more and more dissatisfied with Pater. His work seems fatally external to him.'[50] When, five years later, he came to discuss Hearn's early work, it was to precisely this quality that he objected again. He called the style 'a cumbrous English, stiffened with beauties which do not make it beautiful',[51] and insisted that 'such eloquence rarely has any natural sweet cadence'.[52]

In the two later critical studies this plea for simplicity is enlarged — as it was in the reviews — to include a discussion of means by which to capture the tones of a speaking voice. Thomas's charge against Swinburne that 'he was one of those . . . who seem to shape their thought in order that it may fit a certain favourite type of sentence instead of allowing the thought to govern the form of the sentence'[53] is developed throughout *Pater* into a sustained attack on the absence of speech rhythms:

> Pater has attained an exquisite unnaturalness. He has created a prose of such close pattern and rich material that almost any piece of it is an honest and beauteous sample. . . . It is, however, careful as a rule not to offend the ear, and thus is made a kind of lucid vacuum in which the forms and colours can appear as beyond the purest glass for display.[54]

This castigation of Pater's 'hard and stationary refinement',[55] and the simultaneous emphasis that 'literature has to arrange words in such a manner that they will do all that a speaker can do',[56] embodies the most detailed and strongly phrased of all Thomas's articles of faith. Even by itself it illustrates his anticipation of Frost's poetic techniques, but the long (and usually ignored) perspective of reviews which lies behind it should ensure that his independence is not questioned. Although Frost's public version of their relationship stated that Thomas was his debtor 'not only in verse theory but in inspiration', his private verdict is nearer the truth. Writing to the American poet Grace Walcott Conkling on 28 June 1921, he estimated it in terms which exactly echo the evidence of Thomas's reviews, and his long process of self-discovery in prose:

> You will be careful, I know, not to say anything to exalt either of us at the expense of the other. There's a story going round that might lead you to exaggerate our debt to each other. Anything we may be thought to have in common we had before we met. When Hodgson introduced us at a coffee house in London in 1913 I had written two and a half of my three books[,] he had written all but two or three of thirty. The most our congeniality could do was confirm us both in what we were. There was never a moment's thought about who may have been influencing whom. The least rivalry of that kind would have taken something from our friendship. We were greater friends than almost any two ever were practising the same art.

I don't mean that we did nothing for each other. As I have said we encouraged each other in our adventurous ways. Beyond that anything we did was very practical. He gave me standing as a poet — he more than anyone else, though of course I have to thank Abercrombie, Hueffer, Pound and some others for help too. I dragged him out from under the heap of his own work in prose he was buried alive under. He was throwing to his big perfunctory histories of Marlborough and the like written to order such poetry as would make him a name if he were but given credit for it. I made him see that he owed it to himself and the poetry to have it out by itself in poetic form where it must suffer itself to be admired. It took me some time. I bantered, teased and bullied all the summer we were together at Ledington and Ryton. All he had to do was put his poetry in a form that declared itself. The theme must be the same, the accent exactly the same. He saw it and he was tempted. It was plain that he had wanted to be a poet all the years he had been writing about poets not worth his little finger. But he was afeared (though a soldier). His timidity was funny and fascinating. I had about given him up, he had turned his thoughts to enlistment and I mine to sailing for home when he wrote his first poem. The decision he made in going into the army helped him make the other decision to be a poet in form. And a very fine poet. And a poet all in his own right. The accent is absolutely his own. You can hear it everywhere in his prose, where if he had left it, however, it would have been lost.

You won't quote me in any of this please. It is much too personal. I simply wanted you to know. . . . The point is that what we had in common we had from before we were born . . . don't tell anyone we gave each other anything but a boost.[57]

Frost's 'practical' advice took two distinct forms, both of which were only made effective by his example: advising Thomas to recast prose originals, and complementing his theory of 'thought moments' with his own of 'the sound of sense'. Frost himself properly lays the greater stress on his recommendation to plunder the prose: 'Right at that moment he was writing as good poetry as anybody alive, but in prose form where it did not declare itself. I referred him to paragraphs in his book *In Pursuit of Spring* and told him to write it in verse form in exactly the same cadence.'[58] Thomas, who hardly needed to be told to preserve 'the same cadence', had rejected similar suggestions from his other friends. Bottomley, for example, recorded how he told him that certain passages in *The Heart of England* would be more effective as poetry: 'He replied, "It is strange that you should say this: I spent the night with de la Mare on my way North to you and he said the same thing". I felt sure there was a solution for him on those lines, and that he would find new liberation in verse; and so I urged the experiment on him. He smiled and said "I do not know how".'[59] Advice without approved example was no use to Thomas. But from Frost, with whom he was 'together to the exclusion of every other person and interest',[60] the weight of encouragement broke down barriers which had withheld him in the past. Although he did not turn to *In Pursuit of Spring* in his first poem, it — like those which were to follow — corresponds to an earlier prose passage. The importance of this lies not only in the fact that it enabled him to 'begin over again' and recover his past, but also that it anchored his poems close to prose rhythms which were crucial to 'the sound of sense'.

It was when staying with Frost in Gloucestershire during April and August 1914 that he discovered how closely his ideas resembled Frost's. 'The living part of a poem', Frost explained,

> is the intonation entangled somehow in the syntax, idiom and mean-
> ing of a sentence. It is only there for those who have heard it previ-
> ously in conversation. . . . It goes and the language becomes a dead
> language, the poetry dead poetry. With it go the accents, the stresses,
> the delays that are not the property of vowels and syllables but that
> are shifted at will with the sense. Vowels have length there is no
> denying. But the accent of sense supercedes all other accent, over-
> rides and sweeps it away.[61]

Frost distinguished the 'accent of sense' from free verse by insisting that it is 'only lovely when thrown and drawn and displayed across spaces of the footed line'.[62] Mere free verse was as unrewarding as mere words without an overall sentence sound: 'a sentence is a sound on which other sounds called words may be strung . . . you may string words together without a sentence-sound to string them on just as you may tie clothes together by the sleeves and stretch them without a clothes line between two trees, but — it is bad for the clothes'.[63] As is so often the case, the efficacy of Frost's 'poetic revolution' depended on the adaptation, and not the abandonment of existing conventions. By taking a step forward it was possible to take a step back into the use of a fundamental resource of language:

the sound of sense existed before words, that something in the voice or vocal gesture made primitive man convey a meaning to his fellow before the race developed a more elaborate and concrete symbol of communication in language. . . . thinking more deeply, not in the speculative sense of science and scholarship, he carried out Carlyle's assertion that if you 'think deeply enough you think musically'.[64]

Although it closely resembled Thomas's beliefs in essentials, Frost's theory was more forcibly and confidently argued: it had the authority of practice. But in his response, Thomas immediately showed his under- standing and sympathy, only pausing to warn his friend of the same dangers of over-simplicity that he had found in others: 'I felt I missed some necessary vividness in avoiding mere "poetry",' he wrote in February 1914; 'I hope I was wrong.'[65] And in his appreciations of Frost's second book, *North of Boston* (during August 1914), he gave full play to his familiarity with its intentions. His three reviews are the eloquent culmination of ideas that he had formed alone, and contain an implicit faith in the relationship between the prose of his past and the poetry of his future:

Mr Frost has, in fact, gone back as Whitman and as Wordsworth went back, through the paraphernalia of poetry into poetry again. . . . It is a beautiful achievement, and I think a unique one, as perfectly Mr. Frost's own as his vocabulary, the ordinary English speech of a man accustomed to poetry and philosophy, more colloquial and idiomatic than the ordinary man dares to use even in a letter, almost entirely lacking the emphatic forms of journalists and other rhetori- cians, and possessing a kind of healthy natural delicacy like Words- worth's, or at least like Shelley's, rather than that of Keats.[66]

In the *English Review* he referred to Wordsworth again in order to dis- cuss the retrospectively revolutionary nature of the book:

The new volume marks more than the beginning of an experiment like Wordsworth's, but with this difference, that Mr Frost knows the life of which he writes rather as Dorothy Wordsworth did. That is to say, he sympathises where Wordsworth contemplates. The result is a unique type of eclogue, homely, racy, and touched by a spirit that might, under other circumstances, have made pure lyric on one hand or drama on the other. . . . There are moments when the plain lang- uage and lack of violence make the unaffected verses look like prose,

except that the sentences, if spoken aloud, are most felicitously true
in rhythm to the emotion.[67]

During the months to come, when Thomas defended Frost's ideas to his
friends, he did so in the knowledge that he was maintaining values
which he had always held, and which after sixteen years of definition
had achieved their final form by means of Frost's example and encour-
agement:

> [Frost insists on] what he believes he finds in all poets — absolute
> fidelity to the postures which the voice assumes in the most expressive
> intimate speech. So long as these tones and postures are there he
> has not the least objection to any vocabulary whatever or any inver-
> sion or variation from the customary grammatical forms of talk. In
> fact I think he would agree that if these tones and postures survive in
> a complicated and learned or subtle vocabulary and structure the
> result is likely to be better than if they survive in the easiest form,
> that is in the very words and structures of common speech, though
> that is not easy or prose would be better than it is and survive more
> often. . . . As to my own method I expect it to change if there is
> anything more than a doting replica of youthful eagerness in this
> unexpected ebullition.[68]

II

Thomas's 'unexpected ebullition' began late in 1914. After writing a
prose draft, he completed his first poem, 'Up in the Wind', on 3 Decem-
ber. It was two years since he had written to Bottomley, 'it is too late
now, in these anxious & busy times, to set about trying to write better
than perhaps I was meant to',[69] and only one since he had met Frost.
During that time his already well-developed ideas had been matched by
an intensified search for 'a form that will suit me', and in one appeal to
Frost for confidence he provided a vignette which illuminates the
method of 'Up in the Wind': 'I go on writing something every day,
sometimes brief unrestrained impressions of things lately seen, like a
drover with six newly shorn sheep in a line across a cool weedy road on
market morning and me looking back to envy him and him looking
back at me for some reason which I cannot speculate on. Is this north
of Bostonism?'[70] It is, of course, pure Thomas: the delicately unwound
sentence, the tacit confession of alienation from stable harmony, and
the tone of suggestive bafflement were to become constant elements of

his own poetry from 'Up in the Wind' to 'Out in the Dark'. In addition, this 'brief unrestrained impression' is also entirely characteristic in its use of closely observed detail. As 'The Chalk Pit' and 'The Brook' were to confirm, much of the reverberative richness of Thomas's poems is a result of fidelity to observed facts. The exactitude with which he counts the sheep, records their position in the road, describes the road itself, and gives the reason for their journey, prefigures his remark made six months later: 'I should prefer the truth / Or nothing.' The same scrupulousness governs 'Up in the Wind' and the poem's prose draft illustrates the means by which prose helped to restrain the verse within confines of familiar speech. This is the description of the inn-keeper's daughter at the inn called the White Horse:

> 'I should like to wring the old girl's neck for coming away here.' So said the woman who fetched my beer when I found myself at the inn first. She was a daughter of the house, fresh from a long absence in service in London, a bright wildish slattern with a cockney accent and her hair half down. She spoke angrily. If she did not get away before long, she said, she would go mad with the loneliness. She looked out sharply. All she could see there was nothing but the beeches and the tiny pond beneath them and the calves standing in it drinking, alternately grazing the water here and there and thinking, and at last going out and standing still on the bank thinking.[71]

The extract contains the direct speech which is to be given Frost-like inflection in the poem, but its concluding lines are an example of the pausing sentence which was to become one of Thomas's own poetic hallmarks. These two characteristics share a concern that accurate reporting of aural or visual elements should dictate their structure, and neither loses it in the poem's final draft. To take the Frost-like element first:

> 'I could wring the old thing's neck that put it there!
> A public-house! It may be public for birds,
> Squirrels and suchlike, ghosts of charcoal-burners
> And highwaymen.' The wild girl laughed. 'But I
> Hate it since I came back from Kennington.
> I gave up a good place.'

Here Thomas skilfully demonstrates his understanding of Frost's dictum that 'the sentence well imagined is everything'.[72] The interrupted dialogue, agitated running-on of lines, and rejection of strictly decasyllabic form, perfectly illustrate his adaptation of Frost's intention to 'drag and break the intonation across the metre as waves first comb and then break stumbling on the shingle'.[73] This particular exclamatory style is one that Frost himself regularly interweaves with narrative — as, for example, at the end of 'Home Burial':

> '*You* — oh, you think the talk is all. I must go —
> Somewhere out of this house. How can I make you —'
>
> 'If — you — do!' She was opening the door wider.
> 'Where do you mean to go? First tell me that.
> I'll follow and bring you back by force. I *will*!' —

But the overtly dramatic was foreign to Thomas's nature, and he soon abandoned it in favour of a more reflective tone. Even in the closing lines of 'Up in the Wind' this individual accent can be clearly heard:

> Between the open door
> And the trees two calves were wading in the pond,
> Grazing the water here and there and thinking,
> Sipping and thinking, both happily, neither long.
> The water wrinkled, but they sipped and thought,
> As careless of the wind as it of us.
> 'Look at those calves. Hark at the trees again.'

The subdued and observant cadence, by departing from the stridency of the opening lines with their shower of exclamation marks, reflects in miniature Thomas's development as a poet. Although the general situation of the poem resembles many given by Frost ('A Servant to Servants' and 'The Fear' are typical), it bears an equally strong similarity to scenes throughout his own prose. During the two years which remained to him, he seldom reproduced even these personalised echoes of Frost, and in those which do exist[74] the similarity of phrasing is always subordinate to his individual metrical intentions. Only in 'Up in the Wind' does he 'truly imitate the long blank verse structures he chiefly admired in *North of Boston*',[75] and later in December he told Frost: 'I have been shy of blank verse though (or because) I like it best.'[76] It was a verdict that he repeated in his correspondence with John Freeman: 'I have tried as often as possible to avoid the facilities offered by blank verse and I try not to be long — I even have an ambition to keep under 12 lines.'[77] But while he intuitively assumed a metre, tone of voice, and fragmented sentence structure which were his own, he was simultaneously preoccupied by the dangers of over-simplicity. In one review of *North of Boston* he had asserted that Frost's book was 'poetry because it was better than prose',[78] and thereby rephrased Frost's own distinction between the 'accent of sense' and mere free verse. He had, however, already anticipated this in his study of Pater: 'A mere copy of speech might have a different effect from the spoken words, in the absence of the individual voice.'[79] Both men realised that the animation of speaking tones could not be captured by mere transcription, but must be reflected by 'the interplay of the line with other modes of unification'.[80] In 'Up in the Wind' Thomas consistently interrupts his sentences and the decasyllabic metre itself to achieve this effect.

The danger of too much simplicity was matched, as might be expected, by the risk of too little. As late as 1916 he wrote to Frost: 'There is nothing like the solitude of a solitary lake in early morning, when one is in deep still water. More adjectives here than I allow myself now, and fewer verbs.'[81] And previously, he had written to Bottomley explaining that his poems were 'Perhaps . . . only like doing the best parts of my prose in verse & leaving out the connecting futile parts'.[82] Manuscript corrections to his second poem, 'November Sky', show this struggle to purge himself of his rhetorical instincts. In the first instance he slips into vague posturing, and in the second into inertia. The original lines

> And in amongst them clearly printed
> The foot's seal and the wing's light word

and

> Only odd men (who do not matter)
> Care for the mixture of earth and water

become:

> With foot and wing-tip overprinted
> Or separately charactered

and

> Where dead leaves upward and downward scatter.
> Few care for the mixture of earth and water.

Frost was directly responsible for these alterations. Thomas told him, 'I am glad you spotted "wing's light word". I knew it was wrong and also that many would like it: also "odd men" — a touch nearing facetiousness in it.'[83] But on several later occasions Thomas ridiculed such excesses himself — actually within finished poems. In the first version of 'Sedge-Warblers', for instance, he dreams that there was a time which 'would bear / Another beauty, divine and feminine, / Child to the sun', only to make its luxurious fancifulness appear bogus in comparison to the vigour of faithfully recorded facts:

> And yet, rid of this dream, ere I had drained
> Its poison, quieted was my desire
> So that I only looked into the water,
> Clearer than any goddess or man's daughter,
> And hearkened while it combed the dark green hair
> And shook the millions of the blossoms white
> Of water-crowfoot, and curdled to one sheet
> The flowers fallen from the chestnuts in the park
> Far off.

Thomas's analysis of his mature style is not confined to protestations about its simplicity. Although he realised that a deliberately muted tone ran the risk of going unheard altogether, he admitted in the celebrated last lines of 'Aspens' that it must share the resilience and adaptability of the trees to which it is compared:

> All day and night, save winter, every weather,
> Above the inn, the smithy, and the shop,
> The aspens at the cross-roads talk together
> Of rain, until their last leaves fall from the top.
>
> Out of the blacksmith's cavern comes the ringing
> Of hammer, shoe, and anvil; out of the inn
> The clink, the hum, the roar, the random singing —
> The sounds that for these fifty years have been.
>
> The whisper of the aspens is not drowned,
> And over lightless pane and footless road,
> Empty as sky, with every other sound
> Not ceasing, calls their ghosts from their abode,

A silent smithy, a silent inn, nor fails
In the bare moonlight or the thick-furred gloom,
In tempest or the night of nightingales,
To turn the cross-roads to a ghostly room.

And it would be the same were no house near.
Over all sorts of weather, men, and times,
Aspens must shake their leaves and men may hear
But need not listen, more than to my rhymes.

Whatever wind blows, while they and I have leaves
We cannot other than an aspen be
That ceaselessly, unreasonably grieves,
Or so men think who like a different tree.

The poem — which Frost judged 'the loveliest of them all'[84] — describes what Thomas called 'a personally-conducted tour to the recesses'[85] without any of the disingenuous wonderment that distinguishes his friend's approach to a similar subject in 'The Sound of Trees'. It affirms that poetry comes to him as naturally as leaves to a tree, and demonstrates how, even when tentatively and cautiously described, 'the whisper of the aspens is not drowned', but rises to a final relaxed statement of confidence in his role and ability. This intention to 'whisper' rather than speak aloud as Frost did, was re-emphasised in another self-definition, 'I never saw that land before'. Here too, the use of 'a language not to be betrayed' is only made possible by the fidelity of words to the scene they describe. It is, as Thomas says himself, the same language that 'the trees and birds' use, and entitles him to the knowledge that

> . . . what was hid should still be hid
> Excepting from those like me made
> Who answer when such whispers bid.

In spite of their beautifully judged humility, both 'Aspens' and 'I never saw that land before' contain 'unobtrusive defiance as well as self-deprecation'.[86] And he identifies a similar union of modesty and strength in words themselves. Their potential to be 'light as dreams,/ Tough as oak' depends on the sympathetic handling which he frequently denied them in his prose: 'Words never consent to correspond exactly to any object unless, like scientific terms, they are first killed. Hence the curious life of words in the hands of those who love all life so well that they do not kill even the slender words but let them play on; and such are poets. . . . grown men with dictionaries are as murderous of words as entomologists of butterflies.'[87] This quality of delicate toughness does not simply determine the principal elements of his style, but actually dictates his response to experience. As the previous chapter indicated, he repeatedly creates an equipoise in which idealistic and realistic forces are fleetingly weighed against each other. In his poem 'Two Pewits', he summarises all his linguistic intentions as an endeavour to forge a style suited to keeping all options open and available:

> Under the after-sunset sky
> Two pewits sport and cry,
> More white than is the moon on high
> Riding the dark surge silently;
> More black than earth. Their cry
> Is the one sound under the sky.
> They alone move, now low, now high,
> And merrily they cry
> To the mischievous Spring sky,
> Plunging earthward, tossing high,
> Over the ghost who wonders why
> So merrily they cry and fly,
> Nor choose 'twixt earth and sky,
> While the moon's quarter silently
> Rides, and earth rests as silently.

Thomas had told Eleanor Farjeon that this poem 'had to be clear as glass'[88] if he was to anatomise his poetic temperament accurately, and his intention is dramatised by technical virtuosity. The lines float, soar and wheel just as the birds do themselves, and their concentration of diverse colours, elements and moods exactly reflects his aesthetic. While retaining his sympathy with Frost's theories, he exhibits complete mastery of a more inventive and distilled lyric structure than his friend used, only four months after finishing his first poem.

'Two Pewits' also realises an important difference between their attitudes to life itself. Where Frost habitually rationalises his experience in order to extract a moral from it, Thomas prefers to suggest and qualify, avoiding round conclusions. Instead of offering what Ian Hamilton calls Frost's 'stoic shrug, [his] rugged settling for what is less than perfect'[89] in lines such as 'One could do worse than be a swinger of birches', or

'Earth's the right place for love: I don't know where it's likely to go better', Thomas provides — in 'Liberty', for instance — extended, convoluted sentences which attempt to capture the events described in their full complexity:

> There's none less free than who
> Does nothing and has nothing else to do,
> Being free only for what is not to his mind,
> And nothing is to his mind. If every hour
> Like this one passing that I have spent among
> The wiser others when I have forgot
> To wonder whether I was free or not,
> Were piled before me, and not lost behind,
> And I could take and carry them away
> I should be rich; or if I had the power
> To wipe out every one and not again
> Regret, I should be rich to be so poor.

In 'As the team's head brass' this fastidious thoroughness in his attitude and tone of voice is given definite, organic form. The movement of the plough dictates the structure of his conversation with the ploughman:

> Every time the horses turned
> Instead of treading me down, the ploughman leaned
> Upon the handles to say or ask a word,
> About the weather, next about the war. . . .
> . . . So the talk began —
> One minute and an interval of ten,
> A minute more and the same interval.

The sound of sense in this poem is the sound of qualification, and its accompanying completeness. When action determines speech patterns for Frost it is characteristic that they should be regularly iambic, continuous and unbroken. In 'Mending Wall', for instance, Frost and his neighbour restore the stones to their proper places with the same unavoidable precision as punctuation is placed at the end of his lines:

> I let my neighbour know beyond the hill;
> And on a day we meet to walk the line
> And set the wall between us once again.
> We keep the wall between us as we go.

It is this discrepancy between Frost's regular, relaxed report and Thomas's careful, irregular analysis that summarises a crucial difference between the two poets, and provides the basis for Thomas's developments. In the (mere) eight dialogues among his work, the resemblances to Frost's *North of Boston* are rather of situation than of execution — and even these are absolutely consistent with his previous sixteen years' prose writing. The diligence of his self-analysis, and his development of the sentence as a vehicle for his 'thought moments', constitute a style which is as unique as his character, and which was eloquently summarised by J. C. Squire in his review of Frost's third book, *New Hampshire* (1924):

> Like Thomas, Mr. Frost writes as a musing solitary with a scrutinous eye for rural landscape, a relish for rustic character and vanishing customs; like Thomas his voice is never pitched high: his epithets are never forced, he is impeccably sincere, and he prefers understatements to overstatements. But there is something more than the difference between England and New England that distinguishes the two poets. Thomas had a Celtic melancholy all the more striking in that he indulged it among the warm and lush scenery of Southern England; Mr. Frost has his touches of sadness, but he is harder and soberer, as befits one whose stony, hilly pastures, and struggling farmers have something of the Wordsworth in them.[90]

III

Thomas based his individual stylistic achievements on this simultaneous sympathy with and development from Frost's ideas. Absolute fidelity to the postures of his speaking voice led him, in John Freeman's words 'to impatience of discipline, a revolt against bonds, to which he has earned his right by submission to discipline. Hence in very many of the poems you are aware at once of the submission and the revolt, the very form, the unrest of the poet's style, showing so beautifully the conflict of his mind. The style *is* the man.'[91] While Frost addresses his audience confidently, Thomas's poems seem to be overheard, and as they developed they became increasingly introspective and note-like. In a review of W. H. Hudson's *The Land's End* he had praised this latter quality as one by which the author's presence made itself felt. 'It lets us see', he said, 'the process by which the picture has been made ... it lacks the "trade finish" and is not ashamed of its structure. It reveals with the utmost fairness the character of the man, prejudices and all.'[92] The ability to hint at completeness in full recognition of its elusiveness was fully realised by his third poem, 'March', where the reverberative brevity of each 'thought moment' justifies Leavis's claim that, in his most characteristic work, Thomas seems to be trying 'to catch some shy intuition on the edge of consciousness':[93]

> What did the thrushes know? Rain, snow, sleet, hail,
> Had kept them quiet as the primroses.
> They had but an hour to sing. On boughs they sang,
> On gates, on ground; they sang while they changed perches
> And while they fought, if they remembered to fight:
> So earnest were they to pack into that hour
> Their unwilling hoard of song before the moon
> Grew brighter than the clouds.

The instinctive economy by which Thomas keeps this and other poems close to the very grain and texture of sensuous experience, making them seem — in his own words — 'less works of art than immediate outgrowths of nature',[94] forms an important part of the 'honesty' for which he has been consistently praised. Vernon Scannell's judgment of his 'unflinching emotional honesty'[95] echoes John Moore's verdict that he was 'superlatively honest'[96] and Bottomley's emphasis on his 'fastidious honesty'.[97] His love poems provide an obvious instance of the care that he took to remain absolutely truthful, no matter how disagreeable the truth was, but the strategies they use are found throughout his work. In poem after poem he describes a mood or situation which is then ambushed and forced into precision by modifiers and conditionals. 'Celandine', for instance, finds him opening with an admission that 'Thinking of her had saddened me at first, / Until I saw the sun on the celandines lie / Redoubled', and ends with a qualification that is its echo:

> But this was a dream: the flowers were not true,
> Until I stooped to pluck from the grass there
> One of five petals and I smelt the juice
> Which made me sigh, remembering she was no more,
> Gone like a never perfectly recalled air.

The profusion of negatives, which supports his conditional mood, leads him to tease out his sentences, using the line ends as fixed objects around which he unwinds the thread of his thought, until every nuance has been exposed. But while this means there is a lack of 'any strong gesture or accent'[98] in his poems, it does not signify that they are unplanned and indecisive. His sustained use of litotes, the general use of words beginning un-, im-, or dis-, and his wide-ranging employment of qualified hyperbole, all suggest 'a formidable command of syntactical structure, and the playing of syntax against form . . . [which] is not just a rhetorical figure but a rhetorical strategy'.[99] Just as Thomas's modesty confesses its own strength, so too is this battery of understatement a means by which he establishes a kind of affirmation. 'It rains' is typical in showing his early qualifications developed into a flat denial which then flowers into the possibility of fulfilment:

> And I am nearly as happy as possible
> To search the wilderness in vain though well,
> To think of two walking, kissing there,
> Drenched, yet forgetting the kisses of the rain:
> Sad, too, to think that never, never again,
>
> Unless alone, so happy shall I walk
> In the rain.

In the remainder of the final verse he translates his perceptions into organic terms which constitute an image of such unearthly beauty that all his previous doubts are transfigured into celebration. It provides a moving instance of his suggestive power, and his ability to affirm by means of negatives:

> When I turn away, on its fine stalk
> Twilight has fined to naught, the parsley flower
> Figures, suspended still and ghostly white,
> The past hovering as it revisits the light.

But even this display of rhetorical strategy is strictly contained by his insistence on simplicity. In *The Country*, a year before beginning to write poetry, he had judged that 'When a poet writes, I believe he is often only putting into words what such another old man puzzled out among the sheep in a long lifetime';[100] and as well as encouraging him to suppress excesses of language, this belief also determined his formal structures. Most conspicuous among its effects was his dislike of the sonnet, and in a letter to Jesse Berridge he made clear that his disapproval was aimed at its potential for artifice: 'Personally I have a dread of the sonnet. It must contain 14 lines and a man must be a tremendous poet or a cold mathematician if he can accommodate his thoughts to such a condition. The result is — in my opinion — that many of the best sonnets are rhetoric only.'[101] This assault was continued throughout his reviews; his remark that 'it is almost part of the nature of the sonnet to be solemn, pontifical, unbending'[102] is rephrased in his treatment of sonneteers such as one Lloyd Mifflin, whom he describes as 'a sonneteering animal . . . when he eats a bloater or sees a cat he cannot withhold a sestet at the least'.[103] Thomas himself rigorously avoided the strict form; of the six 'sonnets' he wrote, two are in couplets ('The Wind's Song' and 'A Dream'), two are conventionally Shakespearian ('That girl's clear eyes' and 'It was upon'), and two are semi-Petrarchan ('Some eyes condemn' and 'February Afternoon'). Of all these, however, only the latter maintains a regular decasyllabic line — and even that avoids smooth iambic pentameters — while 'Some eyes condemn' provides clear illustration of the difficulty that he experienced in preserving his characteristic tone of voice within the form. The 'eye' conceit upon which the poem is founded is archly elaborated in the sestet, and his isolation of the words 'one' and 'some' at the end of lines 4 and 10 to meet the requirements of rhyme is, as he said himself to Eleanor Farjeon, 'I suppose, a weakness'.[104]

> Some eyes condemn the earth they gaze upon:
> Some wait patiently till they know far more
> Than earth can tell them: some laugh at the whole
> As folly of another's making: one
> I knew that laughed because he saw, from core
> To rind, not one thing worth the laugh his soul
> Had ready at waking: some eyes have begun
> With laughing; some stand startled at the door.
>
> Others, too, I have seen rest, question, roll,
> Dance, shoot. And many I have loved watching. Some
> I could not take my eyes from till they turned
> And loving died. I had not found my goal.
> But thinking of your eyes, dear, I become
> Dumb: for they flamed, and it was me they burned.

In spite of this sustained avoidance of the sonnet, Thomas's 'ambition to keep under 12 lines' led him to write a large number of poems containing between ten and eighteen lines which seem to suggest that he flirts with the form. Yet the entire emphasis of his work is directed away from artifice. At the same time as he abandoned Frost's dramatic effects, he developed several techniques by which he could capture the inflection and animation of a voice speaking without too palpable a design on the reader. Foremost among these is the recurrent suggestion that his poems are reported, or actual, talk. The implied presence of a speaker frequently gives them an element of drama which is more subdued than Frost's, but which has, nevertheless, the same effect of demanding attention. Paradoxically, their demand is more powerful because it is more muted, as the opening lines of 'Beauty' indicate:

> What does it mean? Tired, angry, and ill at ease,
> No man, woman, or child, alive could please
> Me now.

The rhetorical question lacks the luxuriousness of rhetoric, but introduces the poem as if it were part of a dialogue, and expected an answer. Similarly, 'Adlestrop's' opening ('Yes. I remember Adlestrop —') appears to come in response to a question, and the first lines of 'The Brook' suggest that they are delivered aloud to a group of listeners:

> Seated once by a brook, watching a child
> Chiefly that paddled, I was thus beguiled.

The submerged presence of the phrase 'Once upon a time' establishes a series of pitch patterns which are delicately responsive to the meaning of the narrative and to Thomas's own attitude. This quality is also present in 'The Path': the first full stop of both poems stands as a point after which the speaker draws breath, ready to begin his story: 'Running along a bank, a parapet / That saves from the precipitous wood below / The level road, there is a path.' This structure is repeated at the beginning of many poems — the accent of explanation caught in 'But these things also are Spring's', for example, or the preliminary summary of 'As the team's head brass':

> As the team's head brass flashed out on the turn
> The lovers disappeared into the wood.
> I sat among the boughs of the fallen elm
> That strewed an angle of the fallow . . .

80

In every case the speaking voice seems to steady itself before under-taking its imaginative adventure, securing its accent and its observations within the pale of scrupulous precision.

Such devices (which are corroborated by his use of techniques usually associated with folk-songs and ballads) gain strength from his frequent and subtle collisions between the unit of the sentence and the unit of the line. In 1902, speaking of Liddell's study of English prosody, he has already been seen to have praised the author for speaking of ' "thought moments" instead of "phrases" because "it is important to dissociate them from words and to think of them as groups of notions" '. The same criteria apply in his own poetry: the principal basis for classifica-tion of his rhythm is the fertile irregularity of blank verse. In his study of Pater, he had insisted that if the intimacy of speech was to be repro-duced in literature, so must its variety: 'The rhythms satisfactory to the mere naked ear are of little value; they will be so much sonority or suavity. . . . Here again appears the necessity for the aid of speech in literature. Nothing so much as the writer's rhythm can give the intimate effect "as if he had been talking". Rhythm is of the essence of a sincere expressive style.'[105] The implicit rejection of the foot as the dominant metrical unit, and its accompanying emphasis that the phrase (or series of phrases) should be the ordering principle instead, leads him to take the natural English line not as the five regular feet of the iambic penta-meter, but as eight to twelve syllables which avoid repeating patterns of weak and strong stress. It was this which informed his defence of Frost's verse to his friends. His claims that everyday speech cannot pass unchanged into 'effective' verse, and that a 'complicated and learned and subtle vocabulary and structure' may be compatible with the postures of the voice in intimate speech, are animated by his interpreta-tion of rhythm. And the interaction of irregular speech and strict metre has, as D. W. Harding observes, two possible effects that might at first seem incompatible. 'One is that the metrical set established in the lines may determine the choice between two or more available speech rhythms for the words; the other is that the sense of the words can lead us to adopt one out of several rhythms that can all be reconciled with metre.'[106] But while this emphasises the flexibility that Thomas sought, it also bears out Harding's warning that a precise analysis of rhythm 'can be almost defeatingly difficult'.[107] The 'speculating' move-ment of Thomas's characteristic poem 'Thaw', for example, confuses its own clear divisions into 'thought moments':

Over the land freckled with snow half-thawed
The speculating rooks at their nests cawed
And saw from elm-tops, delicate as flower of grass,
What we below could not see, Winter pass.

The rhythm here, in a phrase that Thomas approvingly quoted from Liddell, is 'not of sounds but of ideas',[108] and illustrates his own contention that if they are 'as it were, absolutely onomatopoeic . . . we have a *dramatic* knowledge of verse'.[109] Take, for instance, the first line:

Over the land / freckled with snow / half-thawed.

Because the division into 'thought moments' is questionable here (should the last one be / 'snow half-thawed'?), it creates the disturbance that Thomas admired. The restlessness which exists between regular metre and the tone of the speaking voice conforms exactly to his shared belief with Frost that 'the accent of sense is only lovely when thrown and drawn and displayed across spaces of the footed line'. But his use of this interrelationship, in spite of his sympathy with Frost's theory, is both more scrupulous and more bold. 'The Signpost' is typical of the way in which his rhythms constantly reflect 'the minuter grain of his countryside and character':[110]

The dim sea glints chill. The white sun is shy,
And the skeleton weeds and the never-dry,
Rough, long grasses keep white with frost
At the hilltop by the finger-post;
The smoke of the traveller's-joy is puffed
Over hawthorn berry and hazel tuft.

A discursive line length here conflicts with the suspense engendered by his strategic avoidance of endstopping, to create an impression of unease which dramatises the dilemma of 'Wondering where he shall journey, O where?' Seventy-six of Thomas's 142 poems are written in this variable blank-verse line, and all of them employ patterns of stress and pause which reflect a mind actually engaged in the act of thinking, rather than offering its concluded thoughts. His rhythm describes the movement of his mind, as well as the sound of its sense.

His insistence that the speaking accent should dictate the rhythm of a poem by pointing its meaning, frequently provided his answer to friends' queries about his poetic technique. When Edward Garnett suggested that he should 'chisel' 'Lob' into evenness, Thomas replied: 'It would be the easiest thing in the world to clean it all up and trim it and have every line straightforward in sound and sense, but it would not really improve it. . . . If you *say* a couplet like

> "If they had mowed their dandelions and sold them
> fairly they could have afforded gold."

I believe it is no longer awkward.'[111] This emphasis on the speaking inflexions of his rhythm, rather than its formal exactitude, was repeated in his opinion that 'the line "England, Old already, was called Merry" looks more eccentric than it is & sounds'.[112] And the intention to preserve a rough-hewn, resourceful simplicity is complemented by his handling of line-endings and sentence lengths. Reviewing D. H. Lawrence's *Love Poems and Others* (1913) he had remarked that 'for some time past it has been understood that verse is not best written in jerks of a line in length',[113] and in his own later practice he frequently gives dramatic emphasis to crucial words by placing them immediately *after* a line-ending. One of his earliest reviewers eloquently identified this trait as 'a certain suspension of emotion that is itself emotional',[114] and in one of his own reviews Thomas made plain his reasons for cultivating it: 'Some scores of times Mr. Swinburne gives way to the trick of using a word, often of only one syllable, as at once the first of a line and the last of a sentence or clause. Used as Shelley uses it in —

> Is this the scene
> Where the old earthquake demon taught her young
> Ruin?

there is no bolder means of laying emphasis on a word.'[115] Characteristically, in his practice of the 'trick' Thomas often subdues the affirmation of emphasis by using a negative word — the division, for instance, in 'Over the Hills': 'Recall / Was vain', or in 'Swedes': 'curled fronds / Unsunned'. And there are also many occasions on which he cautiously negotiates a line-ending only to confront a more leisurely modification to the statement that preceded it. In 'And you, Helen' he is forced to face the qualifications to his own generous impulse:

So many things I would give you
Had I an infinite great store
Offered me and I stood before
To choose.

This tendency to dramatise the natural pause of a line-ending is but one part of the recurring line and sentence structures which organise his poems. At their most characteristic, his sentences serve as long, flexible wires which conduct rhythm through whole poems or parts of poems. And it is not only his speaking cadence that is thus conveyed: the frequent pauses and hesitations convey his state of mind as well as his tone of voice. But even this aspect of his style reconciles opposing forces; while the movement of his verse is consistently cautious, the expertise with which he plays out his sentences suggests confidence, mastery and dexterity. 'Old Man' provides a celebrated instance of this, and so too does 'Rain':

Blessed are the dead that the rain rains upon:
But here I pray that none whom once I loved
Is dying tonight or lying still awake
Solitary, listening to the rain,
Either in pain or thus in sympathy
Helpless among the living and the dead,
Like a cold water among broken reeds,
Myriads of broken reeds all still and stiff,
Like me who have no love which this wild rain
Has not dissolved except the love of death,
If love it be towards what is perfect and
Cannot, the tempest tells me, disappoint.

The superb sweep of the sentence, realising every twist and turn of his thought by its qualifications, internal rhymes and isolated negatives, continually dramatises the tone of his speaking voice and animates an ideal which he had set out ten years earlier: 'We know the beauty of . . . a complex sentence in which the stops are as valuable as the division of a stanza of verse into lines, or as the hedges and littered crags and outcropping rock by which the eye travels up a mountain to the clouds.'[116]

In his study of Pater, Thomas amplified this judgment of 'a complex sentence', and identified it as a principle of unification. His complaint that Pater's sentences 'must be somehow exquisite of themselves',[117] anticipates his own habit of developing their rhythm and cadence through the whole slowly uncoiling length of a poem. But this was not simply a device by which sentences became 'exquisite' of more than themselves; it also contributed to the necessary correspondence between himself and his form. Long before he began writing poetry, he told Bottomley: 'Do you notice how careless of the minutiæ of form I get — long rambling sentences, which I know to be imperfect? I hope it means that I am getting into a truer method & not merely becoming a prose journalist.'[118] Later in his career these prose imperfections had been reformed into two fundamental aspects of his rhetorical strategy. The first, and most conspicuous, is his use of the final, long sentence such as 'Rain' employs. This is frequently preceded by a brief anticipatory clause which stands — like so many of his opening sentences — as a rapidly indrawn breath which is to steady and power his concluding lines. 'Over the Hills' provides a typical example:

> Recall
> Was vain: no more could the restless brook
> Ever turn back and climb the waterfall
> To the lake that rests and stirs not in its nook,
> As in the hollow of the collar-bone
> Under the mountain's head of rush and stone.

Just as his hesitancy was seen to be conveyed, paradoxically, with confidence, so too are the frequently negative statements of his final lines delivered (as here) with a consoling expansiveness and relish of verbal control. It is a reconciliation in formal terms of exactly those opposites that are so often poised against one another in his images. And he repeats this balance in another, related device. Often, instead of prefacing his final sentences with a short, stabilising clause, he concludes them with a brief summarising statement which modifes whatever doubt the poem has expressed. 'Beauty', 'The Mountain Chapel' and 'Swedes' provide obvious examples of this positive emphasis, and even 'The long small room' contains an appreciation of physical awareness which relaxes its mesmerised concentration on approaching death:

> One thing remains the same — this my right hand
>
> Crawling crab-like over the clean white page,
> Resting awhile each morning on the pillow,

Then once more starting to crawl on towards age.
The hundred last leaves stream upon the willow.

The translation of the first line's 'willows in the west' into personalised emblems of mortality is made with such economy that Thomas confessed to Eleanor Farjeon: 'I am worried about the impression that [they] made on you. As a matter of fact I started with that last line as what I was working to. I am only fearing it has a sort of Japanesy suddenness of ending.'[119] It is, however, this 'suddenness' which contains the poem's saving grace. By focusing attention on itself, the line demands that its hopeful as well as its pessimistic qualities be noticed. Although the leaves are few, and thereby suggest the approach of a deathly winter, they are, nevertheless, streaming 'upon' (rather than, say, 'from') the willow. This suggestion of a tenacious, if vulnerable, hold on life is strengthened by the verb 'stream' itself, which carries with it a submerged reference to the stream of life, and so to continuing consciousness. In the face of extreme danger — Thomas had time to write only three more poems — the final line manages to emphasise and preserve a characteristic balance between forces of life and death.

This formal dramatisation of experience is frequently intensified by Thomas's rhyme schemes. As has already been indicated in the discussion of his sonnets, conventions are often established only to be disrupted, and this characteristic is developed even more freely elsewhere. In 'This is no case of petty right or wrong' the opening rhymes *a b c b c d a d* are regimented into strict couplets by the conclusion of the poem, in order to suggest the strengthening of discipline which is demanded of him in time of war. This dispersion and collection of couplets is the most conspicuous of Thomas's widely used collaborations between rhyme and content, and ' "Home" ' ('Fair was the morning') provides a still more subtle and varied example. In the first verse paragraph his 'gladness' and the 'fairness' of his temper, the morning and the place are strengthened by the frequency of rhymes (*a a b c b c*) at the same time as his underlying anxiety is revealed by their increasing unsatisfactoriness: 'and'/'land'; 'made'/'glad'; 'was'/'pass'. The final line, indeed, has to wait until the second verse paragraph to find a rhyme at all; and there, although the other lines marshal themselves into an (incomplete) self-controlled display of couplets, it is not full (*e e d f f*). In the third paragraph these signs of distraction and unease are confirmed by the collapse of his attempt at a regular scheme. As Thomas's mind searches for possible satisfactions in his present condition, it ricochets from rhyme word to rhyme word without finding comfort (*g h h i g j*). It is only when his discussion of the word 'home' itself is succeeded by his consideration of the possible benefits latent in his immediate situation that stability returns. And it returns with such conviction that the last fourteen lines of the poem are in immaculate couplets, so strengthening and unifying in their effect that they overleap even the divisions between paragraphs.

In the previous chapter it was noticed that the benefits of Thomas's search for his 'goal' were attained not after but during his journey towards it. It is precisely this insistence on the values of becoming rather than being that is reflected in his formal practice. In the same way as his expectant sentence structures hold him in suspense, the irregularity of his rhythms and the skilful disruption of regular rhyme schemes prevent him from adopting either the accent or the appearance of conclusiveness. It is this, more than anything else, which distinguishes his poems from Frost's. They remain faithful to beliefs which he had established throughout his writing career, and embody a process of self-discovery which gradually enabled him to realise his unswerving belief that 'in the written word the artist has to make up for all those advantages of tone and look and gesture and other unspoken speech, of which he is deprived, in solitude'.[120]

IV

Thomas's estimate of Frost's influence is, as Frost himself said, 'generous'. With characteristic modesty, he played down his independent formation of verse theories; and with equally characteristic resolution, he never concealed his adaptation of Frost's example. From the evidence of Thomas's reviews, his prose, and the range of his rhetorical strategy, it is clear that Frost stimulated but did not absolutely determine his prosodic arguments or his identity as a poet. But even having insisted that Frost released rather than made Thomas's talent, it remains doubtful whether Thomas would have achieved the same degree of success without one circumstantial accident. In the very week that Thomas arrived in Gloucestershire for his August with Frost, the First World War was declared. Describing his holiday to Eleanor Farjeon, Thomas said that 'we enjoyed many days but with all sorts of mixed feelings'[121] — a remark which hints that it produced exactly the kind of ambivalence that he relished, and suggests that the war gave unprecedented emphasis to the ideas that he and Frost were discussing. Thomas, who for so long had been unable to discover a satisfactory means of self-expression, was offered the best opportunity of attaining it just as the war threatened to deprive him of it. Frost's encouragement had the urgency of a last chance.

When one of Thomas's earliest biographers, John Moore, says that in Gloucestershire he was 'scarcely touched or disturbed'[122] by the war he flies in the face of both poets' accounts. Frost acknowledged that the war made 'some kind of new man and a poet out of him',[123] and Thomas wrote to W. H. Hudson: 'I don't find the war shuts me up. In fact it has given me time to please myself with some unprofitable writing.'[124] As well as complementing Frost's influence in this practical way, its threats also sharpened his feelings for England. Thomas himself realised this, and in his essay 'This England', which became the source of his poem 'The sun used to shine', he explores the interaction of the two forces. Poem and prose share the same paradox of harmony contained in a general context of violence and upset, and are identical in details: the sunlight, the apples, the clumps of wood betony and the 'gate to rest on' all compose an idyllic pastoral into which the war intrudes:

> The sun used to shine while we two walked
> Slowly together, paused and started
> Again, and sometimes mused, sometimes talked
> As either pleased, and cheerfully parted
>
> Each night. We never disagreed
> Which gate to rest on. The to be
> And the late past we gave small heed.
> We turned from men or poetry
>
> To rumours of the war remote
> Only till both stood disinclined
> For aught but the yellow flavorous coat
> Of an apple wasps had undermined,
>
> Or a sentry of dark betonies,
> The stateliest of small flowers on earth,
> At the forest verge; or crocuses
> Pale purple as if they had their birth
>
> In sunless Hades fields. The war
> Came back to mind with the moonrise
> Which soldiers in the east afar
> Beheld then. Nevertheless, our eyes

Could as well imagine the Crusades
Or Caesar's battles. Everything
To faintness like those rumours fades —
Like the brook's water glittering

Under the moonlight — like those walks
Now — like us two that took them, and
The fallen apples, all the talks
And silences — like memory's sand

When the tide covers it late or soon,
And other men through other flowers
In those fields under the same moon
Go talking and have easy hours.

Although Thomas calls the war 'faint' and 'remote', his language subtly conveys its persistent menace: the apple is 'undermined' as if sapped by wasps, the betonies are 'a sentry', and the crocuses are a funereal 'Pale purple as if they had their birth / In sunless Hades fields'. And in both poem and prose the moonrise brings war explicitly to mind, as Thomas imagines soldiers in France watching it appear. The fact that he and Frost 'Could as well imagine the Crusades / Or Caesar's battles' as the present conflict, does not reduce its dangers, but rather suggests that all wars, religious and imperial, ancient and recent, are concentrated in this one, which leads him to 'the forest verge'.

Distance from battle does little to allay his anxiety. While it stresses the value of his and Frost's mutual understanding, it reminds him that their precarious harmony will be erased shortly. In the prose original he diagnoses this knowledge as the patriotism referred to above: 'I was deluged . . . [by] something that overpowered thought. All I can tell is, it seemed to me that either I had never loved England, or I had loved it foolishly, aesthetically, like a slave, not having realised that it was not mine unless I were willing and prepared to die rather than leave it as Belgian women and old men and children had left their country.'[125] The connection between this awakening sense of himself as 'a conscious Englishman' and the poems which followed is regular and intimate. The war freed him from journalism, and intensified the love for England which had been the main theme of his prose books. It combined with the confidence that Frost gave, to break down his inhibiting self-doubt and reconcile his ideal freedom of expression with a full reservoir of material. In order to release the poems, Frost did not introduce new arguments to Thomas, but confirmed those which already existed; and at every point in this process an extraordinary degree of imaginative and personal sympathy provided him with the encouragement he needed to find himself, as he said in a letter of appreciation to Frost, 'engrossed and conscious of a possible perfection as I never was in prose. . . . Still, I won't begin thanking you just yet, though if you like I will put it down now that you are the only begetter right enough.'[126]

CHAPTER FOUR

PATRIOT AND WAR POET

I

Thomas's reputation as a war poet has suffered sixty years of misrepresentation and neglect. Bernard Bergonzi's verdict that 'Very few of [his] poems are actually about the war',[1] John H. Johnston's that he 'refused to let the conflict interfere with [his] nostalgic rural visions',[2] and John Lehmann's that 'he only wrote one poem about the issues of the war',[3] do little more than rephrase the opinion of one of his earliest reviewers: 'Like most of his contemporaries he has too little control over his eyes. ... Or is the new method an unconscious survival of a materialism and naturalism which the tremendous life of the last three years has made an absurdity?'[4] Thomas's reaction to this review is instructive. Writing to Bottomley from France, he asked, 'must I see only Huns on these beautiful hills eastwards?'[5] His question implied a rejection of the same directly documentary approach he scorned in 1914:

> The demand is for the crude, for what everybody is saying or thinking, or is ready to be saying or thinking. I need hardly say that by becoming ripe for poetry the poet's thoughts may recede far from their original resemblance to all the world's, and may seem to have little to do with daily events.[6]

The assumption that war poetry, to be war poetry, must concern itself exclusively with the actual circumstances of battle has blurred the quality of his passionate, but refined, patriotism. Where Wilfred Owen, Isaac

Rosenberg, and Siegfried Sassoon describe the appalling details of the trenches, Thomas examines and cherishes those aspects of the country he had enlisted to defend. In fact, he only wrote one poem in France ('The sorrow of true love'), so quickly was he killed; of his twenty-two months as a soldier, all but forty days were spent training in England. During this time he provided a more balanced, complete and articulate account of his experiences than any given by his contemporaries. It is a many-faceted record, and a unique one, being far removed in circumstance and intention from those handed down by poets who more confidently claimed the title of war poet.

Because all his poetry was written after the outbreak of war, it is all, in an important sense, war poetry. Behind every line, whether mentioned or not, lies imminent danger and disruption. J. W. Haines, who frequently accompanied Thomas and Frost on their walks in Gloucestershire during August 1914, realised this:

> The war tinges many [poems] and directly inspires not a few. Nor was his attitude to the War that of the War Poets in general; he was far older than most of them. He did not embrace it passionately like Rupert Brooke, nor revolt from it as passionately as did Wilfred Owen.[7]

Frost was similarly quick to mention that the war was instrumental in persuading Thomas to begin writing poems; he insisted it 'made some kind of new man and a poet out of him'.[8] Other than in the judgment of his friends, however, he had to wait until 1939 before the war's influence on his work began to be appreciated. During the Second World War soldiers often had to endure long periods of preparation and delay which resembled much of his own military experience. One of them, Alun Lewis, was particularly sympathetic: he realised that Thomas 'did not suffer as Sassoon, Owen or Rosenberg, and was not embittered beyond bearing'.[9] But even Lewis wrote some poems on active service overseas, where the hard facts of conflict were unavoidable, rather than selected and used side by side with other material. This important distinction was wittily made by Philip Larkin during a review of Owen's *Collected Poems* in 1963:

> A 'war poet' is not one who chooses to commemorate or celebrate a war, but one who reacts against having a war thrust upon him: he is chained, that is, to an historical event, and an abnormal one at that. However well he does it, however much we agree that the war

happened and ought to be written about, there is still a tendency for us to withhold our highest praise on the grounds that a poet's choice of subject should seem an action, not a reaction. 'The Wreck of the Deutschland', we feel, would have been markedly inferior if Hopkins had been a survivor from the passenger list.[10]

The circumstances of Thomas's military life, and his poetic beliefs, equipped him to reconcile the paradox of having a war thrust upon him at the same time as he actually chose his subjects. And the essential element in this achievement was his ability to discuss his own circumstances in the historical perspective of other wars.

Where Owen, Rosenberg and Sassoon struggled to express what they saw as the unique horrors of the war to end all wars, Thomas interpreted it as the macabre modern representative of 'the Crusades / Or Caesar's battles'. This phrase — from 'The sun used to shine' — has parallels in his prose books, as well as in other poems. In 'February Afternoon', for example, he describes how:

> Time swims before me, making as a day
>   A thousand years, while the broad ploughland oak
>   Roars mill-like and men strike and bear the stroke
>   Of war as ever, audacious or resigned,
> And God still sits aloft in the array
>   That we have wrought him, stone-deaf and stone-blind.

The realisation that all wars are the same in essentials, no matter how various their outward expression, was stimulated by his penultimate prose book, *The Life of the Duke of Marlborough*, written in 1915. In the blurb, his publisher was quick to point out its topicality: 'The achievements of the First Duke of Marlborough acquire peculiar interest at the present time, when Britain is once more fighting on the fields of Flanders.'[11] But it is the recurrence of war, not mercenary jingoism, which forms Thomas's main preoccupation. His many references to country near the Meuse, for instance, are brought ruthlessly up to date in the prose source for 'The sun used to shine', where modern soldiers are imagined fighting over the same ground. The poem 'Digging' makes this connection explicit. It is the will to destroy which endures, not the individual:

> What matter makes my spade for tears or mirth,
> Letting down two clay pipes into the earth?

The one I smoked, the other a soldier
Of Blenheim, Ramillies, and Malplaquet
Perhaps. The dead man's immortality
Lies represented lightly with my own.

The soldier's immortality depends on the durability of his possessions;
it is a different — and less consoling — aspect of the same capacity for
survival that Thomas admires in landscape and seasonal cycles. The
awareness is shared by Hardy, who at the end of *Far From the Madding
Crowd* refers to the instruments of the Weatherbury band in a phrase
that illuminates Thomas's poem. He describes them as 'venerable worm-
eaten instruments, which had celebrated in their own persons the victor-
ies of Marlborough, under the fingers of the forefathers of those who
played them now'.[12] Thomas's knowledge that he was taking part in an
(admittedly hideous) repetitive process reduced his sense of the
'abnormality' of war, which Larkin argues makes a poet's choice of
subject a reaction, not an action. It freed him to examine his own
involvement by allowing him to introduce material from more pacific
and stable aspects of life, and justifies Lewis's judgment that 'the war
came to him as to his dead ploughman, naturally. He accepted his own
death and, it seems, the death of every fated soldier. Why? Possibly
because he could not write the poetry of supreme anger; possibly
because he was a soldier; possibly because he loved England too well.'[13]

II

The historical perspective of Thomas's war poetry is complemented by
the keen love of England that Lewis mentions, in defining him as an
'active' rather than 'reactive' writer. It was love of a complex and con-
stant character; and because it took poetic form during wartime, it
assumed specifically patriotic qualities. These are usually conveyed with
his habitual reticence, but there is one poem, 'This is no case of petty
right or wrong', in which he adopts a more public tone of voice. In spite
of its outspokenness, the substance of this poem is closely modelled on
the attitudes to English landscape which are described throughout his
prose books. It is the ancient features of England which command his
deepest admiration, although he admits that benefits traditionally
associated with them may be illusory. In *The Happy-Go-Lucky Morgans*,
for instance, one of his alter-egos, Mr Torrance, praises 'the "merry" or
"good old" England of his imagination. He said that from what he could

gather they were merry in the old days with little cause, while today, whatever cause there might be, few persons possessed the ability.'[14] But it is not simply antiquity that Thomas seeks, rather the interconnection of ancient past and immediate present. Another character, Mr Stodham, confirms this:

> Deny England — wise men have done so — and you may find your-
> self some day denying your father and mother — and this also wise
> men have done. Having denied England and your father and mother,
> you may have to deny your own self, and treat it as nothing, a mere
> conventional boundary, an artifice, by which you are separated from
> the universe and its creator. To unite yourself with the universe and
> its creator, you may be tempted to destroy that boundary of your
> own body and brain, and die. He is a bold man who hopes to do
> without earth, England, family and self.[15]

It is this insistence on the value of continuity which counterbalances the persistence of war itself, and it is only maintained by a deliberate refusal to adopt merely jingoistic values, as Mr Stodham's final speech suggests:

> I do not want to shout that our great soldiers and poets are greater
> than those of other nations, but they are ours, they are great, and in
> proportion as we are good and intelligent, we can respond to them
> and understand them as those who are not Englishmen cannot. They
> cannot long do without us or we without them.[16]

This is misunderstood by another character, Higgs, who arrogantly plays 'Rule Britannia', and the narrator is only pacified by hearing 'Land of my Fathers', because it reflects his own, and Mr Stodham's, feelings: 'It was exulting without self-glorification, or any other form of brutality.'[17]

Biographical evidence suggests that 'This is no case of petty right or wrong' was written in reaction to precisely the kind of excessive zeal abominated in Higgs. Eleanor Farjeon gives the necessary facts:

> For love of the dust of his country [Thomas] cried 'God save
> England!' in 1915, as in 1415 he might have cried it at Agincourt.
> His hate-feelings were reserved for the Jingo Press and those who
> used its jargon in argument. His father was among them.[18]

Thomas himself supports this assertion in a letter to Frost describing the Christmas during which he wrote the poem: 'I saw my father . . .

and he made me very sick. He treats me so that I have a feeling of shame that I am alive. I couldn't sleep after it. Nothing much happened. We argued about the war and he showed me that his real feeling when he is not trying to be nice and comfortable is one of contempt.'[19] The unusually angry quality of the poem is explained by this background to its composition, which casts into graphic relief the reasoned rejection of tub-thumping:

> This is no case of petty right or wrong
> That politicians or philosophers
> Can judge. I hate not Germans, nor grow hot
> With love of Englishmen, to please newspapers.
> Beside my hate for one fat patriot
> My hatred of the Kaiser is love true:—
> A kind of god he is, banging a gong.
> But I have not to choose between the two,
> Or between justice and injustice. Dinned
> With war and argument I read no more
> Than in the storm smoking along the wind
> Athwart the wood. Two witches' cauldrons roar.
> From one the weather shall rise clear and gay;
> Out of the other an England beautiful
> And like her mother that died yesterday.
> Little I know or care if, being dull,
> I shall miss something that historians
> Can rake out of the ashes when perchance
> The phoenix broods serene above their ken.
> But with the best and meanest Englishmen
> I am one in crying, God save England, lest
> We lose what never slaves and cattle blessed.
> The ages made her that made us from the dust:
> She is all we know and live by, and we trust
> She is good and must endure, loving her so:
> And as we love ourselves we hate her foe.

Two long essays in *The Last Sheaf*, 'England' and 'Tipperary', reaffirm this distaste for the unduly self-congratulatory: 'Throughout English history you have the two combined inseparably: love of the place where you "have your happiness or not at all", and a more fitfully conscious love of the island, and glory in its glories'.[20] The 'glory in its glories' does not mean a military achievement for Thomas, but a rejoicing in moments of integration with English landscape. It is these which underline the public statement of 'This is no case of petty right or wrong' with more reticent, but no less convinced, records of patriotism.

In order to gauge the full scope and significance of such moments, it is helpful to introduce two other related aspects of Thomas's work. One is his motive in compiling the anthology of patriotic poetry *This England*, and the other is his admiration for Richard Jefferies. *This England*, in intention and execution, illustrates his ideal of war poetry written throughout English history: 'The worst of the poetry being written today is that it is too deliberately, and not inevitably English. It is for an audience: there is more in it of the shouting of rhetorician, reciter or politician than of the talk of friends or lovers.'[21] In discussing two poems included — Coleridge's 'Fears in Solitude' and Blake's 'War Song to Englishmen' — Thomas identified their 'inevitably English' quality as being derived 'from a settled, mystic patriotism, which war could not disturb', rather than being 'bombastic, hypocritical or senseless'.[22] War, in other words, did not introduce so much as intensify the patriotism he admires, and this fact is emphasised in letters referring to the material he needed. It was not, as Eleanor Farjeon initially thought, descriptions of England, but passages which convey its elusive essence: 'I haven't made myself clear about the anthology. It isn't what Dickens "says of England" that I want. Anything that makes us feel England particularly or which we could imagine making a stranger feel it is what I want.'[23] To Bottomley he repeated that antiquity was an important factor, and he bore this out by including a large number of folk-songs and ballads: 'I am not going mainly for the explicitly patriotic. . . . It is to cover the whole of time from the landing of Brutus to the Zeppelins.'[24] From those pieces eventually chosen he crystallised a new meaning of England for himself, and succeeded in compiling a book without any inhibiting references to immediate circumstances. It was war poetry to nourish the present by recovering the best of the past, rather than to warn by mere analysis of the present itself.

Thomas included in *This England* (under the pseudonym Edward Eastaway) two of his own poems which exemplify his general intention as well as specific aspects of his patriotism: 'The Manor Farm' and 'Haymaking'. As his biographer and critic William Cooke points out, by doing this he was 'placing himself in the tradition of writers who had celebrated England, in peace and war. Even the position he gave to his poems is significant. They appear immediately after Coleridge's "Fears in Solitude", which he described . . . as "one of the noblest of patriotic poems", though "no newspaper or magazine, then or now, would print such a poem, since a large part of it is humble".'[25] Both of them define moments full of 'the antiquity and sweetness' of England, and, 'Hay-making' also provides a significant example of Thomas's ability to create an image of balanced contentment:

> After night's thunder far away had rolled
> The fiery day had a kernel sweet of cold,
> And in the perfect blue the clouds uncurled,
> Like the first gods before they made the world
> And misery, swimming the stormless sea
> In beauty and in divine gaiety.
> The smooth white empty road was lightly strewn
> With leaves — the holly's Autumn falls in June —
> And fir cones standing stiff up in the heat.
> The mill-foot water tumbled white and lit
> With tossing crystals, happier than any crowd
> Of children pouring out of school aloud.
> And in the little thickets where a sleeper
> For ever might lie lost, the nettle-creeper
> And garden warbler sang unceasingly,
> While over them shrill shrieked in his fierce glee
> The swift with wings and tail as sharp and narrow
> As if the bow had flown off with the arrow.

Thomas establishes his sense of harmony at once in the poem, by setting it at dawn, then emphasises its union of dark and light by incorporating a similar fusion of temperatures: the 'fiery day' has 'a kernel sweet of cold'. This is followed by melting different seasons into one (in his reference to the holly, whose 'Autumn falls in June'), and the unearthly rarity of the scene is conveyed by the quality of the light that illuminates it. All colours are reduced to their essential tones: the 'perfect blue' of the sky is a simple, original transparency through which appear the white road and the white mill water. This subtle landscaping of the approach to his communion is corroborated by images of endurance or renewal. The water pouring 'happier than any crowd / Of children', the 'little thickets where a sleeper / For ever might lie lost', and the 'unceasing' song of birds all indicate that the potential for ecstasy is as inexhaustible as the landscape in which it recurs. Just as 'Digging' and

'February Afternoon' suggest that cycles of destruction are capable of outlasting individuals, so 'Haymaking' reveals cycles of benefit to have the same capacity.

Later in the poem these images of integration are gradually modified into images of stasis:

> Only the scent of woodbine and hay new-mown
> Travelled the road. In the field sloping down,
> Park-like, to where its willows showed the brook,
> Haymakers rested. The tosser lay forsook
> Out in the sun; and the long waggon stood
> Without its team; it seemed it never would
> Move from the shadow of that single yew.
> The team, as still, until their task was due,
> Beside the labourers enjoyed the shade
> That three squat oaks mid-field together made
> Upon a circle of grass and weed uncut,
> And on the hollow, once a chalk-pit, but
> Now brimmed with nut and elder-flower so clean.
> The men leaned on their rakes, about to begin,
> But still. And all were silent. All was old,
> This morning time, with a great age untold,
> Older than Clare and Cowper, Morland and Crome,
> Than, at the field's far edge, the farmer's home,
> A white house crouched at the foot of a great tree.

Nothing moves but what is most evanescent — 'the scent of woodbine and hay' and among the haymakers 'the tosser lay forsook', the 'long waggon' is immobile without its team, and the team itself relaxes in the shade. The men are, in fact, leaning 'on their rakes, about to begin, / But still', and their paralysed incipience has exactly the same quality of heightened, protracted promise as the lovers in Keats's 'Ode on a Grecian Urn'. The entire scene is poised at the brink of the fulfilment represented by the harvest, without any sign of interruption. It not only summarises all such moments in history by being 'Older than Clare and Cowper, Morland and Crome', but also removes them from time altogether as an invulnerable, ideal manifestation of the England Thomas loved. It is, literally, a picture of immortal perfection:

> Under the heavens that know not what years be
> The men, the beasts, the trees, the implements

> Uttered even what they will in times far hence —
> All of us gone out of the reach of change —
> Immortal in a picture of an old grange.

Such moments are, not surprisingly, uncommon in his work, but they represent the core of his patriotism, as well as the 'goal' he seeks through prose and verse alike. And while their precise character evades analysis even by Thomas himself — he frequently refers to the 'goal' as 'unknown' — a comparison with Richard Jefferies reveals their essential aspects. Thomas regularly chronicled his admiration for Jefferies, and freely admitted his identification with him. As a child, he said, 'anything good or pleasant that I noticed seemed to belong by right to him',[26] just as in later prose writing he found Jefferies's example still before him. 'When a man once gets into Fleet Street he cannot get out,'[27] Jefferies had warned. The influence deriving from youthful idolisation and mature respect took many forms. One, predictably, was occasional similarity in phrasing; the image in these lines from 'Haymaking', for instance —

> The swift with wings and tail as sharp and narrow
> As if the bow had flown off with the arrow

— was not, as Elizabeth Sergeant says, reapplication of a 'fine simile' first told him by Frost's daughter Lesley,[28] but an adaptation of Jefferies's remark about hounds: 'the sinewy back bends like a bow, but a bow that, instead of an arrow, shoots itself'.[29] Less specific resemblances abound in theme rather than in phrasing. Both men so regularly describe vagabond solitaries, gamekeepers' larders, the itinerary of their walks, and rural scenes such as haymaking itself, that the imaginative sympathy between them appears to be as close — and more formative — than that between Thomas and Frost. If it was Frost who, with the war, unlocked Thomas's poetry, it was Jefferies who helped to determine the principal elements of his subject-matter.

For all their significance, these similarities are considerably less important than those which exist between the two men's descriptions of 'moments of everlastingness'. Jefferies's 'power of showing the joy in things'[30] provided Thomas with a yardstick against which his own belief in the regenerative influence of nature could be measured. Thomas was, in fact, reluctant to overplay his experiences of spiritual revelation — 'I ain't a mystic'[31] he told Bottomley — but his friends could not ignore their occurrence. 'The chief reason of the bond uniting us', wrote W. H. Hudson, 'was that we were both mystics in some degree. He was shy of exhibiting it, and either disguised it or attributed it (in his books) to someone he meets or converses with.'[32] Thomas's deep preoccupation with mysticism is nowhere more clearly revealed than in his choice of Jefferies's most transcendent book, *The Story of My Heart*, rather than his novels, as the core of his biographical study. He also gave a prolonged discussion of its manifestations in his introduction to *The Hills and the Vale*. Here, after citing many authorities, he defines it in terms which illuminate the integration described in 'Haymaking': 'the mystic has a view of things by which all knowledge becomes real — or disappears — and all things are seen related to the whole in a manner which gives a wonderful value to the least of them'.[33] In *Light and Twilight* he provides a detailed, and typical, account of its effects:

> I was gathered up with an immortal company, where I and poet and lover and flower and cloud and star were equals, as all the little leaves were equal ruffling before the gusts, or sleeping and carved out of the silentness. And in that company I had learned that I am something which no fortune can touch, whether I be soon to die or long years away. Things will happen which will trample and pierce, but still I shall go on, something that is here and there like the wind, something unconquerable, something not to be separated from the dark earth and light sky, a strong citizen of infinity and eternity. The confidence and ease had become a deep joy; I knew that I could not do without the Infinite, nor the Infinite without me.[34]

Jefferies's own books contain an abundance of equivalent scenes, and as Thomas approvingly relates, their common element is the leading role played by the senses. The following passage from *The Story of My Heart* is characteristic:

> I drew a long breath, then I breathed slowly. My thought, or inner consciousness, went up through the illumined sky, and I was lost in a moment of exaltation. This only lasted a very short time, perhaps only part of a second, and while it lasted there was no formulated wish . . . [but] a deep, strong, and sensuous enjoyment of the beautiful green earth, the beautiful sky and sun . . . [and the thought] that I might have the inner meaning of the sun, the light, the earth, the trees and grass, translated into some growth of excellence, and myself, both of body and of mind; greater perfection of physique, greater perfection of mind and soul; that I might be higher in myself.[35]

Both accounts record an almost identical demand for 'a state of one-ness',[36] but Thomas's heightening of his sensuous responses came to serve an importantly different function. In his poems, he particularises and toughens his insights, and dedicates them to achieving the same kind of 'mystic patriotism' he admired in Coleridge and Blake. Its possession is a triumph of delicacy and reserve.

Thomas also shared with Jefferies a more sombre interpretation of such experiences. One of their central features — the union of all time in a single rapturous moment — involved recalling wars in the past which prefigured the one confronting him in the present. In *The Game-keeper at Home* Jefferies says: 'It is strange to think of, yet it is true enough, that, beautiful as the country is, with its green meadows and graceful trees, its streams and forests and peaceful homesteads, it would be difficult to find an acre of ground that has not been stained with blood. . . . Everywhere under the flowers are the dead.'[37] This was a reflection that Thomas repeatedly singled out for comment: 'Tumuli and earthworks lie on the rising ground . . . so commonly that the youthful Jefferies found it "alive with the dead".'[38] And in his own writing he repeatedly uses landscape to convey the same impression:

> We are not merely twentieth century Londoners or Kentish men or Welshmen. We belong to the days of Wordsworth, of Elizabeth, of Richard Plantagenet, of Harold, of the earliest bands. . . . And of these many folds in our nature the face of the earth reminds us, and perhaps, even when there are no more marks visible upon the land than there were in Eden, we are aware of the passing of time in ways too difficult and strange for the explanation of historian and zoologist and philosopher.[39]

This continual recovery of the dead is an essential aspect of the histori-cal perspective discussed above. Where the buried pipes of 'Digging' testify to the greater durability of objects than individuals, the buried horsemen of 'The Brook', for instance, offer comfort to him in the face of war's threats, by prompting him to forge a link between past, present, and eternity that nothing can break:

> A grey flycatcher silent on a fence
> And I sat as if we had been there since
> The horseman and the horse lying beneath
> The fir-tree-covered barrow on the heath,

> The horseman and the horse with silver shoes,
> Galloped the downs last.

Thomas's poem 'Lob' summarises these attitudes, and also serves as a bridge between his patriotic work and that dealing explicitly with his experience as a soldier. It is 'the apotheosis of all he sought for his *This England* anthology'.[40] As has been shown, the figure of the vagabond solitary who animates the stable qualities inherent in landscape is common throughout his work. In *The Happy-Go-Lucky Morgans*, for instance, he meets one who has Lob's characteristics even without the pressure of war to sharpen them: 'He was pure rustic English. . . . I think he knew men as well as horses; at least he knew everyone in that country, had known them all when he and they were boys. He was a man as English, as true to the soil, as a Ribston pippin.'[41] At the beginning of the poem Lob's own familiarity with the soil is revealed by his physical identification with it; his face is 'sweet as any nut'; literally 'A land face'. At the same time as he conveys this, Thomas also admits that he is in pursuit of precisely those 'inevitably English' qualities on which his patriotism is founded, and re-asserts their elusiveness:

> At hawthorn-time in Wiltshire travelling
> In search of something chance would never bring,
> An old man's face, by life and weather cut
> And coloured, — rough, brown, sweet as any nut, —
> A land face, sea-blue-eyed, — hung in my mind
> When I had left him many a mile behind.

Lob's very resilience is, paradoxically, an important part of his elusiveness, and the first acquaintance that Thomas makes with him occasions another statement of his belief that 'moments of everlastingness' are not susceptible to rational evaluation. The only assessments that can be made of the heart of England are taken by instinct, not scientific investigation, as is suggested in the parenthetical phrase 'by digging':

> 'You see those bits
> Of mounds — that's where they opened up the barrows
> Sixty years since, while I was scaring sparrows.
> They thought as there was something to find there,
> But couldn't find it, by digging, anywhere.'

The entire opening passage in which Thomas repeats this conviction is delivered as recollection, and its consequent sense of imprecision is dramatised by the geographical complexities of the place. Thomas describes how his 'memory could not decide' which among the 'Lurking' villages and lanes was the site of his original meeting with Lob. His difficulties are compounded by the characteristics of the inhabitants; they have 'shot the weathercock' and neglected to 'reap their dandelions' for gold. But this inspired lunacy has a serious aspect: the behaviour of the villagers is no less than an illustration of the origins of folk-tales. The brief history of the 'three Manningfords' and their environs is a telescoped account of a people becoming a culture, and it is swiftly followed by a description of a people becoming their country itself. On his return to the area to search for 'my ancient' — a term which appropriately suggests he is looking for some fundamental, antique aspect of his own personality — Thomas is given directions which record how one of the locals has christened the place with his own life. His Christian name and surname even summarise that paradox of original stasis — and representative exile — (Adam) and mobile transience (Walker) which defines the villages as well as Lob himself:

> To turn back then and seek him, where was the use?
> There were three Manningfords, — Abbots, Bohun, and Bruce:
> And whether Alton, not Manningford, it was
> My memory could not decide, because
> There was both Alton Barnes and Alton Priors.
> All had their churches, graveyards, farms, and byres,
> Lurking to one side up the paths and lanes,
> Seldom well seen except by aeroplanes;
> And when bells rang, or pigs squealed, or cocks crowed,
> Then only heard. Ages ago the road
> Approached. The people stood and looked and turned,
> Nor asked it to come nearer, nor yet learned
> To move out there and dwell in all men's dust.
> And yet withal they shot the weathercock, just
> Because 'twas he crowed out of tune, they said:
> So now the copper weathercock is dead.
> If they had reaped their dandelions and sold
> Them fairly, they could have afforded gold.
>
> Many years passed, and I went back again
> Among those villages, and I looked for men

Who might have known my ancient. He himself
Had long been dead or laid upon the shelf,
I thought. One man I asked about him roared
At my description: ''Tis old Bottlesford
He means, Bill.' But another said: 'Of course,
It was Jack Button up at the White Horse.
He's dead, sir, these three years.' This lasted till
A girl proposed Walker of Walker's Hill,
'Old Adam Walker. Adam's Point you'll see
Marked on the maps.'

After this discreet rehearsal of rural history, Thomas meets someone
who gives him a more accurate description of Lob — the squire's son.
And his report directs the poem into a more obviously patriotic vein.
Superficial resemblances to living villagers are brushed aside in favour of
symbolic significance as the pursuit of an individual is exchanged for the
pursuit of what he represents. Lob's 'inevitably English' quality is des-
cribed by reference to various aspects of country life, and his capacity
for perpetual renewal is suggested by his naming of flowers, birds and
places:

'He is English as this gate, these flowers, this mire.
And when at eight years old Lob-lie-by-the-fire
Came in my books, this was the man I saw.
He has been in England as long as dove and daw,
Calling the wild cherry tree the merry tree,
The rose campion Bridget-in-her-bravery,
And in a tender mood he, as I guess,
Christened one flower Love-in-idleness,
And while he walked from Exeter to Leeds
One April called all cuckoo-flowers Milkmaids.
From him old herbal Gerard learnt, as a boy,
To name wild clematis the Traveller's-joy.
Our blackbirds sang no English till his ear
Told him they called his Jan Toy "Pretty dear".
(She was Jan Toy the Lucky, who, having lost
A shilling, and found a penny loaf, rejoiced.)
For reasons of his own to him the wren
Is Jenny Pooter. Before all other men
'Twas he first called the Hog's Back the Hog's Back.
That Mother Dunch's Buttocks should not lack

Their name was his care. He too could explain
Totteridge and Totterdown and Juggler's Lane:
He knows, if anyone. Why Tumbling Bay,
Inland in Kent, is called so, he might say.'

This catalogue of Lob's achievements bears witness to Thomas's belief that such elements contain a country's oldest and most admirable accumulations of character. It is, as Edna Longley says, a 'beautiful sequence which richly defines the immemorial interaction between man and Nature as well as the role of language in cementing their union. . . . Representing "naturalised" man, he bestows in turn names that humanise Nature.'[42]

In addition to illustrating Lob's role as articulator of the spirit of England, Thomas also includes his role as activator. This is even more significant, since Lob says little 'compared with what he does', and is rudely dismissive of formal education. He will 'buzz / Like a beehive to conclude the tedious fray' of sages, and cut school too, since all the wisdom he needs is contained in the phrase 'Quietness is best'. But it is by coining such proverbs — which are the spoken counterpart of that unchangeable continuum expressed by landscape — that he leads Thomas to celebrate the spirit of England contained in its literature. The authors he praises are themselves either naturalists or those who have included 'the plain, immortal symbols. . . . of a whole countryside'[43] among their work. Appropriately, therefore, Thomas chooses from Shakespeare 'When icicles hang by the wall', and a reference to Herne the Hunter:

'But little he says compared with what he does.
If ever a sage troubles him he will buzz
Like a beehive to conclude the tedious fray:
And the sage, who knows all languages, runs away.
Yet Lob has thirteen hundred names for a fool,
And though he never could spare time for school
To unteach what the fox so well expressed,
On biting the cock's head off, — Quietness is best, —
He can talk quite as well as anyone
After his thinking is forgot and done.
He first of all told someone else's wife,
For a farthing she'd skin a flint and spoil a knife

Worth sixpence skinning it. She heard him speak:
"She had a face as long as a wet week"
Said he, telling the tale in after years.
With blue smock and with gold rings in his ears,
Sometimes he is a pedlar, not too poor
To keep his wit. This is tall Tom that bore
The logs in, and with Shakespeare in the hall
Once talked, when icicles hung by the wall.
As Herne the Hunter he has known hard times.
On sleepless nights he made up weather rhymes
Which others spoilt.'

The passage is an expression of exactly the kind of discreet patriotism preferred in 'This is no case of petty right or wrong', and conforms to his friend John Freeman's judgment that in his poems 'there is no ostentation of love for England, no clamorous apostrophe — there is simply passion, and the name written on his heart'.[44]

The squire's son who describes this fusion of individual, natural and national identity obviously resembles another Wiltshireman, Richard Jefferies. But by praising Lob for possessing these qualities, Thomas also invites the reader to see his (Thomas's) own self as the modern representative of the spirit he celebrates. In the poem's last fifty lines this identification is of especial importance since it involves confronting a uniquely powerful series of threats and dangers. The first direct reference to the war itself is as reticent as the introduction of Lob. By changing his hero's name to 'Hob', Thomas recalls 'old shepherd Hobbe, Crimea veteran'[45] from the essay 'It's a Long Long Way' (itself an accout of the war's effect on English people in the provinces). And this reminiscence is followed at once by a reference to the hog that Hob owns; its unimaginative complacency is of the same quality as the jingoist's:

> . . . 'Hob, being then his name,
> He kept the hog that thought the butcher came
> To bring his breakfast. "You thought wrong", said Hob.'

This sudden undercurrent of violence is not glimpsed again until twenty lines later — when a sinister reference to a giant darkens the poem with an archetypal image of invasion:

> 'And while he was a little cobbler's boy
> He tricked the giant coming to destroy

Shrewsbury by flood. "And how far is it yet?"
The giant asked in passing. "I forget;
But see these shoes I've worn out on the road
And we're not there yet." He emptied out his load
Of shoes. The giant sighed, and dropped from his spade
The earth for damming Severn, and thus made
The Wrekin hill; and little Ercall hill
Rose where the giant scraped his boots.'

Thomas had already given a precise historical perspective to this menace, in an essay which was to be collected in *The Last Sheaf*: 'Napoleon, one hundred years ago, was expected to sail up the Severn and destroy the Forest: now it was feared that the Germans were coming.'[46] The will to destroy is, as he had noticed elsewhere, as tireless and repetitive as the creative instincts he celebrates in the figure of Lob. Until now, Lob's ingenuity and courage have been equal to any threats, but during the final section of the poem, when Thomas adjusts the lens of his attention to focus on the present, the difficulties are seen to be more severe than ever before:

'Do you believe Jack dead before his hour?
Or that his name is Walker, or Bottlesford,
Or Button, a mere clown, or squire, or lord?
The man you saw, — Lob-lie-by-the-fire, Jack Cade,
Jack Smith, Jack Moon, poor Jack of every trade,
Young Jack, or old Jack, or Jack What-d'ye-call,
Jack-in-the-hedge, or Robin-run-by-the-wall,
Robin Hood, Ragged Robin, lazy Bob,
One of the lords of No Man's Land, good Lob, —
Although he was seen dying at Waterloo,
Hastings, Agincourt, and Sedgemoor, too, —
Lives yet. He never will admit he is dead
Till millers cease to grind men's bones for bread,
Not till our weathercock crows once again
And I remove my house out of the lane
On to the road.' With this he disappeared
In hazel and thorn tangled with old-man's-beard.
But one glimpse of his back, as there he stood,
Choosing his way, proved him of old Jack's blood,
Young Jack perhaps, and now a Wiltshireman
As he has oft been since his days began.

The increased gravity is conveyed in the structure of the verse itself; Thomas accelerates the movement of his thought to summarise all Lob's previous trades, names, and qualities. The speed is so headlong that personal names, and the names of flowers and folk-heroes, jostle together until they blur into a compendium of those qualities he had praised earlier. But the procession is abruptly slowed by the reference to 'No Man's Land', in which Thomas updates the original meaning of 'unowned waste land' to embody Lob's present dangers. At first, their significance seems to be reduced by the succeeding account of his experience in historical battles. Indeed, the reiterated suggestion that Lob is as indestructible as the folk-legends he originated is customarily taken to define Thomas's phlegmatic expectancy that England will emerge as unscathed from the present conflict as it did from those which preceded it. Edna Longley, for instance, says that the passage refers to 'the uncrushable spirit of the common soldier still fighting to defend his country'.[47] But Thomas is not so confident. He explicitly says that the continuation of the spirit of England depends upon the survival of its local and original folk characteristics, and yet he has already mentioned how Lob himself has ground up the miller who ground men's bones for flour. The removal of houses 'out of the lane / On to the road', too, would be easily achieved if, as has happened before, 'the road / Approached'. In other words, the durability of many such characteristics is threatened by their principal quality: logical impossibility. Because they are unlikely events themselves, there is no reason to suppose why equally improbable occurrences should not destroy them. Miller, weathercock and moving house have exactly the same properties as Birnham Wood.

This balance of threats and regenerative elements is emphasised by one other facet of 'Lob's' conclusion. The vagabond has the same adaptability as the eponymous hero of George Bourne's *The Bettesworth Book* — who is himself a Lob figure:

> When Bettesworth is done for and his old wagging tongue at length
> still, the same brave qualities . . . will be moulding other men after
> his pattern, controlling their actions, shaping their thoughts, putting
> into their mouths conversations like these, and in them all carrying
> on invisibly these unconscious traditions, habits, instincts, that are
> surely a valuable part of what we think of as the English Race.[48]

A similar capacity for renewal is suggested by Thomas's skilful melting of his own hero back into the landscape with which he was identified at the outset — Lob's beard, for example, confuses itself with the old-man's-beard in the hedge. But the ominous verb 'disappeared', exaggerated at the line-end, has the same finality as that used to describe the departure of the previous solitary to appear in a poem of Thomas's, Jack Noman:

> Bluebells hid all the ruts in the copse.
> The elm seeds lay in the road like hops,
> That fine day, May the twenty-third,
> The day Jack Noman disappeared.

This tension is equivalent to that which occurs in 'Lob'; throughout the conclusion, Thomas is poised between celebration and anxiety. At the same time as he provides a beautifully complete account of his patriotic motives, he also admits that he is fighting for a territory with 'a culture and way of life which, ironically, he knew was disappearing'.[49] The war, he realised, would be the final blow whether it was won or lost, but such certitude did not prevent him from rejoicing in those elements of the ancient culture which remained.

A poem written thirteen months after 'Lob', 'As the team's head brass', discusses these conflicting preoccupations in even more resolute terms:

> As the team's head brass flashed out on the turn
> The lovers disappeared into the wood.
> I sat among the boughs of the fallen elm
> That strewed an angle of the fallow, and
> Watched the plough narrowing a yellow square
> Of charlock. Every time the horses turned
> Instead of treading me down, the ploughman leaned
> Upon the handles to say or ask a word,
> About the weather, next about the war.
> Scraping the share he faced towards the wood,
> And screwed along the furrow till the brass flashed
> Once more.
>   The blizzard felled the elm whose crest
> I sat in, by a woodpecker's round hole,
> The ploughman said. 'When will they take it away?'
> 'When the war's over.' So the talk began —
> One minute and an interval of ten,

A minute more and the same interval.
'Have you been out?' 'No.' 'And don't want to, perhaps?'
'If I could only come back again, I should.
I could spare an arm. I shouldn't want to lose
A leg. If I should lose my head, why, so,
I should want nothing more. . . . Have many gone
From here?' 'Yes.' 'Many lost?' 'Yes, a good few.
Only two teams work on the farm this year.
One of my mates is dead. The second day
In France they killed him. It was back in March,
The very night of the blizzard, too. Now if
He had stayed here we should have moved the tree.'
'And I should not have sat here. Everything
Would have been different. For it would have been
Another world.' 'Ay, and a better, though
If we could see all all might seem good.' Then
The lovers came out of the wood again:
The horses started and for the last time
I watched the clods crumble and topple over
After the ploughshare and the stumbling team.

Just as in 'Blenheim Oranges' the war turned 'young men to dung' — an emblem of decay as well as an agent of fertilisation — Thomas retains the perception of regeneration in the midst of military oppression and agricultural development. Not only does the regular action of the horses (which come close to 'treading me down') call to mind the automatic, menacing movement of a military action — cavalry perhaps — but one of Thomas's alternative titles for the poem was 'The Last Team'.[50] This suggests that he realised the rural order, as it is represented by the plough, was shortly to be upset by mechanical developments, and intensifies the menace of the conclusion:

> . . . for the last time
> I watched the clods crumble and topple over
> After the ploughshare and the stumbling team.

Thomas is leaving for the Front, possibly never to return, and the horses themselves are shortly to be driven off the landscape by agricultural changes. Their 'stumbling' betrays not only their weariness but their obsolescence. These two broad themes of threat and disruption are strengthened by the more obvious elm (which has 'fallen' as if it were a soldier), and a discussion of the ploughman's dead mate, to create at the centre of the poem an analysis of apparently unrelieved chaos and upset. Furthermore, Helen Thomas suggested that this particular pastoral context was itself tainted by an association of ideas she noticed in her husband: 'He loved a good piece of leather', she wrote in *World Without End*, 'and his Sam Browne and high trench-boots shone with a deep clear lustre. The brass, too, reminded him of the brass ornaments we had often admired when years ago we had lived on a farm and knew every detail of a plough-team's harness.'[51]

This catalogue of disruptive elements is, however, balanced against a saving ambiguity in Thomas's conversation with the ploughman. Referring to his companion killed in France they say, with the ploughman beginning:

> 'Now if
> He had stayed here we should have moved the tree.'
> 'And I should not have sat here. Everything
> Would have been different. For it would have been
> Another world.' 'Ay, and a better, though
> If we could see all all might seem good.'

This implication that there is at least the potential for future good in the ashes of the present is paralleled by another: the poem is opened and closed by entrance into and exit from the wood by 'the lovers'. In the poem 'Lovers' itself the 'men in the road' who watch two lovers emerge from a wood agree smilingly that

> 'There are more things than one
> A man might turn into a wood for. . . .'

— acknowledging that their concealment has been for erotic purposes. In *As It Was*, too, Helen Thomas records her own and her husband's penchant for making love in woods.[52] The lovers of 'As the team's head brass' linger throughout the poem as unseen but pervasive presences who have in effect initiated the next generation — the one responsible for employing the potential for good which remains even after the present upheaval. And their overtly regenerative action is dramatised by the plough, which opens the ground prior to the introduction of seed, screwing 'along the furrow till the brass flashed / Once more'. The

destruction which lies at the heart of the poem is thus literally brack-
eted by the promise of rejuvenation, although Thomas acknowledges
that his own future is severely jeopardised by the war. In the discussion
of injuries he might sustain, he includes a tacit anxiety — implied by the
suspense of a line-ending — that his sexual activity will be terminated:

> 'I could spare an arm. I shouldn't want to lose
> A leg. If I should lose my head, why, so,
> I should want nothing more. . . .'

The potency within impotence, the regeneration within destruction, the
hope within apprehension, insists on emerging throughout the poem,
balancing his judgments of war's effects, and endowing them with a
considered maturity. It provides a complete expression of his ability to
suggest alternative interpretations of any given event, and illustrates the
range of his war poetry by relating immediate circumstances to recur-
rent patterns of human and seasonal life.

III

Thomas built a large number of poems dealing explicitly with his own
participation in the war upon the attitudes defined by 'Lob' and 'As
the team's head brass'. It is possible to trace in them his complete
career as a soldier from enlistment, through his response to army life,
to reflections on the possibility of death as he prepares to embark for
France.

In the first of these groups, the poems dealing with enlistment,
Thomas chronicles 'the need to accept, without severe questioning, the
obedient life of a war-time soldier',[53] and describes his need for satisfy-
ing absorption in whatever circumstances present themselves. In 'For
these', written the very day he joined up, he rehearses the pacific,
idealised rural values so frequently espoused by his Georgian contem-
poraries (de la Mare, for instance, in 'I Dream of a Place') only to reject
them in favour of an appeal for active involvement:

> An acre of land between the shore and the hills,
> Upon a ledge that shows my kingdoms three,
> The lovely visible earth and sky and sea,
> Where what the curlew needs not, the farmer tills:

A house that shall love me as I love it,
Well-hedged, and honoured by a few ash-trees
That linnets, greenfinches, and goldfinches
Shall often visit and make love in and flit:

A garden I need never go beyond,
Broken but neat, whose sunflowers every one
Are fit to be the sign of the Rising Sun:
A spring, a brook's bend, or at least a pond:

For these I ask not, but, neither too late
Nor yet too early, for what men call content,
And also that something may be sent
To be contented with, I ask of fate.

The reluctance to define content here amounts almost to self-parody. Struggling to resolve the tension between Frost's invitations to visit America and his clarified sense of patriotic duty, the poem gropes forward as if it were a prayer Thomas did not expect to hear answered. But in spite of his doubts, the rejection of secluded comfort is itself robust. The strength of his resolve to turn away from the sky, garden, birds, and brook of his imagined retirement is measured by the very detail with which he lovingly catalogues them. This step forward into what is unknown in every respect — except that it involves rejecting the chance of ease — is strengthened by the fact that army life forced him to concentrate on the present. Such a distillation of time forms an ironic counterpart to those moments of passionate intensity he shared with Jefferies: 'my state of mind ... is really so entirely preoccupied with getting through the tunnel that you might say I had forgotten there was a sun at either end, before or after this business.'[54] Yet this concentration has its redeeming features. During his career as a prose writer the past and future had repeatedly mocked him with unfulfilled or unfulfillable aspirations. His remark in *Rose Acre Papers* is typical: 'When the world is too much with me, when the past is a reproach harrying me with dreadful faces, and the present a fierce mockery, the future an open grave, it is sweet to sleep'.[55] The reduction of time to a continuous present in which 'I just think about when I shall first go on guard'[56] removed these torments, and the army also appealed to him because it provided exactly the kind of undemanding society he preferred. But it brought unavoidable frustrations as well. ' "Home" ' ('Fair was the morning') illustrates this ambivalence, and two remarks in his correspondence illuminate the genesis of the poem. In the first, to Eleanor Farjeon, he wrote: 'Somebody said something about homesickness the other day. It is a disease one can suppress but not do without under these conditions.'[57] To Frost, he gave a more circumstantial account:

> It is Sunday, always a dreary ruminating day if spent in camp. We got a walk, three of us, one a schoolmaster, the other a gamebreeder who knows about horses and dogs and ferrets. We heard the first blackbird, walked 9 or 10 miles straight across country (the advantage of our uniform — we go just anywhere we like): ate, drank (stout) by a fire at a big quiet inn — not a man to drink left in the village: drew a panorama — a landscape for military purposes drawn exactly with the help of a compass and a protractor, which is an amusement I have quite taken to — they say I am a neo-realist at it.[58]

The movement of the poem itself is based on a similar union of constraint and liberty:

> Fair was the morning, fair our tempers, and
> We had seen nothing fairer than that land,
> Though strange, and the untrodden snow that made
> Wild of the tame, casting out all that was
> Not wild and rustic and old; and we were glad.
>
> Fair too was afternoon, and first to pass
> Were we that league of snow, next the north wind.
>
> There was nothing to return for except need.
> And yet we sang nor ever stopped for speed,
> As we did often with the start behind.
> Faster still strode we when we came in sight
> Of the cold roofs where we must spend the night.
>
> Happy we had not been there, nor could be,
> Though we had tasted sleep and food and fellowship
> Together long.
>
>   'How quick' to someone's lip
> The word came, 'will the beaten horse run home.'
>
> The word 'home' raised a smile in us all three,
> And one repeated it, smiling just so

That all knew what he meant and none would say.
Between three counties far apart that lay
We were divided and looked strangely each
At the other, and we knew we were not friends
But fellows in a union that ends
With the necessity for it, as it ought.

Never a word was spoken, not a thought
Was thought, of what the look meant with the word
'Home' as we walked and watched the sunset blurred.
And then to me the word, only the word,
'Homesick', as it were playfully occurred:
No more. If I should ever more admit
Than the mere word I could not endure it
For a day longer: this captivity
Must somehow come to an end, else I should be
Another man, as often now I seem,
Or this life be only an evil dream.

The poem opens with a panorama of content which prefigures his experience of army comradeship — morning, tempers and land are all 'fair'. And this fusion of mental and natural landscapes is given physical expression by the unifying and 'untrodden snow that made / Wild of the tame'. The snow momentarily restores a 'wild and rustic and old' appearance to the place, and thereby makes it resemble the 'quintessential England' discussed above. Moreover, the fact that 'first to pass / Were we that league of snow, next the north wind' suggests that the walkers are the original, uncompromised possessors of the landscape. Their ownership of it is confirmed by the wind blurring their tracks behind them. It is an action which literally seals them in an exalted, refined state. Thomas acknowledges that practical needs will ensure their return, but this does not impede present enjoyment, which manifests itself in their singing and hurrying 'As we did often with the start behind'. The significance of this phrase emerges when it is recalled that because they must start walking from, and in the end return to, 'the cold roofs' of the camp, their journey will inevitably be circular. Like racehorses (an image developed from the reference to 'the start' in line 10, to 'the beaten horse' in line 16), their appearance of free movement conceals a reality of predetermined constraint. Thomas and his companions are invisibly chained to the beginning of the course of which they walk the extent, by their obligation to fulfil military duties.

The disadvantages of camp life, though real enough, are minimised by the congestion of the line which mentions them: 'Happy we had not been there, nor could be'. This suppression of unhappiness is confirmed by Thomas's attention to benefits inherent in the same context. 'Sleep and food and fellowship' are not simply enumerated, they are intensified and relished by the verb 'tasted'. It is a miniature ascending scale of pleasures which aptly introduce and justify his protracted discussion of 'home'. Of the three walkers, it is Thomas's two companions who first toss the word between them, savouring the irony of its being applied to an army camp. Yet there is a sense in which it is appropriate. In this poem, and in those discussed above, Thomas is reconciled to his patriotic duty, whatever its inconveniences; and until the demands that war makes on him are ended, the camp and his companions define an appreciation of national identity. Between the comforts of domestic homes and the ideal homes of imagination, they constitute a third, which is inadequate in many respects, but admitted to be necessary.

It is, in addition, one which resolves individual differences, however briefly, and forms a unique, practical friendship in which Thomas scrupulously identifies the shortcomings, as well as the virtues:

> Between three counties far apart that lay
> We were divided and looked strangely each
> At the other, and we knew we were not friends
> But fellows in a union that ends
> With the necessity for it, as it ought.

The nervous balance of their relationship is as fine as their interpretation of the word 'home'. In his letters, he expanded on the reasons for this, employing the same terminology as he did in the poem. The day before it was written he had said to Frost: 'here I have to like people because they are more my sort than the others, although I realise at certain times they are not my sort at all and will vanish away after the war. What almost completes the illusion is that I can't help talking to them as if they were friends.'[59] But by the time he embarked for France he had made it clear that it was not simply the quality of his comrades' characters which made friendship difficult. It was rather that he was reluctant to form ties which would almost certainly be broken painfully: 'I don't want *friends* here', he told Bottomley, 'I should be too introspective or too happy to meet the circumstances.'[60]

The tacit suggestion of a perfect state of friendship, from which these fall short, emphasises the similarly missed ideal of home. But Thomas — only now speaking for the first time — refuses to visualise this clearly:

> Never a word was spoken, not a thought
> Was thought, of what the look meant with the word
> 'Home' as we walked and watched the sunset blurred.
> And then to me the word, only the word,
> 'Homesick', as it were playfully occurred:
> No more.

The ideal is deliberately left as blurred as the sunset, lest it should make the reality unbearable. Another poem, 'Liberty', confirms this interpretation of the passage. Freedom to do nothing but imagine an unattainable utopia has no attraction for him: 'There's none less free than who / Does nothing and has nothing else to do, / Being free only for what is not to his mind, / And nothing is to his mind.' It is precisely because he realises that to juxtapose perfection with reality is to stimulate his appreciation of both, that he closes the poem by describing himself as 'half in love with pain'. In 'Home', therefore, as the soldiers return to camp, Thomas allows the musing movement of his mind to release 'the word, only the word, / "Homesick" ' to intensify his enjoyment of its opposite. The hesitant speech is exactly in keeping with his deliberate, slow pondering of its meaning. As with 'Adlestrop' ('the name'), or 'the name, only the name' of 'The Word', he registers a hiatus between the word 'home' and the associations it has for him, but carefully avoids upsetting the relationship he has created between ideal and real:

> If I should ever more admit
> Than the mere word I could not endure it
> For a day longer.

The poem's conclusion enlarges the significance of this balance. The last four lines subtly join military and moral life into a symbol of captivity which refers back to his frustrations as a prose writer:

> . . . this captivity
> Must somehow come to an end, else I should be
> Another man, as often now I seem,
> Or this life be only an evil dream.

Thomas's historical appraisal of war, and his relative good fortune in having time to write during his training, enabled him to describe life in the army as a continuation, rather than a denial, of much previous experience. And he is not blind to the personal cost it involves — indeed, he suggests that the necessary suppression of ideals threatens to produce a radical alteration of character. In letters to Frost, as in the poem itself, he realised that, as a soldier, he risked misrepresenting himself just as thoroughly as he had done during his sixteen years as a 'doomed hack'. 'Am I indulging in the pleasure of being someone else?' he asked; and he noted with wry amusement that 'My disguises increase, what with spurs on my heels, and hair on my upper lip.'[61]

This ability to record the war as part of a continuous process, which affects the civilian as much as the soldier, is more obviously evident in the large number of poems concerned with its influence beyond the confines of military society. In 'The Cherry Trees' and 'In Memoriam [Easter 1915]', for example, he concentrates, like A. E. Housman, on emblems of pastoral pleasure (flowers and cherry blossom) which the war has caused to be neglected:

> The cherry trees bend over and are shedding
> On the old road where all that passed are dead,
> Their petals, strewing the grass as for a wedding
> This early May morn when there is none to wed.

The compressed quatrains of both poems have the quality of maxims which realise the domestic aspect of the deprivations recorded by Owen in France. Instead of mutilated corpses there is an absence of any humans at all — only the motifs of peace sinisterly unused. Those poems which do mention war by name operate in a similarly reticent but comprehensive manner. Often, as in 'Blenheim Oranges', a single reference to the war provides an urgency which ripples through the entire poem. 'Wind and Mist' also illustrates this. Its interlocutor's primary concern is to analyse his sense of simultaneous alienation from, and desire to communicate with, the natural world; but the threat war poses to his possessing any natural world at all intensifies his longing:

> 'If you like angled fields
> Of grass and grain bounded by oak and thorn,
> Here is a league. Had we with Germany
> To play upon this board it could not be
> More dear than April has made it with a smile.'

Behind the insubstantiality of wind and mist lies the involved sensuality
he demands, and it is this which the war clarifies. The paradoxical
process of endearment by jeopardy is confirmed and expanded in 'The
Owl'. Here, three months before enlisting, Thomas appears to chastise
himself for the comfort he enjoys compared to soldiers:

> Downhill I came, hungry, and yet not starved;
> Cold, yet had heat within me that was proof
> Against the North wind; tired, yet so that rest
> Had seemed the sweetest thing under a roof.
>
> Then at the inn I had food, fire, and rest,
> Knowing how hungry, cold, and tired was I.
> All of the night was quite barred out except
> An owl's cry, a most melancholy cry
>
> Shaken out long and clear upon the hill,
> No merry note, nor cause of merriment,
> But one telling me plain what I escaped
> And others could not, that night, as in I went.
>
> And salted was my food, and my repose,
> Salted and sobered, too, by the bird's voice
> Speaking for all who lay under the stars,
> Soldiers and poor, unable to rejoice.

In this poem the sense of guilty escape actually stimulates his enjoy-
ment. As Vernon Scannell points out, 'the word "salted" certainly
means "flavoured" or "spiced", but at the same time less comfortable
connotations are involved: the harshness of salt, the salt in the wound,
the taste of bitterness, and of tears'.[62]

The connection between soldiers and poor in 'The Owl' reaffirms the
correspondence between military and civilian life. Thomas's war poems
are concerned with all circumstances of disruption, past and present,
and have particular but not exclusive reference to the First World War.
In 'A Private', for example, the ploughman who slept outdoors nightly
'At Mrs Greenland's Hawthorn Bush' rediscovers many circumstantial
details of the place, including its secrecy, 'Where now at last he sleeps /
More sound in France'. The similarites are even more evident in an
earlier draft of the poem:

A labouring man lies hid in that bright coffin
Who slept out many a frosty night and kept
Good drinkers and bedmen tickled with his scoffing
'At Mrs Greenland's Hawthorn bush I slept.'[63]

Here the 'bright coffin' that the ploughman's corpse lies in recalls the bright coffin of air itself, just as it does in Andrew Young's poem 'A Dead Mole': 'Your body lies here stout and square / Buried within the blue vault of the air'.[64] Like 'The Cherry Trees', 'A Private' conveys the extent of its grief by poignantly withholding itself from any kind of extreme statement. It is compressed 'into *almost* impersonal and epigrammatic sharpness'.[65]

In 'Tears' Thomas employs another method of releasing emotion under restraint. The title itself warns of an ambiguity that the poem expands: tears of pleasure and sadness fall almost indistinguishably as he passes from remembering

When twenty hounds streamed by me, not yet combed out
But still all equals in their rage of gladness

to watching

Soldiers in line, young English countrymen,
Fair-haired and ruddy, in white tunics.

Both sights are accompanied by the stillness appropriate to a moment of contentment, but both reluctantly deny it. The uniformity of hounds and soldiers suggests a partially unveiled threat which is emphasised by Thomas's identification of the latter as 'countrymen'. The visual shock of their red faces, dramatised by fair hair and white tunics, prefigures the bloodstains which will shortly blot out the values of Lob's England which they represent. It is entirely in character with the rest of his war poems that 'Tears' should struggle to preserve a balanced response and not, in honesty, be able to prevent it tilting towards a confession of imminent tragedy.

This emphasis is confirmed by the group of four poems describing Thomas's reaction to 'the trumpet [which] blows for everything'.[66] In the first of them, 'Cock-Crow' (only the fourth poem he wrote after enlisting), his enthusiasm for military life is tightly reined:

Out of the wood of thoughts that grows by night
To be cut down by the sharp axe of light, —
Out of the night, two cocks together crow,
Cleaving the darkness with a silver blow:
And bright before my eyes twin trumpeters stand,
Heralds of splendour, one at either hand,
Each facing each as in a coat of arms:
The milkers lace their boots up at the farms.

The crowing cocks are transformed by his pun on 'blow' into 'twin trumpeters' which, although wilfully stylised, strengthen his resolve by cutting down the shadows of uncertainty. Nevertheless, he refuses to become intoxicated by their summons, and it is a beautifully evocative, pacific, pastoral action to which he turns in the end: 'The milkers lace their boots up at the farms.'

The second poem, 'Bugle Call', expands on this reluctance to be seduced by the trumpet call. His phrasing draws attention to the fact that its notes occur in the Last Post as well as in Reveille:

'No one cares less than I,
Nobody knows but God
Whether I am destined to lie
Under a foreign clod,'
Were the words I made to the bugle call in the morning.

But laughing, storming, scorning,
Only the bugles know
What the bugles say in the morning,
And they do not care, when they blow
The call that I heard and made words to early this morning.

The trumpets' refusal to divulge the meaning of their own notes suggests at once the danger which lies behind their call; the romance of Rupert Brooke's 'foreign field' is replaced by the bathetic and heavily rhymed 'foreign clod' as death's seal. And the discrepancy between idealised and likely circumstances of death represents a criticism of cavalier responses to military action which, in the third 'bugle poem' — 'The Trumpet' — receives its subtlest treatment. Perhaps because of this, it has suffered several dramatic misreadings. Paul Fussell's comment is typical: ' "The Trumpet" inverts the terms of the standard aubade in order to encourage enlistment. Dawn is conceived as a signal to action rather than as the last hurried moment for dalliance.'[67] Even Thomas's friend J. W. Haines called it one 'of the most stirring war songs that poet ever uttered'.[68] In fact, the full and characteristic ambivalence of the poem is lost unless some credence is given to these opinions. It begins with an invitation to 'Rise up, rise up' and salute the happy morn, with what appears to be a deliberately straightforward echo of Housman's 'Reveille'.[69] But this enthusiasm is checked in at least two places:

> Rise up, rise up,
> And, as the trumpet blowing
> Chases the dreams of men,
> As the dawn glowing
> The stars that left unlit
> The land and water,
> Rise up and scatter
> The dew that covers
> The print of last night's lovers —
> Scatter it, scatter it!

In the third line Thomas suggests that by abolishing men's 'dreams', the trumpets also puncture their innocent ideals, and open their eyes to a war in which it is necessary to scatter the harmony represented by lovers. In other words, the poem explores exactly the same hiatus between the trumpet's enthralling invitation and Thomas's dubious response as 'Bugle Call'. And in the second verse this becomes clearer still:

> While you are listening
> To the clear horn,
> Forget, men, everything
> On this earth newborn,
> Except that it is lovelier
> Than any mysteries.
> Open your eyes to the air
> That has washed the eyes of the stars
> Through all the dewy night:
> Up with the light,
> To the old wars;
> Arise, arise!

123

Here 'the clear horn' persuades Thomas to forget all modern aspects of the earth, and remember that, in essence, 'it is lovelier / Than any mysteries'. He is not asking that he should be filled with military fervour at all, but that he should be reminded of the stable England which is the core of his patriotism. At the same time, he encourages the trumpet to erase the individual character of the present conflict so that, as he responds to his duty, he is not flattered into thinking he is taking part in a war to end all wars, but knows it is an interminable process of destruction. It is for this reason that he describes himself as summoned 'to the old wars' and not, say, to the Somme. War, the poem affirms, is an inalienable condition of mankind, and if it is to be endured, the individual soldier must define clearly his motives for participation. And those motives are not so much an obsessive commitment to immediate circumstances as a love for what is as old as war itself: the unbreakable and untranslatable bond between a race and the quintessence of its country.

Thomas has no illusions that even this analysis of warfare, and his patriotism, will help to preserve his life. In the last of the trumpet group, he faces up to the possibility of his own death even more candidly. This poem, as a remark to Eleanor Farjeon illustrates, disposes of ironic masks and tongue-in-cheek interpretations of the bugle note, 'Now I have actually done still another piece which I call "Lights Out",' he said. 'It sums up what I have often thought at that call. I wish it were as brief — two pairs of long notes.'[70] In fact the poem is five short notes in which he poises himself between waking and sleeping, and between the trumpet's summons to self-sacrifice and his natural instinct for life. The labyrinthine course between these alternatives is perfectly dramatised by the tortuous sentence structure:

> I have come to the borders of sleep,
> The unfathomable deep
> Forest, where all must lose
> Their way, however straight
> Or winding, soon or late;
> They can not choose.
>
> Many a road and track
> That since the dawn's first crack
> Up to the forest brink
> Deceived the travellers,
> Suddenly now blurs,
> And in they sink.

Here love ends —
Despair, ambition ends;
All pleasure and all trouble,
Although most sweet or bitter,
Here ends, in sleep that is sweeter
Than tasks most noble.

There is not any book
Or face of dearest look
That I would not turn from now
To go into the unknown
I must enter, and leave, alone,
I know not how.

The tall forest towers:
Its cloudy foliage lowers
Ahead, shelf above shelf:
Its silence I hear and obey
That I may lose my way
And myself.

Here, like a drowning man, Thomas summarises his life in scenes connected by the image of a road. But this device, which recurs throughout his writing career, leads him to the prospect of unconscious nullity, and not to the chance of new beginnings. His certainty that the trumpet signals his death is so absolute that even his attempts to balance the appeal of death against his recoil from it are of no avail. Love and despair, pleasure and trouble, are reduced to the same blank 'sleep that is sweeter / Than tasks most noble'. When, in the penultimate verse, the opportunity of choice returns, it only brings him closer to death. And yet, paradoxically, his decision to 'turn from' the known and 'go into the unknown' amounts to a faint affirmation of life. By having a choice at all, he is momentarily reminded of his identity before the final obedient entrance into the forest where he will lose it irredeemably. During this transformation from known to unknown, the guiding image of the road is replaced by silence, and possibilities of self-discovery are smothered by the certainty of self-effacement. It is the moving culmination of all Thomas's trumpet poems, and of his whole life's journey.

IV

'Lights Out' is not an elegantly phrased Romantic longing for escape, but a realistic assessment of Thomas's chances of survival. And the conclusions it reaches are discussed in so many of his other poems that it is possible to examine his attitude to death in considerable detail. His characteristic response in the prose books is a desire for release from human frustrations which is forestalled by his wish to retain consciousness. This tension is apparent throughout the contemplation of suicide in his story 'The Attempt', and is also present in this passage from *The South Country*:

> the poverty of death is such that we cannot hope from it . . . a gift
> of contemplation from afar, cannot hope even that once out of the
> world we may turn round and look at it and feel that we are not of
> it anymore, nor hope that we shall know ourselves to be dead and be
> satisfied.[71]

Death was not, as Alun Lewis said (speaking more of himself than of Thomas), 'the ultimate response that he, despite himself, desired'.[72] It was a realistically assessed, and repeatedly rejected, backdrop to his existence, which stimulated and flavoured his pleasure in living.

A poem explicitly concerned with Thomas's reaction to the future, 'Fifty Faggots', illuminates this ambivalence. It was written on 13 May 1915, and sent to Frost two days later with the query '[Is it] *north* of Boston only?'[73] He need not have worried; it is entirely characteristic of himself in form and meaning:

> There they stand, on their ends, the fifty faggots
> That once were underwood of hazel and ash
> In Jenny Pinks's Copse. Now, by the hedge
> Close packed, they make a thicket fancy alone
> Can creep though with the mouse and wren. Next Spring
> A blackbird or a robin will nest there,
> Accustomed to them, thinking they will remain
> Whatever is for ever to a bird:
> This Spring it is too late; the swift has come.
> 'Twas a hot day for carrying them up:
> Better they will never warm me, though they must
> Light several Winters' fires.

The faggots stored to heat him for 'several Winters', although cut down and destined to endure for only a limited time, are immediately taken to be permanent by the blackbird and robin, who think 'they will remain / Whatever is for ever to a bird'. And to start with, Thomas also supposes that his own sense of dislocation from customary life-cycles does not deny the chance of adapting to different, military circumstances. But the tacit suggestion that 'Whatever is for ever to a bird' is not for ever to himself undermines his confidence. In the second half of the poem, as his attention fixes on the faggot pile itself, his anxiety about surviving the new situation increases. The logs constitute a prophecy in which the possibility of loss overshadows his hopes:

> Before they are done
> The war will have ended, many other things
> Have ended, maybe, that I can no more
> Foresee or more control than robin and wren.

A year after sending the poem to Frost, Thomas referred to it again, in such a way as to suggest that the balance of loss inherent in gain, and gain in loss, should have been tilted even more emphatically towards uncertainty:

the future is less explorable than usual, and I don't take it (the future) quite seriously. I find myself thinking as if there wasn't going to be no future. This isn't perversity. I say I find myself doing so. On the other hand it may be I am just as wrong as when I wrote about those fifty faggots. I thought that one simply had to wait a very long time. I wonder if it is pleasanter to be Rupert Brookeish.[74]

Thomas had seven months left to live when he wrote this, and during that time his hopes of survival shrank dramatically. In recording his progress towards death, he continually employs images of roads and travellers; but instead of initiating self-discovery as they did in 'The Other' or 'The Bridge', they describe a gradual progress towards extinction. In one of his finest poems, actually called 'Roads' and written on 22 January 1916, he maps this transformation. It unites three themes: the description of roads themselves, of the gods who inhabit them, and of their role as guides leading him to France. These are deftly intertwined to form a single strand, and it is one that he commented on himself in *The Icknield Way*: 'I could not find a beginning or an end of the Icknield Way. It is thus a symbol of mortal things with their beginnings and ends always in immortal darkness.'[75] Not only does the poem summarise his career, it also redefines his feelings for England; the roads are not modern means of transport but, as it were, veins running through the body of that ancient English landscape which was the ground of his patriotism. They are the Icknield Way, the Ridgeway, the Pilgrims' Way and 'the mountain ways of Wales'.

In the opening verse Thomas blends these literal and symbolic qualities, introducing the 'invisible' gods who are to join with the ghosts of the dead returning from France at the close. Their spectral presence haunts the entire poem, bracketing it, and quickening his realisation that roads possess the paradoxical quality which forms the basis of his contentment. Their simultaneous manifestation of transience and permanence is immediately apparent:

> I love roads:
> The goddesses that dwell
> Far along invisible
> Are my favourite gods.
>
> Roads go on
> While we forget, and are
> Forgotten like a star
> That shoots and is gone.

Travellers and roads depend on each other for their existence: 'If we trod [them] not again', they would sink back into their original landscape. Even at night

> They are lonely
> While we sleep, lonelier
> For lack of the traveller
> Who is now a dream only.

But just as roads 'fade / So soon' and yet 'so long endure', the sleeping traveller also embodies a duality. He is not only dreaming himself, but is the roads' own dream of all those who preceded him. It is this apprehension of mutable stability that enlarges Thomas's role in the poem from an individual to a representative, seeking for what in *The Icknield Way* he called 'the mystery of the road'.[76] Not surprisingly, his search encourages him to complete his unravelling of the paradoxes he has already discovered. In stanza 6, for instance, roads are seen as a thread connecting dawn and dusk. But their function is not simply to connect two opposites, it is to suggest that both are present in the same moment:

> From dawn's twilight
> And all the clouds like sheep
> On the mountains of sleep
> They wind into the night.

These lines offer an example of Thomas's writing at its most suggestive and concentrated. The journey is now conceived as a temporal rather than a physical one, and the 'dawn's twilight' from which it begins contains two opposite times of day (morning and evening) reconciled in one. This union is strengthened by the following image of sheep. The 'And' beginning the line in which it occurs implies that 'the clouds like sheep' are seen at dawn. But dawn itself has already been compared to dusk, and sheep are counted to send people to sleep, not to awaken them. The clouds also confuse the physical with the temporal world. The primary sense of the image is clearly that the fluffy cumulus clouds resemble unshorn sheep, yet in the following line — 'On the mountains of sleep' — the clouds *become* rather than simply ornament the mountains. The close similarity between the key words 'sheep' and 'sleep' contributes to this, but it is substantiated by the fact that clouds resemble mountains as often as they do sheep. (Compare Thomas's line 'The sunset piled / Mountains on mountains of snow and ice in the west' in 'March'.) In other words, by running the unpunctuated lines into one another here, he transforms insubstantial things, clouds and sleep, into substantial things, sheep and mountains, and vice versa, until their proper character is in doubt. And the effect of this is to reduce time and place to a single, concentrated moment which sanctions the visionary, Bunyanesque glimpse of Heaven and Hell in the succeeding stanza:

> The next turn may reveal
> Heaven: upon the crest
> The close pine clump, at rest
> And black, may Hell conceal.

Although this stanza provides the allegorical climax of the poem, he avoids drawing a firm conclusion about the nature of the goal to which he is advancing. It is only when he descends from this vantage point to reaffirm his affection for roads that the destination which awaits him begins to become apparent.

Thomas has now sufficiently educated the reader into the symbolic aspects of his images to deal more openly with them. It is as if stanzas 8 and 9 began the poem again, repeating its essence exactly, but expanding it. 'I love roads' (line 1) becomes 'Often footsore, never / Yet of the road I weary' (lines 29-30), and the invisible gods (lines 2-4) become 'Helen of the roads':

> Often footsore, never
> Yet of the road I weary,
> Though long and steep and dreary
> As it winds on for ever.
>
> Helen of the roads,
> The mountain ways of Wales
> And the Mabinogion tales,
> Is one of the true gods.

This greater specificity (and the attractively coincidental personalisation of Helen — his wife's name as well as the heroine of *The Dream of Maxen*) licenses the long discussion of gods and the dead which occupies the remainder of the poem. With characteristic compression, he immediately endows them with palpable reality by a skilfully ambiguous deployment of syntax. Helen is one of the gods

> Abiding in the trees,
> The threes and fours so wise,
> The larger companies,
> That by the roadside be,
>
> And beneath the rafter
> Else uninhabited
> Excepting by the dead;
> And it is her laughter
>
> At morn and night I hear
> When the thrush cock sings
> Bright irrelevant things,
> And when the chanticleer

> Calls back to their own night
> Troops that make loneliness
> With their light footsteps' press,
> As Helen's own are light.

But this greater specificity brings no allegorical vision — only an asser-
tion that Helen's presence embraces his existence by becoming audible
at dawn and dusk. Yet she is not entirely comforting. Although she is
graceful (her footsteps 'are light') and apparently happy (it is by 'laugh-
ter' that she reveals herself), she cannot dispel Thomas's uneasy sense
that he is shortly to join her company of ghosts. This anxiety is empha-
sised by the details of dawn and dusk with which her laughter is associ-
ated. Both are heralded by birdsong (a thrush at night and a cock at
morning), and Thomas usually imagines birds as the articulators of a
comforting 'essentially English' quality. In 'Sedge-Warblers', for inst-
ance, they are heard 'Wisely reiterating endlessly / What no man learnt
yet, in or out of school', and in 'Under the Wood' their song is interpre-
ted as the modern version of a tune echoing back to the time when — as
he says in 'The Manor Farm' — 'This England, Old already, was called
Merry':

> The thrushes' ancestors
> As sweetly sung
> In the old years.

But in 'Roads' the thrush brings none of these rewards. The burden of
its song is described as 'irrelevant', so complete is the claim that Helen's
reminder of mortality has on his attention. This denial of hope is con-
firmed by the fact that the cock crow

> Calls back to their own night
> Troops that make loneliness
> With their light footsteps' press.

Thomas sees clearly that the ghosts' night lies behind his own human
day, darkening his apparent freedom from care. And in the following
verse this threat, so gradually and delicately introduced, becomes fixed
and actual. 'Troops' of ghosts become marching troops of war:

> Now all roads lead to France
> And heavy is the tread
> Of the living; but the dead
> Returning lightly dance.

He knows that his own death is more than likely to occur soon, but his mesmerised fascination with the dead, and his insistence on their graceful freedom, removes any sense of shock from his response. Throughout the poem he has so consistently mingled substance and insubstantiality, permanence and transience, and dawn and dusk, that by its conclusion his own physical presence seems indistinguishable from the ghosts who 'keep me company / With their pattering'. It is this blurring of the barrier between life and death which explains why he should so passively accept 'Whatever the road bring / To me or take from me'. And in the final stanza its consequence is movingly clarified. The dead are seen

> Crowding the solitude
> Of the loops over the downs,
> Hushing the roar of towns
> And their brief multitude.

The focus of his attention turns from country to town, and from silence to hubbub, in an appropriately summarising final sweep. Under the delicate, pattering footsteps of the dead, his life, and the life of entire communities, is smothered. It is the poem's one consolation that to cross the boundary between life and death is to join the company of 'one of the true gods'. With them, he imagines that he will gain freedom from mortal restrictions.

Throughout poems written later in 1916, Thomas's imaginative progress from life to after-life becomes distinctly less sanguine. To the certainty of extinction in 'Roads' is added a despairing recognition that no correspondence can exist between life and death. His original balance of death's attractions and life's demands is replaced by a chilling certainty of annihilation. The simultaneous decay and regeneration of 'Digging' (written on 4 April 1915), for instance, in which he had said:

> It is enough
> To smell, to crumble the dark earth,
> While the robin sings over again
> Sad songs of Autumn mirth

is upset by the repeated statement that no recovery is possible. The traveller of 'The Green Roads' (written on 28 June 1916) 'has never come back' from the forest of death, and in 'The Dark Forest' itself (written on 1, 5 and 10 July 1916), Thomas categorically denies any chance of communication between the living and the dead:

> The forest foxglove is purple, the marguerite
> Outside is gold and white,
> Nor can those that pluck either blossom greet
> The others, day or night.

In early poems, like 'The Other', forests are often introduced to describe a trackless region in which he seeks his proper identity and purpose. But in the two poems mentioned above, as in 'Lights Out', they represent a state of imminent unconsciousness.

'The Green Roads' illustrates his technique of blending symbol and reality in its record of fascinated hopelessness.

> The green roads that end in the forest
> Are strewn with white goose feathers this June,
>
> Like marks left behind by some one gone to the forest
> To show his track. But he has never come back.
>
> Down each green road a cottage looks at the forest.
> Round one the nettle towers; two are bathed in flowers.
>
> An old man along the green road to the forest
> Strays from one, from another a child alone.
>
> In the thicket bordering the forest,
> All day long a thrush twiddles his song.
>
> It is old, but the trees are young in the forest,
> All but one like a castle keep, in the middle deep.
>
> That oak saw the ages pass in the forest:
> They were a host, but their memories are lost,
>
> For the tree is dead: all things forget the forest
> Excepting perhaps me, when now I see
>
> The old man, the child, the goose feathers at the edge of
> the forest,
> And hear all day long the thrush repeat his song.

These rangy couplets show Thomas, like Theseus, following an Ariadne's thread of white goose feathers. It is June, and the roads are green, but these suggestions of promise and discovery are strictly ironic: instead of travelling away from a labyrinthine maze, he is approaching one. His destination is not the result of having made a bad choice and taken the wrong road. It is now *'each* green road' that leads to the forest, just as *'all* roads lead to France' in 'Roads' itself. The approach to this unavoidable conclusion is lined with emblems suggesting the forest's ruthless inclusiveness. Even the cottages are humanised, so that their windows facing the forest appear to pay it hypnotised attention. And from their interiors, it draws an old man and a child — young men are significantly absent — to leave them poised 'at the edge'. It is this point that Thomas reaches in the conclusion of 'Lights Out', but in the central passage of 'The Green Roads' he identifies some of the forest's characteristics more accurately. His observation that 'It is old, but the trees are young ... / All but one like a castle keep, in the middle deep' insists that nullity will prolong itself infinitely. It also, as Edna Longley says, suggests that 'the dead oak ... concentrates a sense of the fathomless oblivion that can engulf man and his history'.[77] In other words, the end of his journey is the very essence of unconsciousness, where even unconsciousness itself will be forgotten. But in spite of this final overthrow of the wish to preserve his humanity, there is no sense of revolt in the poem. Its tone is so resigned that, like the thrush's song at the forest's brink, it seems less a creative denial of death than a weary failure to prevent its approach. The bird may, like those in 'Sedge-Warblers', be endlessly reiterating wisdom, but Thomas's hope in its capacity for renewal has crumbled.

In 'Out in the Dark' Thomas's clear-sighted knowledge that what awaits him will replace physical pleasures with a vacuum receives its final utterance. The poem was written at High Beech in Epping Forest, on his last leave before embarkation, and in a letter to Eleanor Farjeon he said 'it is really Baba [Myfanwy, his second daughter] who speaks, not I. Something she said put me onto it.'[78] But in spite of the poem being, in a sense, a dramatic monologue, it stands as a conclusion to his own progress towards death:

> Out in the dark over the snow
> The fallow fawns invisible go
> With the fallow doe;
> And the winds blow
> Fast as the stars are slow.

Stealthily the dark haunts round
And, when a lamp goes, without sound
At a swifter bound
Than the swiftest hound,
Arrives, and all else is drowned;

And I and star and wind and deer
Are in the dark together, — near,
Yet far, — and fear
Drums on my ear
In that sage company drear.

How weak and little is the light,
All the universe of sight,
Love and delight,
Before the might,
If you love it not, of night.

In *The Happy-Go-Lucky Morgans* he had adopted a similar stance to that which he takes in this last poem: 'I went over again to the window and looked out. In a flash I saw the outer world of solitude, darkness and silence, waiting eternally for its prey.'[79] The novel's interpretation of the dark as a hunter is continued and amplified in the poem. In the first verse its menace is emphasised by the fact that the deer he sees are without their stag, and therefore seem especially vulnerable, etched starkly against the snow. It is a pitiable but not a pathetic sight; an important part of its effect is the transformation of a Christmas-card scene (the poem was written on 24 December 1916) into one of desolating reality. This image of hunting is developed in the second stanza, and at the same time the poem rises to an expansively symbolic plane: the dark which arrives 'At a swifter bound / Than the swiftest hound' picks up a subterranean echo of hunting in line 6 — 'Stealthily the dark haunts round' — to combine ghostly and preying qualities. In fact, the dark actually seals him within itself, in a moment of integration which is the deathly counterpart of those he sought in the natural world:

And I and star and wind and deer
Are in the dark together, — near
Yet far.

Here Thomas penetrates the void of death, rather than the essence of

England, and its black, timeless conditions are momentarily prefigured. Even the star is in the dark, as if to suggest it is either extinguished or giving light which is now also black. It is from this platform of imaginative pre-creation that he delivers, in the last and finest stanza, his summary of the poem which is also a summary of all those discussed above:

> How weak and little is the light,
> All the universe of sight,
> Love and delight,
> Before the might,
> If you love it not, of night.

In *The Happy-Go-Lucky Morgans*, faced with a similar prospect, he 'had even a feeling that he would rather not discover it, that if he were to enter it . . . he might not return, never stand out in the dark again and look up at the house'.[80] In 'Out in the Dark' there is no such appeal for the retention of consciousness. The stanza is spoken as if from the dark already, four months before the actual date of his death.

'Out in the Dark' is the culmination of those poems in which Thomas watches himself brought to the very edge of destruction, and it also concludes his wide-ranging analysis of military life. From discussions of his patriotism, through enlistment and the company of soldiers, to his own imminent death, he responds with characteristic and scrupulous honesty. The set-pieces of battle are absent, but their place is taken by a historical perspective which enables him to minimise the individual character of his own conflict, and write poems as true to the effect of all wars as they were to his own particular circumstances. Their choice of subject is an action, not a reaction, and because of this there are no grounds, in Larkin's phrase, 'to withhold our highest praise'. But also because of this, and because of their reticence, they have seldom received their proper due. Thomas himself realised that the war helped to release his poetry, and formed one of its principal themes, but he refused even to increase the sales of his first (posthumous) collection of poems by writing what was 'too deliberately and not inevitably English'. The note in which he insisted on this was quoted by his publisher Roger Ingpen in a letter written to Frost two weeks after he had been killed. It stands now as a monument to the discreet and understated character of his poetry:

I beg you not to make use of my situation, as a publisher might be tempted to, now or in the event of any kind of accident to me, to advertise the book.[81]

CHAPTER FIVE

FRIEND AND COUNTRYMAN

I

Thomas's distinction as a war poet is his ability to interpret the conflict of 1914-18 as the particularly horrendous manifestation of a more general historical process. He did not see it as an isolated event, but as one which dramatised long-standing tensions, and intensified existing challenges to the structure and distribution of society. By deciding to enlist, he knew that he was contributing to these forces working for change, and realised they would not end when an Armistice was signed. In his poem 'Fifty Faggots' he admitted the future was something 'I can no more / Foresee or more control than robin and wren'. One reason for his percipience was that long periods of training prevented him from concentrating exclusively on the compelling details of the Front Line. But it was not only this circumstantial fact which enlarged the range and resonance of his war poetry. For many years he had preached that 'by becoming ripe for poetry the poet's thoughts may recede far from their resemblance to all the world's', and he never deviated from this belief in practice. His most common strategy is to refract thoughts about military life through his observations of Nature — 'Lob', 'As the team's head brass', ' "Home" ' ('Fair was the morning') and 'Roads' are obvious examples. But the significance of such poems does not lie simply in their subtle portrayals of his experience as a soldier. They also point out that the disruption associated with the war had begun long before it broke out, and was nowhere more evident than in their own setting: the countryside. It is tempting to think of 1914 as an absolute division between the stable, sunlit Edwardian world and the world which will never know 'such innocence again'. But Thomas — like many of his contemporaries — was well aware that profound changes had been noticeable long before that date. As far as he was concerned, the most important consequence was that small rural communities were threatened as towns expanded. These developments are documented throughout his prose, and a brief summary of his attitude towards them illuminates a recurrent theme in his poetry. Even when not mentioned directly, they are largely to blame for the acute sense of isolation which affected his relationship with his country, his friends and his family. In analysing this feeling he produced a body of work which is, perhaps, not as clearly unified as his war poetry; but it is no less impressive, and no less far-reaching in its implications.

Born in Lambeth and brought up in Wandsworth, Thomas felt that his 'accidentally Cockney nativity' made him 'neither townsman nor countryman'.[1] And when he and his wife left London in 1901, he could not escape the disorientating influence of the suburbs entirely. He moved house six times before joining up in 1915, restlessly attempting — and failing — to find stability. Thirty years earlier, it had been possible for Hardy to praise Casterbridge for having no 'transitional intermixture of town and down. . . . The farmer's boy could sit under his barleymow and pitch a stone into the office window of the town clerk.'[2] But Thomas found it increasingly difficult to get far enough from the suburbs for feelings of 'security'.[3] Memories of their permanent impermanence continued to harass him, and his prose books abound with references to their steadily increasing size and menace:

> The new people were a mysterious, black-liveried host, the grand-
> children of peers, thieves, gutter-snipes, agricultural labourers,
> artisans, shopkeepers, professional men, farmers, foreign financiers,
> an unrelated multitude. . . . Well did they keep their secrets, this
> blank or shamefaced crowd of discreetly dressed people who might
> be anywhere tomorrow.[4]

The most detailed assault on the dehumanising effect of this enforced vagrancy is made by Thomas's double in *The South Country*. He is a man who lives 'in Wandsworth in a small street newly built',[5] works as a clerk in an office during the winter, and comes to the country during the summer to help with harvesting. His attempt to restore harmony between himself and the natural world has obvious parallels with Thomas's, and also like Thomas he regretfully admits that nothing can

alter the legacy of his upbringing. As well as compromising his relation-
ship with the country, it prevents him from communicating with people,
since — as a child — 'the roar in which all played a part developed into a
kind of silence'.[6] The silence of the suburbs is the silence of 'I built
myself a house of glass', and those who make it are trapped in a bind of
conscious deprivation:

> London was hot and dry, and would have been parched, cracked and
> shrivelled had it been alive instead of dead. . . . The plane trees were
> like so many captives along the streets, shackled to the flagstones,
> pelted with dust, humiliated, all their rusticity ravished though not
> forgotten.[7]

As might be expected, the double's inability to discover the 'heart of
England' means that he is barred from those traditions which are its
social manifestations. And the feelings of 'superfluousness' which this
provokes are tragically dramatised towards the end of the book. Thomas
sees him taking part in a procession of the unemployed, and realises
that he 'by no means could . . . have been made to express more feeble-
ness, more unbrotherliness, more lack of principle, purpose or control'.[8]

Thomas's knowledge that the circumstances of his birth could not be
altered just by moving into the country simultaneously intensified and
frustrated his search for ideal communion with English landscape. Eight
of his prose works are topographical studies, two are biographies of
Richard Jefferies and George Borrow, and many of his essays are
descriptive. Yet their tone is distinctly more reflective and melancholic
than any used by previous rural writers. They tend to concentrate on
the 'domination and destruction of Nature'[9] rather than continuing the
kind of relaxed celebration typified by Isaak Walton and Gilbert White.
Until well into the nineteenth century, it was relatively easy to cross
what Hardy called the 'mathematical line'[10] between town and country,
and even as late as 1883 Jefferies could call a book *Nature Near London*
without any sense of irony. But towards the end of his career, Jefferies
had begun to evolve the preoccupations which authors such as Hardy,
George Bourne, W. H. Hudson and Thomas himself were to develop.
His 'communal suggestiveness'[11] (as W. J. Keith terms it) was gradually
replaced by the personalisation contained in the very title of *The Story
of My Heart*. This shift in emphasis suggests a breakdown in corporate
identity which was confirmed elsewhere. Hardy, for instance, recorded
the 'increasingly nomadic habit'[12] of villagers, and their loss of 'peculi-
arities as a class',[13] and Bourne complained that his own rural commun-

ity was 'passing out of the hands of its former inhabitants. They are being crowded into corners and are becoming aliens in their own home.'[14]

Thomas's identification with Jefferies — as has already been mentioned — was remarkably strong. His literary ambitions were fostered by spending many childhood holidays in the Wiltshire of which Jefferies had written, and his early mentor, the tramp 'Dad' Uzzell, bore an obvious resemblance to the solitaries in his hero's work. But while the young Jefferies had been able to find England more or less as unspoiled as he wished, it was the compromised world of his later work that Thomas found most familiar. The double of *The South Country* discusses its hazards when, on revisiting a childhood haunt, he discovers that 'a road had been made alongside of it, and the builder's workmen going to and fro had made a dozen gaps in the hedge and trodden the wood backward and forward and broken down the branches and made it noisome'.[15] The poignancy of this scene, of course, is that it represents the destruction of his personal past, and stamps him (and Thomas through him) as one of 'those modern people who belong nowhere'.[16] In their most extreme form, desecrations such as this prompted Thomas to believe that when he turned from town to country, he merely left one form of isolation for another. In the former it was caused by the — as he felt — heartless compromise of suburbia; in the latter he found that communities were often poised, in Bourne's words, between 'two civilisations, one of which has lapsed, while the other has not come [their] way'.[17] Bourne identified latter-day enclosures as the main cause of this. Their effect, he said, was 'like knocking the keystone out of an arch. The keystone is not the arch, but, once it is gone, all sorts of forces, previously resisted, begin to operate towards ruin, and gradually the whole structure crumbles down.'[18] The disappearance of communal economic practice encouraged competitiveness, and this in turn led to the abandonment of time-honoured practices that earlier rural writers had praised. It left the labourers not only 'shut out from [their] countryside and cut off from [its] resources',[19] but also exiled them from their past with 'only some derelict habits left'.[20]

Thomas's response to similar evidence and experience is characteristically unostentatious. Confronted with proof of Bourne's judgment that the traditional rural culture was largely 'forgotten',[21] he either describes his own sense of isolation as an example of a general condition, or projects it onto characters who appear in his work. Tramps and gypsies are particularly frequent manifestions of it — no doubt largely because his long and regular walking tours gave him a special affinity with them. The strength of such figures lies in the fact that instead of searching for harmony with a particular place, they enjoy a mobile life which entitles them to feel at home everywhere. They are 'the simplest, kindest, and perhaps the wisest of men, indifferent to mobs, to laws, to all of us who are led aside, scattered and confused by hollow goods'.[22] But even their kind of admired independence is vulnerable. The threat of extinction which has already been noticed in poems like 'Lob', 'The New Year' and 'Man and Dog', is also discussed throughout the prose — most noticeably when Thomas mourns the lack of surviving common land:

> those lone wayside greens, no man's gardens, measuring a few feet
> wide but many miles in length — why should they be used either as
> receptacles for the dust of motorcars or as additions to the property
> of the landowner who happens to be renewing his fence? They used
> to be as beautiful and cool and fresh as rivers, these green sisters of
> the white roads — illuminated borders of many a weary tale. But
> now, lest there should be no room for the dust, they are turning
> away from them the gypsies who used to camp there for the night.[23]

At worst, the eventual fate of rural solitaries was to be 'driven from parish to parish, and finally [to] settle down as squalid degenerate nomads in a town where they lose what beauty and courage they had'.[24] And the best was not much better, since the loss of traditional common land kept them in a state of permanent insecurity. Their plight was all the more tragic because signs of their former harmony survived to mock them. This, from *The South Country*, is a typical scene: 'the common is small; it is bounded on every side by roads, and on one by a row of new mean houses; there is a golf-house among the tumuli, in one place a large square has been ploughed and fenced by a private owner'.[25] The same sense of being tantalised by a vanished ideal is a crucial element of Thomas's own reaction to the countryside. As early as 1902, in *Horae Solitariae*, he admitted 'I could have wept that my senses were not chastened to celestial keenness, to understand the pipits as they flew',[26] and four years later he recorded a similar experience in *The Heart of England* while describing a field of poppies:

> Something in me desired them, might even seem to have long ago
> possessed and lost them, but when thought followed vision, as,
> alas! it did, I could not understand their importance, their distance

142

from my mind, their desirableness, as of a far-away princess to her
troubador. . . . Had I offended against the commonwealth of living
things that I was not admitted as an equal to these flowers? Why
could they not have vanished and left me with my first vision,
instead of staying and repeating that it would be as easy to draw
near to the stars as to them?[27]

In falling thus far short of this ambition, Thomas achieved what he was
to praise in Jefferies — 'the most ancient discovery of the theologians —
that man stands apart from the rest of created things'.[28] The only con-
clusion, he realised, was to renew unsatisfactory human relationships,
and attempt to retain the same 'great hope' that Jefferies possessed. 'It
is man that is supreme in mans' world', Jefferies insisted. 'Let us give
way to our virtues and energies, and cease to look for help apart from
man.'[29]

II

In all Thomas's poetry, the vulnerability of this 'great hope' is nowhere
given more dramatic form than in 'Wind and Mist', which was written on
1 April 1916. Specifically, it describes a house built for him at Wick
Green on the extreme edge of a high plateau overlooking the village of
Steep. It was, in Helen Thomas's words, a home they 'could not love.
. . . There was nothing in that exposed position to protect us from
the wind, which roared and shrieked in the wide chimneys, nor have I
ever heard such furious rain as dashed vindictively against our windows.
. . . Often a thick mist enveloped us, and the house seemed to be stand-
ing on the edge of the world, with an infinity of white rolling vapour
below us.'[30] It was here that Thomas suffered a nervous breakdown in
1911, and he returned to it in imagination four years later, using the
'intolerable swishing'[31] of the elements to describe his psychological
disturbance. The wind, by violently possessing 'my past and the past of
the world', alienates him from himself and his family; and the mist, by
obliterating the earth, exiles him from the natural world.

The poem begins by resembling the blank verse dialogues in Frost's
North of Boston, but quickly develops a symbolism which is entirely
individual. Indeed, the symbols dwarf the speakers as completely as the
weather is to obscure the house. When Thomas and the stranger who
addresses him are introduced, the landscape reduces them to apparently
disembodied voices:

> They met inside the gateway that gives the view,
> A hollow land as vast as heaven. 'It is
> A pleasant day, sir.' 'A very pleasant day.'
> 'And what a view here . . .'

Thomas's (the second speaker's) taciturnity stands in stark contrast to the frank denunciations of wind and mist he is to make later. At this early stage it is the stranger who is loquacious, and like the romantic fantasist of 'The Chalk Pit' he cannot confine himself to telling 'the truth / Or nothing' about what he sees:

> 'Had we with Germany
> To play upon this board it could not be
> More dear than April has made it with a smile.
> The fields beyond that league close in together
> And merge, even as our days into the past,
> Into one wood that has a shining pane
> Of water. Then the hills of the horizon —
> That is how I should make hills had I to show
> One who would never see them what hills were like.'

Thomas's criticism of this fancifully ornate speech is implied by his silence. And at several points the stranger's banality is self-evident: he realises that the war stimulates his appreciation of England, but by envisaging the chequered fields as part of a game — a chess board, perhaps — he misrepresents the gravity of his circumstances. A similar error of judgment is apparent when he says that 'the hills of the horizon' are 'how I should make hills had I to show / One who would never see them what hills were like'. His determination to notice only what is flawlessly beautiful renders his account incomplete. The scene appears to be pacific, but is capable, as Thomas soon points out, of extreme hostility:

> 'I have seen that house
> Through mist look lovely as a castle in Spain,
> And airier. I have thought: " 'Twere happy there
> To live." And I have laughed at that
> Because I lived there then.' 'Extraordinary.'
> 'Yes, with my furniture and family
> Still in it, I, knowing every nook of it
> And loving none, and in fact hating it.'

This discrepancy between attractive appearance and desolating reality was one he had commented on before. While living at Berryfield Cottage — his home from December 1906 until he moved to Wick Green in December 1909 — he had written to Bottomley: 'We are now become people of whom passers-by stop to think: How fortunate are they within those walls. I know it. I have thought the same myself as I came to the house & forgot it was my own.'[32] In 'Wind and Mist' the same illusion is seen with distinctly less equanimity. It provokes a barely controlled account of loneliness and anxiety:

> 'Doubtless the house was not to blame,
> But the eye watching from those windows saw,
> Many a day, day after day, mist — mist
> Like chaos surging back — and felt itself
> Alone in all the world, marooned alone.
> We lived in clouds, on a cliff's edge almost
> (You see), and if clouds went, the visible earth
> Lay too far off beneath and like a cloud.
> I did not know it was the earth I loved
> Until I tried to live there in the clouds
> And the earth turned to cloud.'

These heavily repetitive lines reproduce the agitation of Thomas's mind by illustrating its self-destructive circuitousness when alienated from reality. The clouds (mentioned five times in six lines) do not simply conceal the earth but actually replace it. And when the stranger reminds him that he had ' "a garden / Of flint and clay" ', he angrily rejects any idea that it might have consoled him:

> 'The flint was the one crop that never failed.
> The clay first broke my heart, and then my back;
> And the back heals not.'

Thomas's response suggests that the world around him has been reduced to a fraction of itself — the garden — without any diminution of its burdens. They smother him just as thoroughly as the mist threatens to evaporate him. The same inability to find happiness is reintroduced in the following lines: childbirth, instead of being a cause for celebration, is seen entirely in terms of the increased pressure it will bring to bear on domestic life:

> 'Never looked grey mind on a greyer one
> Than when the child's cry broke above the groans.'

The signs of possible rejuvenation in this scene are quickly passed over as Thomas turns his attention from mist to wind:

> 'I had forgot the wind.
> Pray do not let me get on to the wind.
> You would not understand about the wind.
> It is my subject, and compared with me
> Those who have always lived on the firm ground
> Are quite unreal in this matter of the wind.
> There were whole days and nights when the wind and I
> Between us shared the world, and the wind ruled
> And I obeyed it and forgot the mist.
> My past and the past of the world were in the wind.
> Now you will say that though you understand
> And feel for me, and so on, you yourself
> Would find it different. You are all like that
> If once you stand here free from wind and mist:
> I might as well be talking to wind and mist.'

The emphasis on wind here is as strong as that on mist had been, but it describes social rather than natural isolation. Because all those 'who have always lived on the firm ground / Are quite unreal in this matter of the wind', their advice and comfort is no use to him. As a result, Thomas's anxiety mounts — though instead of prompting him to retreat into himself altogether, it leads him to scorn all those who say they 'Would find it different'. And while this might seem to complete the poem's account of his loneliness, it also indicates a return of confidence in his ability to survive without the support of people or nature. In addition, by telling the stranger, 'I might as well be talking to wind and mist,' he changes the original elemental danger of these two forces to mere personal vapidness. It is a transformation which shows that he has proved himself equal to his rigorous trials, and hints that he has valued them as a means of discovering the resourcefulness of his own spirit:

> 'I want to admit
> That I would try the house once more, if I could;
> As I should like to try being young again.'

This conclusion does not lead him to expect a future continually blessed by social and natural integration, but it is, nevertheless, mutedly optimistic. In *Beautiful Wales*, after a similar trial, he had simply admitted 'the effort was unsuccessful, and I rose hurriedly, and left the village behind'.[33] In 'Wind and Mist' he is prepared to undergo the experience again, in the knowledge that he possesses sufficient reservoirs of strength to endure and even benefit from it.

The cautious balance of optimism and resignation which ends 'Wind and Mist' depends on the assumption that isolation from nature is the result of particular and reversible circumstances. But discussions of his place in human society lack such potential consolation. Throughout his life he insisted that 'each of us is alone . . . [and] every piece of ground where a man stands is a desert island with footprints of unknown creatures all round its shore.'[34] His most detailed analysis of this belief occurs in *The Happy-Go-Lucky Morgans*, and it illuminates all those poems concerned with the same experience. One of the main characters in the book, Mr Aurelius, is described by Thomas – in a phrase that Chekhov, among others, had done much to popularise – as a 'superfluous man'. Although he was based on 'Charles Dalmon, the poet'[35] according to Thomas's brother Julian, his attributes are remarkably like his creator's:

The superfluous are those who cannot find society with which they are in some sort of harmony. The magic circle drawn round us all at birth surrounds these in such a way that it will never overlap, far less become concentric with, the circles of any other in the whirling multitudes. The circle is a high wall guarded as if it were a Paradise, not a Hell . . . or it is no more than a shell border round the garden of a child, and there is no one so feeble but he can slip over it, or shift it, or trample it down, though powerless to remove it. Some of these weaker ones might seem to have several circles enclosing them, which are thus upset or trampled one by one as childhood advances. Everybody discovers that he can cross their borders. They do not retaliate. These are the superfluous who are kept alive to perform the most horrible or most loathsome tasks.[36]

It is this divisive 'magic circle' that Thomas's 'chiefly pathetic memories of the Suburbs'[37] had done so much to create. Poems like 'I built myself a house of glass' and 'What will they do?' obviously refer to its existence, and the same sense of exclusion is also evident in his love poetry. But where, towards the end of his life, his frustration was intensified by ruthless analysis of his own and other people's shortcomings, as a young man it sprang from different origins. Throughout his prose, he persistently idealised women: they appear to offer the perfect society he wants, knows to be illusory, but cannot quite bring himself to discountenance. His longing is often increased because these figments of his romantic imagination correspond to all that is best in the natural world. *Rest and Unrest* is typical in describing a girl who is 'akin to the spirit abroad on many days that had awed or harried me with loveliness . . . in all places where Nature had stung me with a sense of her own pure face'.[38] This attitude, like so many others, is illuminated by a comparison with Jefferies, whose presentation of women as the 'supreme expression of natural beauty'[39] is frequently as mawkish. Felise, for instance, the heroine of *The Dewy Morn*, is shown early in the novel with her 'frame drooped, as the soul, which bears it up, flowed outwards, feeling to grass, and flower, and leaf, as the swimmer spreads the arms abroad, and the fingers feel the water. She sighed with deep content, dissolving in the luxurious bath of beauty.'[40] The main consequence of this 'dissolution' is not so much a 'divine correspondence'[41] between herself and nature, as the eradication of any trace of individual personality. And in describing all such female characters created by Jefferies, Thomas tacitly admitted that his own youthful ideal was similarly vague and wraith-like: 'In women [Jefferies] found the beauty he saw and loved in Nature, as if . . . they were made, as Blodeuwedd was made by Gwydion, of the blossoms of the oak and the blossoms of the broom and the blossoms of the meadow-sweet, but with an added solemnity as of the mountains and of light upon great waters.'[42] Equally insubstantial creatures traipse through Thomas's prose. Paradoxically, their elevation to 'another world, ever at hand, ever unavoidable, ever mysterious'[43] stems from the belief he shared with Jefferies that 'Women are more earthly than men, more directly and practically connected with the circumstances and foundations of life'.[44] Eleanor Farjeon identifies just such a character in the story 'At the End of the Day', of whom Thomas says:

> Had she leaped out of the earth or out of the sky to express in human shape the loveliness of the hour, she could not have been made otherwise by a sculptor god — solemn and joyous and proud with the pride of things that are perfect and know it not, yet have as it seems attendant spirits offering them praise and courtliness wherever they go. No princess barbarically and multitudinously escorted

could have walked with greater magnificence.[45]

Such figures, Eleanor Farjeon says, 'are the key to one of Edward's dreams, to attain which would destroy it, the dream of a "thing impossible and marvellous". He wanted no more than to behold it at a distance.'[46] While this judgment is amply justified by his prose, Thomas's poems regularly show him struggling to overcome the distance between himself and women, rather than simply accepting and welcoming it. There are, undoubtedly, some in which he is content to revere rather than communicate — the 'Beautiful, swift and bright one' of 'Song' ('The clouds that are so light') is a girl of the same 'exquisite combination of wildness and meekness'[47] as that in his story 'The Fountain'. But towards the end of his life, he usually presents those he admires as complex images of isolation, and does not simply maroon them in 'another world from mine'.[48]

On a number of occasions, Thomas suggests that the tradition of love poetry increases his difficulties by reminding him of ideals it has celebrated in the past. In 'The Unknown', for instance, his repeated emphasis on the word 'poet' indicates that its subject may be the Muse itself — 'inspiration as well as aspiration'.[49] This poem, however, like 'These things that poets said', only introduces the convention of 'the impossible she' to make clear that he cannot sympathise with it entirely. The greater his temptation to idealise, the more honestly sceptical he becomes:

> She is most fair,
> And when they see her pass
> The poets' ladies
> Look no more in the glass
> But after her.
>
> On a bleak moor
> Running under the moon
> She lures a poet,
> Once proud or happy, soon
> Far from his door.
>
> Beside a train,
> Because they saw her go,
> Or failed to see her,
> Travellers and watchers know
> Another pain.

The simple lack
Of her is more to me
Than others' presence,
Whether life splendid be
Or utter black.

I have not seen,
I have no news of her;
I can tell only
She is not here, but there
She might have been.

She is to be kissed
Only perhaps by me;
She may be seeking
Me and no other: she
May not exist.

Here the 'pale glorious face'[50] which appears so often in Thomas's prose books is admitted to be a shadowy fiction. And this denial of false ideals is even more explicit in the 'household'[51] poems addressed to his family. As they strip away imprecision, they abandon the pursuit of perfection to discuss less exalted hopes with scrupulous honesty. The first of them, 'P.H.T' (written on 8 February 1916), is especially stark and outspoken. Drawing on memories of his father as someone who treated him 'so that I have a feeling of shame that I am alive',[52] Thomas admits 'I may come near loving you / When you are dead', but realises that 'not so long as you live / Can I love you at all'. Such a dismissal of mutual affection, and the acknowledgment that hostility will outlast life itself, is moderated in 'No one so much as you'. This was written three days later, and replaces the complete absence of love with a wary recognition that it exists in another, if not himself. Edna Longley follows R. George Thomas's lead in asserting that the poem is addressed to Thomas's mother.[53] But the suggestion that his wife might be a more likely candidate is corroborated by the internal evidence of 'And you, Helen'. Both poems share the same tone of rueful regret, and both criticise the severity of his self-restraint:

I at the most accept
Your love, regretting
That is all: I have kept
A helpless fretting

> That I could not return
> All that you gave
> And could not ever burn
> With the love you have,
>
> Till sometimes it did seem
> Better it were
> Never to see you more
> Than linger here
>
> With only gratitude
> Instead of love —
> A pine in solitude
> Cradling a dove.

In the main body of the 'household' poems, this painfully austere diction is replaced by a delight in sensuous language. It creates a sense of unity which is supplemented by their shared reference to place-names taken from the vicinity of Hare Hall training camp in Essex, where they were written between 29 March and 9 April 1916. They also have a common concern to express 'desirable human attributes in terms of the countryside'[54] — but while the women of the prose books actually dissolved themselves into natural scenery, so close was their identification with it, here the lovingly catalogued details release the character of the person addressed. This is itself a measure of the tenderness the sequence contains; it suggests that for the first time Thomas felt no hesitation in showing affection. To say so, however, oversimplifies the poems considerably: each one depends on a system of exchange which qualifies their generous impulse. In the first, 'If I should ever by chance' (which was dedicated to 'my elder daughter', Bronwen), the qualifications are muted. Thomas offers to buy 'Codham, Cockridden, and Childerditch, / Roses, Pyrgo and Lapwater', and decides:

> The rent I shall ask of her will be only
> Each year's first violets, white and lonely,
> The first primroses and orchises —
> She must find them before I do, that is.

This condition introduces a number of others which run throughout the series. And their steadily increased gravity associates the poems, as Edna Longley points out, with 'fairy gifts in folk lore. Various techniques reinforce this traditional element: sing-song rhythms, exaggerated feminine rhymes, incantatory refrains.'[55] In other words, Thomas redeploys the principles on which he based 'Lob'; the traditions to which he refers are acknowledged to contain unlikely difficulties, and these threaten to frustrate his good intentions.

In the second poem, 'If I were to own', his reservations are even more apparent — though at first the terms of the exchange seem simple enough. Thomas will give his son, Merfyn, another tract of landscape for an appropriately pastoral rent:

> If I were to own this countryside
> As far as a man in a day could ride,
> And the Tyes were mine for giving or letting, —
> Wingle Tye and Margaretting
> Tye, — and Skreens, Gooshays, and Cockerells,
> Shellow, Rochetts, Bandish, and Pickerells,
> Martins, Lambkins, and Lillyputs,
> Their copses, ponds, roads, and ruts,
> Fields where plough-horses steam and plovers
> Fling and whimper, hedges that lovers
> Love, and orchards, shrubberies, walls
> Where the sun untroubled by north wind falls,
> And single trees where the thrush sings well
> His proverbs untranslatable,
> I would give them all to my son
> If he would let me any one
> For a song, a blackbird's song, at dawn.

This offer is doubly valuable because it includes many elements of the countryside that Thomas especially admired. They are gathered up in such a way as to provide the poem with the quality of a will. The plovers which 'fling and whimper' recall those of 'Two Pewits', and the thrush which 'sings well / His proverbs untranslatable' promises to pass on the 'pure thrush word' of 'The Word'. It is for this reason, perhaps, that the poem's first condition is exacting, compared to any in 'If I should ever by chance'. The rent Thomas proposes to charge his son is developed, even as it is announced, from 'a song' (with its connotations of 'a nominal fee'), to a particular bird's song (a blackbird's), and finally to one gained at a specific time (dawn). The exigencies of this are compounded by a further clause, which insists that having rented land and birds to his son

> He should have no more, till on my lawn
> Never a one was left, because I
> Had shot them to put them into a pie, —
> His Essex blackbirds, every one,
> And I was left old and alone.

This suggestion that Merfyn will abandon him in old age diverts the poems still further from their course of gentle benevolence. But while Thomas honestly assesses the difficulties of their relationship, he is careful to accept the blame for jeopardising his son's inheritance. The price he pays is apparent in the poem's closing lines. He reverses the roles of giver and receiver, and commits himself to providing a rent which he knows to be beyond his capabilities:

> Then unless I could pay, for rent, a song
> As sweet as a blackbird's, and as long —
> No more — he should have the house, not I:
> Margaretting or Wingle Tye,
> Or it might be Skreens, Gooshays, or Cockerells,
> Shellow, Rochetts, Bandish, or Pickerells,
> Martins, Lambkins, or Lillyputs,
> Should be his till the cart tracks had no ruts.

In the third poem — addressed to his 'daughter the younger', Myfanwy — these tensions appear at first to have been replaced by affectionate straightforwardness. But like Philip Larkin's 'Born Yesterday', 'What shall I give' establishes itself as a benediction only to founder on qualifications:

> What shall I give my daughter the younger
> More than will keep her from cold and hunger?
> I shall not give her anything.

The gifts of landscape he offered his other children are denied to Myfanwy, because he knows that — in the long run — they will leave her 'no richer than the queen / Who once on a time sat in Havering Bower'. (Or, in other words, trapped and destitute, like Joanna the widow of Henry IV, who died there.) But this determination to curb his generosity is itself contradicted in the final lines. Instead of providing her with the 'lumber' of 'many acres', he offers something less extensive but more valuable:

> Steep and her own world
> And her spectacled self with hair uncurled,
> Wanting a thousand little things
> That time without contentment brings.

In the two preceding poems, as well as elsewhere, Thomas mourns his failure to enjoy the present. But by promising Myfanwy close familiarity with her home at the village of Steep, he gives her the chance of relishing every immediate moment. And this is accompanied by an even more precious opportunity — namely, the stability to discover the strengths and weaknesses of her own personality. The rewards of such a gift are self-evident, but their full significance is not developed until the final poem, 'And you, Helen':

> And you, Helen, what should I give you?
> So many things I would give you
> Had I an infinite great store
> Offered me and I stood before
> To choose. I would give you youth,
> All kinds of loveliness and truth,
> A clear eye as good as mine,
> Lands, waters, flowers, wine,
> As many children as your heart
> Might wish for, a far better art
> Than mine can be, all you have lost
> Upon the travelling waters tossed,
> Or given to me. If I could choose
> Freely in that great treasure-house
> Anything from any shelf,
> I would give you back yourself,
> And power to discriminate
> What you want and want it not too late,
> Many fair days free from care
> And heart to enjoy both foul and fair,
> And myself, too, if I could find
> Where it lay hidden and it proved kind.

Here the fairy-tale quality of the poems addressed to his children is replaced by a frank appraisal of human possibilities and limitations. As it unfolds, Thomas admits that his own frustrated pursuit of self is bound to compromise his ability to give and receive affection. Even if he could 'find' where his true identity 'lay hidden', he suspects that it would not be worthy of Helen. Taken together, these restrictions seem to close the poem — and the series — on a note of resigned lovelessness. But in spite of their shortcomings, his feelings have a few faintly encouraging aspects. For one thing, he has replaced the wraiths of his prose with sympathetically human beings; and for another, he has realised — in a phrase from 'These things that poets said' — that 'I, loving not, am different'. Both amount to proof that he has freed himself from the tyranny of false ideals, and both (notwithstanding his remarks to the contrary) indicate a growth in self-knowledge. Feelings of 'superfluousness' haunted him until the end of his life, but by admitting that the best love he could offer was a mixture of generosity and distrust, he created a common ground between himself and his wife, to which he always returned, and which she never deserted:

> there were to come dark days when his brooding spirit shut me out
> in a lonely exile, and my heart waited too eagerly to be let into the
> light again. . . . But this was to come, and it was only now and then
> that I had hints of this darkness in his soul, this fierce unrest which
> beyond all found peace in nature, but not in me. Alone he had to be
> in his agony, but when he emerged from it, exhausted by God knows
> what bitter contest, he looked for me and needed me, and our love
> was always the firm ground on which we stood secure and that no
> storm ever swept away.[56]

III

Thomas's sense of isolation from his family, and his difficulties in finding an ideal 'heart of England', may be regarded as a legacy of his 'accidentally Cockney nativity'. But the conditions of his upbringing also helped to produce several other, less obviously related themes in his poetry. Among the most important are those concerned with the gulf between past and present, age and youth, and language and experience. They all derive from his knowledge that the suburbs had denied him the chance of permanent integration and stability. This realisation did not, however, rule out the possibility of contentment altogether, and throughout his career Thomas attempted to develop a cast of mind and speech which would register even the most fleeting satisfactions. But his capacity to enjoy them depended on his ability to 'partake' of the

present 'as if he were eating ripe fruit',[57] and when this proved imposs-
ible, it prompted him to take refuge in nostalgia. In his prose books,
despair of the immediate moment often encouraged him to idealise the
past so completely and regularly that it intensified the very feelings of
isolation he intended to overcome. His description of a vanished Golden
Age in *The South Country* is typical. He imagines a world where 'ambi-
tion, introspection, remorse had not begun', and admits that his efforts
to restore it 'glorify it exceedingly and it becomes like a ridge of the
far-off Downs, transfigured in golden light, so that we in the valley sigh
at the thought that where we have often trod is heaven now'.[58] Thomas
was, of course, well aware that this kind of transformation was counter-
productive, but it was only towards the end of his life that he managed
to discipline what he called his 'melting moods for what we cannot
reach'.[59] His poetry consistently juxtaposes the ideal past with the
troublesome present, and thereby creates a balance in which the merits
of each are fully appreciated. 'The Unknown Bird' eloquently illustrates
this technique:

> Three lovely notes he whistled, too soft to be heard
> If others sang; but others never sang
> In the great beech-wood all that May and June.
> No one saw him: I alone could hear him
> Though many listened. Was it but four years
> Ago? or five? He never came again.
>
> Oftenest when I heard him I was alone,
> Nor could I ever make another hear.
> La-la-la! he called, seeming far-off —
> As if a cock crowed past the edge of the world,
> As if the bird or I were in a dream.
> Yet that he travelled through the trees and sometimes
> Neared me, was plain, though somehow distant still
> He sounded. All the proof is — I told men
> What I had heard.
>
>   I never knew a voice,
> Man, beast, or bird, better than this. I told
> The naturalists; but neither had they heard
> Anything like the notes that did so haunt me
> I had them clear by heart and have them still.

Four years, or five, have made no difference. Then
As now that La-la-la! was bodiless sweet:
Sad more than joyful it was, if I must say
That it was one or other, but if sad
'Twas sad only with joy too, too far off
For me to taste it.

In his prose, Thomas had often used unseen singing birds as symbols of his fugitive ideal. But one passage in particular, from *The Last Sheaf*, anticipates 'The Unknown Bird' by exploring the conflict between his aspirations and his restrictive daily commitments: 'For half a minute [the bird] sang, changed his perch unseen and sang again, his notes as free from the dust and heat as the cups of the marigolds, and as soft as the pale white-blue sky, and as dim as the valley into whose twilight he was gathered, calling fainter and fainter as I drew towards home.'[60] In the poem, this tension is resolved into an acknowledgment that the perfect and real, if combined, allow Thomas to get the best of both worlds. Although the bird appears to taunt him by being 'unknown' and 'too soft to be heard / If others sang', its elusiveness does not lead him to doubt its existence. Instead, it offers him a fruitful union of opposites — of nearness and distance — which is reproduced in the ambiguous joyful sadness of its song.

Far from encouraging him to indulge in utopian speculation, Thomas's memory organises this reconciliation. He preserves former happiness without forgetting that orthodox naturalists have never come across 'Anything like the notes that did so haunt me'. In doing so, he includes a qualification which prevents him from 'glorifying' the past: his insistence that 'I alone could hear' the bird implies that it represents a highly personalised kind of fulfilment. And because of this he realises — like Keats in the 'Ode to a Nightingale' — that he would be escaping responsibilities by abandoning himself to it entirely. Once this has been borne in on him, the poem closes in terms which are more obviously an echo of Wordsworth than of Keats. Without offering the bogus pleasure of impossible ideals, the bird flashes on Thomas's 'inward eye', and enables him to experience past happiness without compromising the present:

> ... I cannot tell
> If truly never anything but fair
> The days were when he sang, as now they seem.
> This surely I know, that I who listened then,

Happy sometimes, sometimes suffering
A heavy body and a heavy heart,
Now straightway, if I think of it, become
Light as that bird wandering beyond my shore.

Thomas's hard-won certainty that fulfilment could only be achieved by reconciling 'sadness' and 'joy' characterises all his mature work. But there is one important theme in both prose and verse which does not illustrate this belief: childhood. His own and other people's infancy, as the furthest point to which memory can penetrate, is consistently seen as the period of most intense harmony with the social and natural world. Like almost all his Romantic forebears, he argues that it allows a wisdom denied to adults — even though this is sometimes more evident in retrospect than at the time. 'I confess to remembering little joy', he wrote in 1909,

> but to much drowsy pleasure in the mere act of memory. . . . I recall green fields, one or two whom I loved in them, and though no trace of such happiness as I had remains, the incorruptible tranquillity of it all breeds fancies of great happiness. I recall many scenes . . . I do not recall happiness in them, yet the moment I return to them in fancy I am happy. Something like this is also true of much later self-conscious years. I cannot — I am tempted to — allow what then spoiled the mingling of the elements of joy to reappear when I look back. The reason, perhaps, is that only an inmost true self that desires and is in harmony with joy can perform these long journeys, and when it has set out on them it sheds those gross incrustations which were our curse before.[61]

Throughout Thomas's prose, children appear to be exempt from such 'gross incrustations'. In *Rest and Unrest*, for instance, he describes a young girl, Mary, in phrases which closely resemble 'If I should ever by chance': she 'always finds the violets first. You see she is so little that she looks the flowers in their faces almost.'[62] This ability to 'grasp the infinite'[63] as a matter of course is discussed at greater length in *The South Country*. Here Thomas sees two children proving the correspondence between past and present which is a necessary aspect of the stability he seeks himself:

> As I look . . . I think of such a child and such a playmate that lived two thousand years ago in the sun and once as they played each set

a foot upon the soft clay of a tile that the tile maker had not yet burned hard and red. The tile fell in the ruins of a Roman city in Britain, was buried hundreds of years in the ashes and flowering mould, and yesterday I saw the footprints in the dark red tile, two thousand years old.[64]

As an adult, Thomas can record such correspondence, but his self-consciousness alienates him from the children's experience. This loss of vision, and the torments which accompany it, are strikingly similar to Wordsworth's and Coleridge's, as a short story in *Rest and Unrest*, 'The First of Spring', illustrates. The heroine, Alice Lacking, is alert to the possibility of harmony between herself and the spring scenery which surrounds her. But in endeavouring to feel rather than merely imagine it, she is forced to dismiss her attempt as 'an unsatisfied desire, a worship without a skilled priest, nay! without a god even'.[65] When this disappointment prompts her to reconsider her childhood, and 'the bliss which she had in those days not recognised',[66] she realises that it is precisely the mature ability to analyse happiness which prevents her from experiencing it:

> She still enjoyed many things, but not as before; she had a sense of something postponed; but the next day or perhaps the next the veil would be lifted that had fallen insidiously, a veil of huge, dim, unintelligible things, of mere greyness, having nothing to do with life.[67]

This concern with the frustrations of adult self-consciousness illuminates Thomas's poem 'The Path', which was written on 26 March 1915, five years after 'The First of Spring' had been published. By defining a middle-ground between the threatening 'precipitous wood' and the familiar normality of the 'level road', the path reconciles opposing forces in a stable balance. Adults, however, do not appreciate this: only children are able to take the opportunities that it represents:

> Running along a bank, a parapet
> That saves from the precipitous wood below
> The level road, there is a path. It serves
> Children for looking down the long smooth steep,
> Between the legs of beech and yew, to where
> A fallen tree checks the sight: while men and women
> Content themselves with the road and what they see
> Over the bank, and what the children tell.

The path, winding like silver, trickles on,
Bordered and even invaded by thinnest moss
That tries to cover roots and crumbling chalk
With gold, olive, and emerald, but in vain.
The children wear it. They have flattened the bank
On top, and silvered it between the moss
With the current of their feet, year after year.
But the road is houseless, and leads not to school.
To see a child is rare there, and the eye
Has but the road, the wood that overhangs
And underyawns it, and the path that looks
As if it led on to some legendary
Or fancied place where men have wished to go
And stay; till, sudden, it ends where the wood ends.

Throughout the poem, children occupy the path, while 'men and women / Content themselves with the road and what they see / Over the bank'. Thomas clearly admires this youthful impatience with the second-hand, but he is careful to point out its vulnerability. The path is originally described as running along 'a parapet', and is later said to be 'invaded' by creeping, parasitical moss. This use of terms appropriate to military action — the 'fallen tree', too, like the 'fallen elm' of 'As the team's head brass', carries with it a sense of 'fallen in battle' — intensifies the menace of the surrounding wood. But having stressed this danger, Thomas goes on to insist that the children are more than a match for its encroachments. Like those who marked the tile in *The South Country*, these seem capable of infinite renewal, and are so closely identified with their path that they 'wear it' as if they not only pressed it down but actually assumed it, like clothing. These two factors appear to indicate that Thomas believes the future will continue to provide opportunities for harmonious fulfilment. But the closing lines of the poem are less sanguine. By saying that 'To see a child is rare there' — whether on road or path — he recalls previous warnings about the fugitive nature of his ideal. Furthermore, he shows no signs of taking the path himself — however necessary he admits it to be, and however exactly he recognises its benefits. And it is not only adult self-consciousness which prevents him. His final references to the wood make it seem less like a manageable threat than a deathly and cavernous forest similar to the one in 'Lights Out'. Indeed, it almost commands his complete attention — and when the path does appear it seems to lead 'to some legendary / Or fancied place' rather than a haven of stability. It is a transformation which suggests that Thomas, unlike the children, cannot hope to prolong his perception of harmony indefinitely. To do so would mean escaping into fantasy, and destroying the balance upon which his chances of happiness depend.

In 'The Path', Thomas insists that the harmony he vainly struggles to realise is freely available to children. The same belief is contained in a number of other poems, but it is often stated with a reticence which belies its importance. In 'The Brook' it is a child's voice which 'raised the dead' and discovers what Thomas 'felt, yet never should have found / A word for'; in 'The Penny Whistle' it is a small boy who, 'playing / On a whistle an olden nursery melody, / Says far more than I am saying'; and in 'Good-night' it is 'the noise of man, beast, and machine' which prevails:

> But the call of children in the unfamiliar streets
> That echo with a familiar twilight echoing,
> Sweet as the voice of nightingale or lark, completes
> A magic of strange welcome.

This lack of ostentation perfectly matches the inspirational wisdom that children possess. Their very discretion emphasises the fact that Thomas's ideal evades precise analysis. But while they make no attempt to define it themselves — so entirely proper does it seem — Thomas persistently tries and fails. In 'The Other', 'I never saw that land before' and 'Some eyes condemn', he falls back on the familiar imprecision of 'goal', and elsewhere he uses phrases of similar vagueness — 'a season of bliss unchangeable' or 'something I was waiting for'. And in the many poems which show birds, rather than children, expressing the stability he seeks, he categorically states that such powers of articulation are denied him: sedge-warblers, typically, reiterate 'What no man learnt yet, in or out of school'.

As has already been pointed out, this preoccupation with the inexpressible was developed by a large number of Thomas's Romantic predecessors, and was restated by most of his modernist successors. It testifies to the fact that a sense of linguistic isolation frequently dictates the form and strategy of his poetry. In 'I never saw that land before', for instance, he suggests that language must approach 'moments of everlastingness' as gingerly as the moments themselves are fleeting. While he reminisces about an admired, secluded valley, he acknowledges that the breeze which defined the spirit of the place 'hinted all and nothing spoke'. But this kind of revelation is enough for him to realise 'some goal', provided he responds with equally tactful suggestiveness:

> . . . if I could sing
> What would not even whisper my soul
> As I went on my journeying,
>
> I should use, as the trees and birds did,
> A language not to be betrayed;
> And what was hid should still be hid
> Excepting from those like me made
> Who answer when such whispers bid.

Thomas's attempts to let Nature 'speak for herself as far as the medium of words can make it possible'[68] prevents the subtleness of language and experience from being betrayed. Yet he knew such precise sympathy was almost impossible to maintain. However lightly observed, palpable physical facts cannot hope to share the extreme delicacy of his occasional moments of harmony. Because, as he said himself, they are 'probably inexpressible',[69] any attempts to apprehend them sensuously were likely to misrepresent them. But he also realised that one sense — that of smell — was appropriately elusive, and he exploited it with rewarding frequency. Judging by the evidence of his prose, his sensitivity to smell was particularly acute. A diary entry in his first book, *The Woodland Life*, records 'deep-red blossom clusters on the ash; odorous of the earth or of peeling bark',[70] and similar perceptions abound elsewhere. In *The Heart of England*, for example, he describes how 'The air smells like a musty white wild rose; coming from the west it blows gently, laden with all the brown and golden savours of Wales and Devon and Wiltshire and Surrey which I know, and the scent lifts the upper lip so that you snuff deeply as a dog snuffs'.[71] This kind of imaginative nourishment is recovered throughout his poetry. In 'The Word' he hears the thrush singing:

> While perhaps I am thinking of the elder scent
> That is like food, or while I am content
> With the wild rose scent that is like memory. . . .

And in 'Celandine', he is unable to communicate with the past 'Until I stooped to pluck from the grass there / One of five petals and I smelt the juice'. These frail scents exactly reflect the quality of his ideal, and provide him with a pattern of illumination similar to Wordsworth's 'spots of time'. One of their most concentrated appearances is made in 'Digging', which contains a graphic expression of faith in their power and significance:

> Today I think
> Only with scents, — scents dead leaves yield,
> And bracken, and wild carrot's seed,
> And the square mustard field;
>
> Odours that rise
> When the spade wounds the roots of tree,
> Rose, currant, raspberry, or goutweed,
> Rhubarb or celery;
>
> The smoke's smell, too,
> Flowing from where a bonfire burns
> The dead, the waste, the dangerous,
> And all to sweetness turns.
>
> It is enough
> To smell, to crumble the dark earth,
> While the robin sings over again
> Sad songs of Autumn mirth.

The opening lines of 'Digging' inaugurate a fine sensuous catalogue which affirms that scents are stimulatingly regenerative. Not only does the smell of 'dead leaves' encourage his intuitive reflections, but the bonfire upon which they are thrown 'burns / The dead, the waste, the dangerous, / And all to sweetness turns.' What appears to be destructive is purgative, and what is exhausted becomes a means of continuation. It is this paradox which allows him to achieve a sense of communion in the final stanza. The knowledge of simultaneous decay and regeneration in the season itself is corroborated by the song of the robin. Its fusion of diverse elements — its sad mirth — establishes a balance which allows Thomas to overcome the potentially isolating effects of language. It is literally 'enough' to smell the earth in order to achieve the communion he seeks.

If 'Digging' exemplifies Thomas's belief that nothing but the most discreet formal and sensuous strategies are capable of realising his ideal,

'Old Man' animates all the distractions which threaten to frustrate them. Although only the fourth poem he wrote, it summarises the effect that memory, children, scent and language have on his place in the social and natural world. Chronologically speaking it is a prophecy, but its uniquely inclusive scope makes it an equally appropriate conclusion. The first prose draft was written on 17 November 1914, nearly three weeks before the poem was finished, but that draft was itself based on childhood and adult memories. Thomas's autobiography contains what is probably the earliest source, in its description of a London friend's back garden where 'I first saw dark crimson dahlias and smelt bitter crushed stalks in plucking them. As I stood with my back to the house among the tall blossoming bushes I had no sense of any end to the garden between its brown fences. There remains in my mind a greenness, at once lowly and endless.'[72] Several years later, another friend, Bottomley, inadvertently started the sequence of events which was to produce the poem when he sent Thomas a cutting of the herb called 'old man'. In time Thomas was to tell him, 'The Old Man or Lad's-Love you gave me is now a beautiful great bush at my study door.'[73] Helen Thomas confirms this precise context. In her account of Yewtree Cottage (where they moved in 1913), she noted: 'By the only door into the house we planted the herbs which [Edward] so loved. Rosemary, thyme, lavender, bergamot and old man were there, all direct descendants of our first country garden, which we had propagated from cuttings each time we moved.'[74] A further step towards the poem — the connection between smelling the 'bitter crushed stalks' of the dahlias as a child and the later act of plucking the 'bitter' herb as an aid to memory — was taken in *The South Country*. Describing 'many scenes' from his childhood, Thomas recalls 'a church and churchyard and black pigs running down from them towards me in a rocky lane — lad's-love and tall, crimson, bitter dahlias in a garden — the sweetness of large, moist yellow apples eaten out of doors — children'.[75] One of the children he sees in this passage is walking 'down a long grassy path in an old garden',[76] and is 'content only to brush the tips of the flowers with her outstretched hands'.[77] For her, Thomas imagines, 'there was no end to the path',[78] and he watches her 'gravely walk on into the shadow and into Eternity, dimly foreknowing her life's days'.[79] This acknowledgment that the pursuit of childhood memories is a pursuit of happiness, and that the child's absorption in the present gives her a sense of stability, provided the basis for 'Old Man'. Moreover, the prose also contains a submerged paradox which was to be crucially developed later.

The girl's experience is both limited and defined by the shadows which surround her, and by the fact that her goal recedes as she advances towards it. As was to be the case with Thomas himself, her 'content' is the result of exploration rather than attainment.

The poem's paradoxical foundation is established in the opening lines:

> Old Man, or Lad's-love, — in the name there's nothing
> To one that knows not Lad's-love, or Old Man,
> The hoar-green feathery herb, almost a tree,
> Growing with rosemary and lavender.
> Even to one that knows it well, the names
> Half decorate, half perplex, the thing it is:
> At least, what that is clings not to the names
> In spite of time. And yet I like the names.

This hiatus between the herb's names and 'the thing it is' reaffirms Thomas's belief that language cannot adequately re-create the object that it describes. The 'thisness' of the herb, and the memories to which it is a means of access, hover so close to the edge of consciousness that any attempt to articulate them risks destroying their elusive nature. But this loss is offset by Thomas's gain in realising that the plant's principal characteristics are paradoxical. The proper names — their age and youth — initiate a series of reconciled opposites that define the one context in which harmony becomes possible. The same balance is evident in its appearance: the 'hoar-green' colouring blends faded antiquity with youthful health, and its being 'almost a tree' — with its suggestion of transition — reconciles the states of maturity and immaturity. Like the names, these qualities 'Half decorate, half perplex' Thomas by enlarging the herb's significance: as he stands watching, in middle age, he remembers his own past while looking forward to the child's future. His hopes of recalling 'something out of [his] youth'[80] are increased by the fact that the old man is placed between rosemary and lavender. The former's connotations of rememberance, and the latter's of preservation, combine to shelter the old man's potential harmony.

In this first stanza Thomas erects a platform upon which to build the main burden of the poem. The contradictory names of the herb have become, in Marie Quinn's words, 'an image of the speaker's goal, because to retrieve past time is also to conquer the discreteness of time, to live in the past and present simultaneously'.[81] But in addition to this, the names have established him in a catalogue of distinct age groups ranging from the old man of the title to the child on whom he now concentrates his attention. Here too a paradox is implicit. While the gradations of age emphasise the remorseless passage of time, they also suggest a regenerative, cyclical movement. Child, adult and 'old man' discover that their patterns of experience are repeated when they look back:

> The herb itself I like not, but for certain
> I love it, as some day the child will love it
> Who plucks a feather from the door-side bush
> Whenever she goes in or out of the house.

Thomas's original examination of the hiatus between 'thing' and name is here subtly enlarged to accommodate the discrepancy between his attitude to the herb itself and the consoling memories that it inspires. Their value has so far only been conveyed by 'hints and whispers', and his emphatic escalation of 'like' to 'love' is made while realising that he cannot entirely repossess the harmony they embody. Only the child has a pure and simple sense of integration with her surroundings:

> Often she waits there, snipping the tips and shrivelling
> The shreds at last on to the path, perhaps
> Thinking, perhaps of nothing, till she sniffs
> Her fingers and runs off. The bush is still
> But half as tall as she, though it is as old;
> So well she clips it. Not a word she says. . . .

So complete is her absorption and sympathy with the herb that she undertakes a literally physical process of identification with it. She shares its age, and trims it regularly as if to keep it a child like herself. And this outward harmony is complemented by evidence of an internal, invisible sympathy. By 'perhaps / Thinking, perhaps of nothing', and by saying 'not a word', the child exemplifies the same rapt, wordless communion described by Thomas in 'Digging'. 'It is enough' for her to sniff the shreds, just as it was 'enough' for him 'To smell, to crumble the dark earth': both states make the need for verbal expression redundant, and deny the possibility that language will betray them.

Thomas's appreciation of the rarity of the child's experience is made even more evident in the following lines:

> . . . I can only wonder how much hereafter
> She will remember, with that bitter scent,
> Of garden rows, and ancient damson-trees
> Topping a hedge, a bent path to a door,
> A low thick bush beside a door, and me
> Forbidding her to pick.

The child has in fact 'run off' by now, and Thomas's memory is free to ponder her future. But he does so knowing that he cannot imitate her silent communion; although he shares her intuitive knowledge that 'the ultimate language is that of the thing',[82] he is unable to use it. His 'Forbidding her to pick' is stern proof of this: it replaces 'hints and whispers' with forthright disapproval. If this is the audible sign of his isolation, its inward effects are explored in the lines which follow:

> As for myself,
> Where first I met the bitter scent is lost.
> I, too, often shrivel the grey shreds,
> Sniff them and think and sniff again and try
> Once more to think what it is I am remembering,
> Always in vain. I cannot like the scent,
> Yet I would rather give up others more sweet,
> With no meaning, than this bitter one.

Where the child was content with 'perhaps / Thinking, perhaps of nothing', Thomas wrestles with the fugitive 'meaning' of the scent. As he pulls the leaves from the herb, the repetitiveness of his actions conveys a sense of frustrated bafflement. But this does not prevent him from introducing a few more hopeful signs. The present tense of 'am remembering' suggests that the mere operation of memory produces some — albeit unspecified — results. This promise is strengthened by the admission that 'I would rather give up others more sweet, / With no meaning, than this bitter one'. The confession indicates clear knowledge of his own shortcomings, and emphasises his reluctance to settle for less elusive — and less rewarding — goals.

In the poem's final stanza, however, these potential pleasures are overshadowed:

> I have mislaid the key. I sniff the spray
> And think of nothing; I see and I hear nothing;

> Yet seem, too, to be listening, lying in wait
> For what I should, yet never can, remember:
> No garden appears, no path, no hoar-green bush
> Of Lad's-love, or Old Man, no child beside,
> Neither father nor mother, nor any playmate;
> Only an avenue, dark, nameless, without end.

The original location of the herb's scent has already been described as 'lost', but its disappearance is here translated into incontrovertible, concrete terms. By saying he has 'mislaid the key', Thomas recalls the fact that the bush itself is 'door-side', and that one of the things the child might remember is 'a bent path to a door'. It is as if the bush — which was touched by the child 'Whenever she [went] in or out of the house' — actually facilitated her passage from one state (indoors/outdoors) to another (outdoors/indoors). All the apartments of experience, and all the divisions of time, were available to her, whereas for Thomas there is no free access. The past, in terms of his image, is locked to him, and so is the harmony he once enjoyed there. When he repeats the mnemonic of his former happiness by sniffing the spray, it is not the absorbed and receptive 'nothing' of the child that he sees, but merely a shadowy telescopic view of emptiness. His failure is exacerbated by the very insistence of his longing for success. Not only is he looking and listening, but even 'lying in wait' — as if to ambush 'what I should, yet never can, remember'. His anxious self-consciousness is aggravated by his knowledge of what to expect, were it possible to realise his ambition.

Because Thomas is trying to reproduce, rather than originate, a sense of integration, his closing account of natural and social isolation is a tormenting mixture of visible and invisible qualities. This is most obviously apparent in the superb closing line: customary expectations that an avenue should lead towards a specific place are rebuffed by a vacant darkness. It is, however, an avenue 'without end'. While this suggests that his search for harmony will repeatedly be compromised, it also contains at least the potential for fulfilment. As Edna Longley says, 'despite the poem's overt statements, it has itself explored and illuminated as much of the avenue as is humanly and imaginatively possible'.[83]

In the role that it assigns to children, in its restless exploration of the discrepancy between the name for a thing and its essential qualities, in its extraordinarily full and delicate response to scents, and in its discussion of memory, 'Old Man' summarises every theme and technique that Thomas used in his pursuit of wholeness. It is, as Frost said, 'the flower of the lot',[84] and movingly defines the sense of isolation which compromised Thomas's relationship with landscape, family and friends. It also illustrates the changes that he underwent when he abandoned prose for poetry. In the former, his feelings of 'superfluousness' provoked him into single-minded pursuit of an impossible ideal. The circumstances of his suburban childhood, and his failure to find a satisfactory rural society, encouraged him to cultivate a destructively nostalgic cast of mind. Although he battled to overcome it during his long career as 'a doomed hack', it was only in the last two years of his life that his flight from reality was checked. His discovery of a medium better suited to express the full range of his personality — including its 'modern scepticism'[85] — did not blunt his desire for perfection, but forced him to realise that he could only possess it in full knowledge of the hardships it strove to transcend. It is this determination to reconcile the conflict between real and ideal that justifies his repeated use of paradox, animates the figure of the double, and explains the function of interlocutors in his narrative poems. He consistently ridicules his original misguided assumption that 'the thing it is' will be better revealed by 'a tale' than 'the truth / Or nothing'. And the change of heart was not simply his salvation as a man: it also produced the special excellences of his poetry. With the most delicate sensuous sympathy, it clarifies all that is 'ungraspable in the very nature of words, and memory, and consciousness'.[86] The elusiveness is so scrupulously reflected in the disarmingly low-keyed tone of voice that it is easy to understand why he has suffered undue neglect. But his refusal to let language betray his vision, and his use of 'the minor modes' to make insights of 'major psychological subtlety',[87] entitle him to a prominent and permanent place in the history of twentieth-century literature.

NOTES

INTRODUCTION

1 *Times Literary Supplement*, 21 June 1917, p. 299.
2 Quoted in Michael Reck, *Ezra Pound: A Close-Up* (London, 1968), p. 14.
3 Stephen Spender, *Love Hate Relations* (London, 1974), p. 106.
4 Edward Thomas, *Poems and Last Poems*, ed. Edna Longley (London, 1973), p. 10. (Hereafter cited as *Poems and Last Poems*.)
5 John Moore, *The Life and Letters of Edward Thomas* (London, 1939), p. 165. (Hereafter cited as *Letters*.)
6 *New Weekly*, 9 May 1914, p. 249.
7 *Letters from Edward Thomas to Gordon Bottomley*, ed. R. George Thomas (London, 1968), p. 233. (Hereafter cited as *Letters to Gordon Bottomley*.)
8 *Daily Chronicle*, 7 June 1909. Edward Thomas's reviews in University College Library, Cardiff, vol. 4, p. 113. (Hereafter cited as UCC.)
9 *Daily Chronicle*, 23 November 1909. UCC, vol. 4, p. 135.
10 Edward Thomas, *Maurice Maeterlinck* (London, 1911), p. 21.
11 Quoted in *Imagist Poetry*, ed. Peter Jones (Harmondsworth, Middlesex, 1972), p. 135.
12 *Times Literary Supplement*, 29 March 1917, p. 151.
13 Gordon Bottomley, 'A Note on Edward Thomas', *Welsh Review*, vol. IV, no. 3 (September 1945), p. 177.
14 Edward Thomas, *The Heart of England* (London, 1906), p. 226.
15 *The Oxford Book of Modern Verse*, ed. W. B. Yeats (Oxford, 1936), p. xiii.
16 *Morning Post*, 23 December 1907. UCC, vol. 3, p. 56.
17 Edward Thomas, *The South Country* (London, 1909), p. 241.
18 *Bookman*, November 1909. UCC, vol. 1, p. 106.
19 The other adapts the traditional ballad 'In Amsterdam There Dwelt a Maid'.
20 Edward Thomas, *Celtic Stories* (Oxford, 1911), pp. 127-8.
21 Quoted by Edna Longley in 'Edward Thomas and the "English" Line', *New Review*, vol. 1, no. 11 (February 1975), p. 8.

22   Robert Graves and Laura Riding, *A Survey of Modernist Poetry* (London, 1927), p. 112.

23   Altogether five *Georgian Poetry* anthologies were published by Harold Munro from his Poetry Bookshop — in 1912, 1915, 1917, 1919 and 1922. The hard core of poets included Lascelles Abercrombie, Gordon Bottomley, Rupert Brooke, W. H. Davies, Walter de la Mare, John Drinkwater, W. W. Gibson, Ralph Hodgson and John Masefield.

24   Edward Marsh, Prefatory Note to *Georgian Poetry* (London, 1912).

25   *Daily Chronicle*, 5 November 1912. UCC, vol. 6, p. 89.

26   *Daily Chronicle*, 26 November 1903. UCC, vol. 2, p. 131.

27   Robert H. Ross, *The Georgian Revolt* (London, 1967), pp. 145-6.

28   Ibid., p. 257.

29   Philip Hobsbaum, 'The Road Not Taken', *Listener*, vol. 66 (13 November 1961), p. 860.

30   Lascelles Abercrombie, 'Poetry and contemporary Speech', *English Association Pamphlet*, no. 27 (February 1914), p. 7.

31   *Daily Chronicle*, 30 August 1905. UCC, vol. 2, p. 83.

32   *Daily Chronicle*, 5 November 1912. UCC, vol. 5, p. 89.

33   Christopher Hassall, *Edward Marsh, Patron of the Arts* (London, 1959), p. 422.

34   Quoted in William Cooke, *Edward Thomas: A Critical Biography* (London, 1970), p. 87. (Hereafter cited as *Biography*.)

35   'A New Poet', *Daily News and Leader*, 22 July 1914, p. 7.

36   Ibid., p. 7.

37   F. R. Leavis, *New Bearings in English Poetry* (London, 1932), p. 69.

CHAPTER 1: BIOGRAPHICAL

1   Fuller accounts may be found in William Cooke, *Edward Thomas: A Critical Biography* (London, 1970); Helen Thomas, *As It Was* and *World Without End* (London, 1956); and R. George Thomas, *Edward Thomas* (Cardiff, 1972).

2   Helen Thomas, *As It Was* and *World Without End* (London, 1956, reissued 1972), p. 23. (Hereafter cited as *World Without End*.)

3   Philip Henry Thomas, *A Religion of this World: A Selection of Positivist Addresses* (London, 1913), p. 7.

4   Quoted in H. Coombes, *Edward Thomas: A Critical Study* (London, 1956), p. 31.

5   John Moore, *Letters*, p. 277.

6   Ibid., p. 306.

7   Edward Thomas, *The Childhood of Edward Thomas* (London, 1938), p. 135. (Hereafter cited as *Childhood*.)

8   Helen Thomas, *World Without End*, p. 26.

9   Ibid., p. 22.

10   Ibid., p. 38.

11   Bodleian Library, MS Eng. Lett. c. 280, p. 124.

12   Helen Thomas, *World Without End*, p. 82.

13   *Letters to Gordon Bottomley*, p. 51.

14 In addition to Elses Farm, Thomas also rented a cottage-cum-study half a mile away.

15 *Letters to Gordon Bottomley*, p. 107.

16 John Moore, *Letters*, p. 76.

17 Helen Thomas, *World Without End*, p. 115.

18 Q. D. Leavis, 'Lives and Works of Richard Jefferies', *Scrutiny*, vol. VI, no. 4 (March 1938), p. 436.

19 Edward Thomas, *Beautiful Wales* (London, 1905), p. 144.

20 Helen Thomas, *World Without End*, p. 99.

21 John Moore, *Letters*, p. 171.

22 Helen Thomas, *World Without End*, p. 84.

23 *Letters to Gordon Bottomley*, p. 104.

24 Robert P. Eckert, *Edward Thomas: A Biography and a Bibliography* (London, 1937), p. 126. (Hereafter cited as *A Biography*.)

25 John Moore, *Letters*, p. 171.

26 Helen Thomas, *World Without End*, pp. 148-9.

27 Helen Thomas, *Time & Again* (Manchester, 1978), p. 63.

28 John Moore, *Letters*, p. 180.

29 *Letters to Gordon Bottomley*, p. 226.

30 Eleanor Farjeon, *Edward Thomas: The Last Four Years* (London, 1958), p. 13. (Hereafter cited as *Edward Thomas*.)

31 Helen Thomas, *Time & Again*, p. 93.

32 Robert Frost, *Selected Letters*, ed. Lawrance Thompson (London, 1965), p. 217.

33 Lawrance Thompson, *Robert Frost: The Early Years 1874-1915* (London, 1967), p. 463.

34 'Robert Frost', *New Weekly*, 8 August 1914, p. 249.

35 John Moore, *Letters*, p. 220.

36 Ibid., p. 170.

37 Quoted in William Cooke, *Biography*, p. 81.

38 Edward Thomas, *The Last Sheaf* (London, 1928), pp. 100-1.

39 *Letters to Gordon Bottomley*, pp. 242-3.

40 Eleanor Farjeon, *Edward Thomas*, p. 81.

41 Helen Thomas, *Time & Again*, pp. 149-50.

42 'Edward Thomas's Letters to W. H. Hudson', *London Mercury*, vol. II, no. 10 (August 1920), pp. 439-40.

43 *Letters to Gordon Bottomley*, p. 245.

44 Eleanor Farjeon, *Edward Thomas*, p. 154.

45 Edward Thomas, *The Last Sheaf*, p. 221.

46 *Letters to Gordon Bottomley*, p. 269.

47 In June 1916 Thomas was given a £300 grant, instead of a Civil List Pension, as well.

48 John Moore, *Letters*, p. 255.

49 Eleanor Farjeon, *Edward Thomas*, p. 155.

50 Gordon Bottomley, 'A Note on Edward Thomas', *Welsh Review*, vol. IV, no. 3 (September 1945), p. 177.

51 John Moore, *Letters*, p. 240.

52 Helen Thomas, *Time & Again*, p. 126.

53 John Moore, *Letters*, p. 255.
54 *The Collected Poems of Edward Thomas*, ed. R. George Thomas (Oxford, 1978), p. 472.
55 DCL, Edward Thomas to Robert Frost, 6 March 1917.
56 Edward Thomas, *Selected Poems*, ed. Edward Garnett (Newtown, Montgomeryshire, 1972), p. x.
57 Quoted in William Cooke, *Biography*, pp. 99-100.
58 There is some debate about the exact circumstances of Thomas's death. A full discussion of it may be found in ibid., pp. 268-70.

CHAPTER 2: DOUBLE VISION

1   John Moore, *Letters*, p. 221.
2   Ibid., p. 133.
3   Ibid., p. 103.
4   Edward Thomas, *The Happy-Go-Lucky Morgans* (London, 1913), p. 122.
5   John Moore, *Letters*, p. 76.
6   *Letters to Gordon Bottomley*, p. 104.
7   John Moore, *Letters*, p. 172.
8   Israel Levine, *The Unconscious* (London, 1923), p. 159.
9   Morton Prince, *The Dissociation of a Personality* (London, 1906), p. 3.
10 Ibid., p. 22.
11 *Letters to Gordon Bottomley*, p. 129.
12 Ibid., p. 140.
13 Eleanor Farjeon, *Edward Thomas*, p. 13.
14 Edward Thomas, *Light and Twilight* (London, 1911), pp. 120-1.
15 R. D. Laing, *The Divided Self* (Harmondsworth, Middlesex, 1975), p. 86.
16 Ralph Tymms, *Doubles in Literary Psychology* (Cambridge, 1949), p. 55.
17 Oscar Wilde, *The Picture of Dorian Gray* (Harmondsworth, Middlesex, 1971), p. 143.
18 Ibid., p. 74.
19 R. L. Stevenson, *The Strange Case of Dr Jekyll and Mr Hyde* (London, 1896), p. 107. (Hereafter cited as *Jekyll and Hyde*.)
20 Morton Prince, *The Dissociation of a Personality*, p. 2.
21 Edgar Allan Poe, *William Wilson* in *The Complete Poems and Stories of Edgar Allan Poe*, ed. Arthur Hobson Quinn and Edward H. O'Neill (New York, 1958), vol. I, p. 282.
22 Robert P. Eckert, *A Biography*, p. 11.
23 Ibid., p. 11.
24 Edward Thomas, *The South Country* (London, 1909), p. 73.
25 Ibid., p. 78.
26 Ibid., p. 75.
27 Ibid., p. 75.
28. Ibid., p. 78.
29 Ibid., p. 86.
30 Ibid., p. 78.
31 Edward Thomas, *The Happy-Go-Lucky Morgans*, p. 122.
32 Ibid., p. 127.

33 Edward Thomas, *The South Country*, p. 85.

34 Edward Thomas, *The Last Sheaf*, p. 55.

35 Ibid., p. 52.

36 Ibid., p. 55.

37 Edward Thomas, *The Icknield Way* (London, 1913), p. 280.

38 Ibid., pp. 280-1.

39 R. L. Stevenson, *Jekyll and Hyde*, p. 19.

40 Edward Thomas, *In Pursuit of Spring* (London, 1914), pp. 119-20.

41 Ibid., p. 140.

42 Ibid., p. 141.

43 Ibid., p. 220.

44 Ibid., p. 282.

45 Edward Thomas, *Childhood*, p. 115.

46 Quoted in R. George Thomas, *Edward Thomas*, p. 39.

47 John Moore, *Letters*, p. 326.

48 Edward Thomas, *Selected Poems*, ed. Edward Garnett, p. vi.

49 Edward Thomas, *Poems and Last Poems*, ed. Edna Longley, p. 164.

50 Edward Thomas, *Light and Twilight*, pp. 124-5.

51 See also Thomas Hardy's poem 'He Follows Himself'.

52 H. Coombes, *Edward Thomas: A Critical Study*, p. 219.

53 James Hogg, *The Private Memoirs and Confessions of a Justified Sinner* (London, 1824), p. 364.

54 Otto Rank, *The Double: A Psychoanalytic Study* (Chapel Hill, North Carolina, 1971), pp. 16-17.

55 Joseph Conrad, 'The Secret Sharer', *'Twixt Land and Sea* (London, 1947), p. 125.

56 Edward Thomas, *In Pursuit of Spring*, p. 127.

57 Ibid., p. 127.

58 See Chapter 5, pp. 158-61.

59 Edward Thomas, *Poems and Last Poems*, ed. Edna Longley, p. 166.

60 R. D. Laing, *The Divided Self*, p. 91.

61 Edward Thomas, *The Heart of England* (London, 1906), pp. 61-2.

62 Ibid., p. 37.

63 Edward Thomas, *Light and Twilight*, p. 31.

64 Edward Thomas, *The Icknield Way*, p. 245.

65 Edward Thomas, *In Pursuit of Spring*, p. 210.

66 Ibid., p. 287.

67 Edward Thomas, *The South Country*, p. 152.

68 Edward Thomas, *Poems and Last Poems*, ed. Edna Longley, p. 169.

69 R. L. Stevenson, *Jekyll and Hyde*, p. 137.

70 Mary Shelley, *Frankenstein or The Modern Prometheus* (Oxford English Texts, London, 1969), p. 149.

71 Edward Thomas, *Poems and Last Poems*, ed. Edna Longley, p. 169.

72 H. Coombes, *Edward Thomas: A Critical Study*, p. 201.

73 *Letters to Gordon Bottomley*, p. 53.

74 Ibid., p. 160.

75 Eleanor Farjeon, *Edward Thomas*, p. 13.

76 Edward Thomas, *Light and Twilight*, p. 164.

77   *Letters to Gordon Bottomley*, p. 174.
78   The same is true of the prose; see *The South Country*, p. 25; *The Heart of England*, pp. 37-8; and *The Last Sheaf*, p. 206.
79   Robert Frost, *The Poetry of Robert Frost*, ed. Edward Connery Latham (London, 1971), 'Waiting', p. 14, l. 9.
80   Edward Thomas, *Poems and Last Poems*, ed. Edna Longley, p. 216.
81   Edward Thomas, *Beautiful Wales*, p. 38.
82   John F. Danby, 'Edward Thomas', *Critical Quarterly*, vol. 1, no. 4 (Winter 1959), p. 313.

CHAPTER 3: THE SOUND OF SENSE

1   Eleanor Farjeon, *Edward Thomas*, p. 37.
2   See William Cooke, *Biography*, pp. 182-6.
3   Edward Thomas, *Selected Poems*, ed. Edward Garnett, p. xiii.
4   John Moore, *Letters*, p. 210.
5   Quoted in Elizabeth Sergeant, *Robert Frost: The Trial by Existence* (New York, 1961), p. 209.
6   Edward Garnett, 'Edward Thomas', *Dial*, vol. 64, no. 760 (14 February 1918), p. 135.
7   Edward Thomas, *Collected Poems*, ed. Walter de la Mare (10th impression, London, 1969), p. 6. A fact referred to by Sara Huntingdon in her unpublished MA thesis, 'A Study of the Literary Relations of Robert Frost and Edward Thomas' (Ohio State University, 1938). Bodleian Library MS Eng. Lett. d. 677.
8   Conrad Aiken, review of *Poems*, *Dial*, vol. 64, no. 765 (25 April 1918), p. 405.
9   Louis Untermeyer, review of *Last Poems*, *North American Review*, vol. 209, no. 2 (February 1919), p. 263.
10   Eleanor Farjeon, *Edward Thomas*, pp. 55-6.
11   Edward Thomas, *The Happy-Go-Lucky Morgans*, p. 127.
12   Lawrance Thompson, *Robert Frost: The Early Years 1874-1915* (London, 1967), p. 464.
13   Elizabeth Sergeant, *Robert Frost: The Trial by Existence*, p. 135.
14   Lawrance Thompson, *Robert Frost: The Years of Triumph 1915-1938* (London, 1971), p. 94.
15   Bodleian Library, MS Eng. Lett. d. 281, p. 76.
16   DCL, Edward Thomas to Robert Frost, 6 June 1914.
17   Quoted in Lawrance Thompson, *Robert Frost: The Years of Triumph*, p. 506.
18   Lawrance Thompson, *Robert Frost: The Early Years*, p. 225.
19   William James, *The Will to Believe* (New York, 1897), p. 51.
20   Lawrance Thompson, *Robert Frost: The Early Years*, p. 427.
21   Ibid., p. 241.
22   William James, *Psychology: Briefer Course* (New York, 1892), p. 149.
23   *Daily Chronicle*, 5 September 1912. UCC, vol. 5, p. 89.
24   DCL, Edward Thomas to Robert Frost, 19 May 1914.
25   Lawrance Thompson, *Robert Frost: The Early Years*, p. 267.
26   Robert Frost, *Selected Letters*, p. 217.
27   DCL, Edward Thomas to Robert Frost, 3 May 1915.

28   DCL, ibid., 3 October 1915.
29   *Daily Chronicle*, 27 August 1901. UCC, vol. 1, p. 27.
30   *Bookman*, January 1908. UCC, vol. 2, p. 93.
31   *Daily Chronicle*, 1 January 1907. UCC, vol. 4, p. 1.
32   *Daily Chronicle*, 5 December 1902. UCC, vol. 1, p. 15.
33   *Week's Survey*, Summer 1904. UCC, vol. 1, p. 134.
34   *Daily Chronicle*, 17 January 1906. UCC, vol. 3, p. 28.
35   *Daily Chronicle*, 18 September 1902. UCC, vol. 1, p. 95.
36   *Week's Survey*, 20 September 1902. UCC, vol. 3, p. 4.
37   *Bookman*, October 1904. UCC, vol. 2, p. 79.
38   Lawrance Thompson, *Robert Frost: The Early Years*, p. 418.
39   *Letters to Gordon Bottomley*, p. 57.
40   Edward Thomas, *Poems and Last Poems*, ed. Edna Longley, p. 143.
41   *Letters to Gordon Bottomley*, p. 194.
42   Ibid., pp. 223-4.
43   Bodleian Library, MS Eng. Lett. d. 281, p. 76.
44   Edward Thomas, *Childhood*, p. 145.
45   Edward Thomas, *The Last Sheaf*, pp. 19-20.
46   DCL, Edward Thomas to Robert Frost, 19 May 1914.
47   Robert Frost, *Selected Letters*, p. 140.
48   Bodleian Library, MS Eng. Lett. c. 280, p. 93.
49   Edward Thomas, *Rose Acre Papers* (London, 1904), p. 108.
50   *Letters to Gordon Bottomley*, p. 138.
51   Edward Thomas, *Lafcadio Hearn* (London, 1912), p. 43.
52   Ibid., p. 48.
53   *Daily Chronicle*, 9 September 1909. UCC, vol. 5, p. 61.
54   Edward Thomas, *Walter Pater* (London, 1913), pp. 219-20.
55   Ibid., p. 118.
56   Ibid., p. 210.
57   William Cooke, 'Elected Friends: Robert Frost and Edward Thomas', *Poetry Wales*, vol. 13, no. 4 (Spring 1978), pp. 22-3.
58   Quoted in Elizabeth Sergeant, *Robert Frost: The Trial by Existence*, p. 136.
59   Gordon Bottomley, 'A Note on Edward Thomas', *Welsh Review*, vol. IV, no. 3 (September 1945), p. 172.
60   Quoted in Elizabeth Sergeant, *Robert Frost: The Trial by Existence*, p. 136.
61   Robert Frost, *Selected Letters*, p. 167.
62   Ibid., pp. 171-2.
63   Quoted in Lawrance Thompson, *Robert Frost: The Early Years*, p. 434.
64   Quoted in Robert S. Newdick, 'Robert Frost and the Sound of Sense', *American Literature*, vol. 9 (November 1937), pp. 292-3.
65   DCL, Edward Thomas to Robert Frost, 24 February 1914.
66   Edward Thomas, review of *North of Boston*, *New Weekly*, 8 August 1914, p. 249.
67   Edward Thomas, review of *North of Boston*, *English Review*, vol. 18, no. 1 (August 1914), pp. 142-3.
68   John Moore, *Letters*, pp. 328-9.
69   *Letters to Gordon Bottomley*, p. 220.
70   DCL, Edward Thomas to Robert Frost, 19 May 1914.

71 'The White Horse', LML (quoted in *The Collected Poems of Edward Thomas*, ed. R. George Thomas, p. 436).

72 Robert Frost, *Selected Letters*, pp. 124-5.

73 Quoted in Lawrance Thompson, *Robert Frost: The Early Years*, p. 435.

74 See William Cooke, *Biography*, pp. 199-200.

75 Edward Thomas, *Poems and Last Poems*, ed. Edna Longley, p. 402.

76 DCL, Edward Thomas to Robert Frost, 15 December 1914.

77 John Moore, *Letters*, p. 326.

78 Edward Thomas, review of *North of Boston*, *Daily News and Leader*, 22 July 1914, p. 7.

79 Edward Thomas, *Walter Pater*, p. 205.

80 D. W. Harding, *Words into Rhythm* (Cambridge University Press, 1976), p. 71.

81 DCL, Edward Thomas to Robert Frost, 15 August 1916.

82 *Letters to Gordon Bottomley*, p. 245.

83 DCL, Edward Thomas to Robert Frost, 15 December 1914.

84 Quoted in Lawrance Thompson, *Robert Frost: The Years of Triumph*, p. 90.

85 Eleanor Farjeon, *Edward Thomas*, p. 147.

86 Edward Thomas, *Poems and Last Poems*, ed. Edna Longley, pp. 290-1.

87 Edward Thomas, *Feminine Influence on the Poets* (London, 1910), pp. 85-6.

88 Eleanor Farjeon, *Edward Thomas*, p. 134.

89 Robert Frost, *Selected Poems*, ed. Ian Hamilton (Harmondsworth, Middlesex, 1973), p. 18.

90 J. C. Squire, review of *New Hampshire*, *London Mercury*, vol. 10, no. 57 (July 1924), p. 317.

91 John Freeman, 'Edward Thomas', *New Statesman*, vol. X, no. 240 (10 November 1917), p. 133.

92 *Bookman*, August 1908. UCC, vol. 5, p. 133.

93 F. R. Leavis, *New Bearings in English Poetry*, p. 69.

94 *Daily Chronicle*, 12 September 1910. UCC, vol. 5, p. 96.

95 Vernon Scannell, *Edward Thomas*, Writers and their Work, no. 163 (London, 1962), p. 21.

96 John Moore, *Letters*, p. 75.

97 *Letters to Gordon Bottomley*, p. 7.

98 F. R. Leavis, *New Bearings in English Poetry*, p. 69.

99 Edna Longley, 'Larkin, Edward Thomas and the Tradition', *Phoenix*, nos 11-12 (Autumn and Winter 1973-4), p. 82.

100 Edward Thomas, *The Country* (London, 1913), pp. 8-9.

101 John Moore, *Letters*, p. 284.

102 *Daily Chronicle*, 15 December 1907. UCC, vol. 3, p. 51.

103 *Daily Chronicle*, 17 October 1905. UCC, vol. 3, p. 88.

104 Eleanor Farjeon, *Edward Thomas*, p. 198.

105 Edward Thomas, *Walter Pater*, p. 218.

106 D. W. Harding, *Words into Rhythm*, p. 25.

107 Ibid., p. 8.

108 *Week's Survey*, 20 September 1902. UCC, vol. 3, p. 4.

109 UCC, ibid.

110 Edward Thomas, *Poems and Last Poems*, ed. Edna Longley, p. 403.

111 Edward Thomas, *Selected Poems*, ed. Edward Garnett, p. xi.
112 Ibid., p. viii.
113 *Bookman*, April 1913. UCC, vol. 5, p. 124.
114 Review of *Collected Poems*, *Times Literary Supplement*, no. 975 (23 September 1920), p. 614.
115 *Bookman*, May 1908. UCC, vol. 4, p. 130.
116 *Academy*, 23 September 1905. UCC, vol. 3, p. 41.
117 Edward Thomas, *Walter Pater*, p. 107.
118 *Letters to Gordon Bottomley*, p. 120.
119 Eleanor Farjeon, *Edward Thomas*, p. 221.
120 *Morning Post*, 12 November 1908. UCC, vol. 5, p. 31.
121 *Letters to Gordon Bottomley*, p. 238.
122 John Moore, *Letters*, p. 211.
123 Robert Frost, *Selected Letters*, p. 193.
124 'Edward Thomas's letters to W. H. Hudson', *London Mercury*, vol. II, no. 10 (August 1920), p. 145.
125 Edward Thomas, *The Last Sheaf*, p. 221.
126 DCL, Edward Thomas to Robert Frost, 15 December 1914.

CHAPTER 4: PATRIOT AND WAR POET

1 Bernard Bergonzi, *Heroes' Twilight* (London, 1965), p. 85.
2 John H. Johnston, *English Poetry of the First World War* (Princeton, New Jersey, 1964), p. 128.
3 John Lehmann, *The Open Night* (London, 1952), p. 82.
4 Unsigned review of *An Annual of New Poetry* (London, 1917), *Times Literary Supplement*, 29 March 1917, p. 151.
5 *Letters to Gordon Bottomley*, p. 283.
6 Edward Thomas, 'War Poetry', *Poetry and Drama*, vol. II, no. 8 (December 1914), p. 342.
7 Bodleian Library, MS Eng. Lett. c. 281, p. 142.
8 Robert Frost, *Selected Letters*, p. 193.
9 Alun Lewis, review of *The Trumpet and Other Poems*, *Horizon*, vol. 3, no. 13 (January 1941), p. 80.
10 Philip Larkin, review of *The Collected Poems of Wilfred Owen* (London, 1966), *Listener*, vol. 70 (10 October 1963), p. 561.
11 Dust jacket of Edward Thomas, *The Life of the Duke of Marlborough* (London, 1915).
12 Thomas Hardy, *Far from the Madding Crowd* (New Wessex Edition, London 1974), p. 424.
13 Alun Lewis, *Horizon*, vol. 3, no. 13, p. 80.
14 Edward Thomas, *The Happy-Go-Lucky Morgans*, p. 220.
15 Ibid., p. 222.
16 Ibid., pp. 223-4.
17 Ibid., p. 224.
18 Eleanor Farjeon, *Edward Thomas*, p. 180.
19 DCL, Edward Thomas to Robert Frost, 2 January 1916.
20 Edward Thomas, *The Last Sheaf*, p. 103.

21 Edward Thomas, 'Anthologies and Reprints', *Poetry and Drama*, vol. II, no. 8 (December 1914), p. 384.

22 Edward Thomas, 'War Poetry', *Poetry and Drama*, vol. II, no. 8, pp. 342-4.

23 Eleanor Farjeon, *Edward Thomas*, p. 116.

24 *Letters to Gordon Bottomley*, p. 243.

25 William Cooke, *Biography*, pp. 215-16.

26 *British Country Life in Autumn and Winter*, ed. Edward Thomas (London, 1909), p. 128.

27 Richard Jefferies, *Amaryllis at the Fair* (London, 1887), p. 217.

28 Elizabeth Sergeant, *Robert Frost: The Trial by Existence*, p. 135.

29 Richard Jefferies, *The Amateur Poacher* (London, 1879), p. 100.

30 H. Coombes, *Edward Thomas: A Critical Study*, p. 65.

31 *Letters to Gordon Bottomley*, p. 152.

32 W. H. Hudson, Introduction to Thomas's *Cloud Castle* (London, 1922), p. vi.

33 Richard Jefferies, *The Hills and the Vale* (London, 1909), p. xxix.

34 Edward Thomas, *Light and Twilight*, p. 51.

35 Richard Jefferies, *The Story of My Heart* (London, 1883), pp. 181-2.

36 Edward Thomas, *Richard Jefferies* (London, 1909), p. 59.

37 Richard Jefferies, *The Gamekeeper at Home* (London, 1878), p. 67.

38 Edward Thomas, *Richard Jefferies*, p. 7.

39 Edward Thomas, *The South Country*, p. 152.

40 William Cooke, *Biography*, p. 216.

41 Edward Thomas, *The Happy-Go-Lucky Morgans*, pp. 148-9.

42 Edward Thomas, *Poems and Last Poems*, ed. Edna Longley, p. 243.

43 Edward Thomas, *The Heart of England*, p. 226.

44 John Freeman, 'Edward Thomas', *New Statesman*, vol. X, no. 240 (10 November 1917), p. 134.

45 Edward Thomas, *The Last Sheaf*, p. 138.

46 Ibid., p. 136.

47 Edward Thomas, *Poems and Last Poems*, ed. Edna Longley, p. 252.

48 George Bourne, *The Bettesworth Book* (London, 1901), pp. 324-5.

49 Jon Silkin, *Out of Battle* (London, 1972), p. 88.

50 Eleanor Farjeon, *Edward Thomas*, p. 144.

51 Helen Thomas, *World Without End*, pp. 177-8.

52 Ibid., pp. 40-1.

53 R. George Thomas, *Edward Thomas*, p. 50.

54 John Moore, *Letters*, p. 264.

55 Edward Thomas, *Rose Acre Papers*, p. 107.

56 John Moore, *Letters*, p. 229.

57 Eleanor Farjeon, *Edward Thomas*, p. 188.

58 DCL, Edward Thomas to Robert Frost, 5 March 1916.

59 DCL, ibid.

60 *Letters to Gordon Bottomley*, p. 280.

61 DCL, Edward Thomas to Robert Frost, 19 October 1916.

62 Vernon Scannell, *Edward Thomas*, p. 20.

63 Bodleian Library, MS. Eng. Lett. c. 281, p. 220.

64 Andrew Young, *The Collected Poems of Andrew Young*, ed. Leonard Clark (London, 1950), p. 280.

65   Jon Silkin, *Out of Battle*, p. 97.

66   Eleanor Farjeon, *Edward Thomas*, p. 214.

67   Paul Fussell, *The Great War and Modern Memory* (New York, 1975), p. 59.

68   Bodleian Library, MS. Eng. Lett. c. 281, p. 142.

69   Cf. 'Reveille', lines 5-8:

> Wake: the vaulted shadow shatters,
>   Trampled to the floor it spanned,
> And the tent of night in tatters
>   Straws the sky-pavilioned land.

70   Eleanor Farjeon, *Edward Thomas*, p. 218.

71   Edward Thomas, *The South Country*, p. 216.

72   Alun Lewis, *Horizon*, vol. 3, no. 13 (January 1941), p. 80.

73   DCL, Edward Thomas to Robert Frost, 15 May 1915.

74   DCL, ibid., 9 September 1916.

75   Edward Thomas, *The Icknield Way*, p. vii.

76   Ibid., p. vii.

77   Edward Thomas, *Poems and Last Poems*, ed. Edna Longley, p. 358.

78   Eleanor Farjeon, *Edward Thomas*, p. 237.

79   Edward Thomas, *The Happy-Go-Lucky Morgans*, pp. 238-9.

80   Ibid., p. 239.

81   DCL, Roger Ingpen to Robert Frost, 17 April 1917.

CHAPTER 5: FRIEND AND COUNTRYMAN

1   John Moore, *Letters*, p. 277.

2   Thomas Hardy, *The Mayor of Casterbridge*, New Wessex Edition (London, 1975), p. 59.

3   Edward Thomas, *Horae Solitariae* (London, 1902), p. 108.

4   Edward Thomas, *The South Country*, pp. 65-6.

5   Ibid., pp. 74-5.

6   Ibid., p. 90.

7   Ibid., pp. 88-9.

8   Ibid., p. 92.

9   W. J. Keith, *The Rural Tradition* (Hassocks, Sussex, 1975), p. 193.

10   Thomas Hardy, *The Mayor of Casterbridge*, p. 116.

11   W. J. Keith, *The Rural Tradition*, p. 146.

12   Thomas Hardy, 'The Dorsetshire Labourer', *The Personal Writings of Thomas Hardy*, ed. Harold Orel (London, 1967), p. 181.

13   Ibid., p. 180.

14   George Bourne, *Change in the Village* (London, 1912), p. 17.

15   Edward Thomas, *The South Country*, p. 80.

16   Ibid., p. 7.

17   George Bourne, *Change in the Village*, p. 226.

18   Ibid., pp. 130-1.

19   Ibid., p. 133.

20   Ibid., p. 126.

21   Ibid., p. 115.
22   Edward Thomas, *The South Country*, p. 254.
23   Ibid., pp.256-7.
24   Ibid., p. 257.
25   Ibid., p. 265.
26   Edward Thomas, *Horae Solitariae*, p. 123.
27   Edward Thomas, *The Heart of England*, pp. 79-80.
28   Edward Thomas, *Richard Jefferies*, p. 190.
29   Ibid., p. 190.
30   Helen Thomas, *World Without End*, p. 133.
31   *Letters to Gordon Bottomley*, p. 206.
32   Ibid., p. 126.
33   Edward Thomas, *Beautiful Wales*, p. 177.
34   Edward Thomas, *The Heart of England*, p. 132.
35   Bodleian Library, MS Eng. Lett. d. 282, p. 31.
36   Edward Thomas, *The Happy-Go-Lucky Morgans*, pp. 49-50.
37   *Letters to Gordon Bottomley*, p. 135.
38   Edward Thomas, *Rest and Unrest* (London, 1910), p. 143.
39   Edward Thomas, *Richard Jefferies*, p. 233.
40   Richard Jefferies, *The Dewy Morn* (London, 1884), p. 6.
41   Edward Thomas, *Richard Jefferies*, p. 227.
42   Ibid., p. 224.
43   Edward Thomas, *Feminine Influence on the Poets*, p. 4.
44   Ibid., p. 49.
45   Edward Thomas, *Light and Twilight*, p. 54.
46   Eleanor Farjeon, *Edward Thomas*, p. 67.
47   Edward Thomas, *Rest and Unrest*, p. 140.
48   Ibid., p. 139.
49   Edward Thomas, *Poems and Last Poems*, ed. Edna Longley, p. 325.
50   Edward Thomas, *Horae Solitariae*, p. 184.
51   *Letters to Gordon Bottomley*, p. 266.
52   DCL, Edward Thomas to Robert Frost, 2 January 1916.
53   Edward Thomas, *Poems and Last Poems*, ed. Edna Longley, p. 323.
54   Ibid., p. 331.
55   Ibid., p. 331.
56   Helen Thomas, *World Without End*, p. 47.
57   Edward Thomas, *Beautiful Wales*, p. 75.
58   Edward Thomas, *The South Country*, pp. 126-7.
59   Ibid., p. 127.
60   Edward Thomas, *The Last Sheaf*, p. 64.
61   Edward Thomas, *The South Country*, p. 127.
62   Edward Thomas, *Rest and Unrest*, p. 25.
63   Edward Thomas, *Light and Twilight*, p. 3.
64   Edward Thomas, *The South Country*, pp. 17-18.
65   Edward Thomas, *Rest and Unrest*, p. 8.
66   Ibid., p. 12.
67   Ibid., p. 15.
68   John Lehmann, *The Open Night*, p. 84.

69   *Letters to Gordon Bottomley*, p. 41.
70   Edward Thomas, *The Woodland Life* (London, 1897), p. 233.
71   Edward Thomas, *The Heart of England*, p. 95.
72   Edward Thomas, *Childhood*, pp. 15-16.
73   *Letters to Gordon Bottomley*, p. 201.
74   Helen Thomas, *World Without End*, pp. 144-5.
75   Edward Thomas, *The South Country*, p. 127.
76   Ibid., p. 140.
77   Ibid., p. 140.
78   Ibid., p. 140.
79   Ibid., p. 140.
80   C. Day Lewis, 'The Poetry of Edward Thomas', *Essays by Divers Hands*, vol. XXVIII (London, 1956), p. 86.
81   Marie Quinn, 'The Personal Past in the Poetry of Thomas Hardy and Edward Thomas', *Critical Quarterly*, vol. XVI, no. 1 (Spring 1974), p. 22.
82   John F. Danby, 'Edward Thomas', *Critical Quarterly*, vol. I, no. 4 (Winter 1959), p. 315.
83   Edward Thomas, *Poems and Last Poems*, ed. Edna Longley, p. 155.
84   Robert Frost, *Selected Letters*, p. 209.
85   William Cooke, *Biography*, p. 125.
86   John F. Danby, 'Edward Thomas', *Critical Quarterly*, vol.I, no. 4, p. 313.
87   Ibid., p. 313.

BIBLIOGRAPHY

1 Books by Edward Thomas consulted

a Poems

Haymaking and *The Manor Farm* by 'Edward Eastaway' in *This England* (Oxford University Press, London, 1915), pp. 111-12.

Six Poems by 'Edward Eastaway' (The Pear Tree Press, Flansham, Sussex, 1916).

Eighteen poems by 'Edward Eastaway' in *An Annual of New Poetry* (Constable, London, 1917).

Poems (Selwyn & Blount, London, 1917).

Last Poems (Selwyn & Blount, London, 1918).

Collected Poems, with a foreword by Walter de la Mare (Selwyn & Blount, London, 1920).

Selected Poems, edited and introduced by Edward Garnett (The Gregynog Press, Newtown, Montgomeryshire, 1927).

Collected Poems (Ingpen & Grant, London, 1928).

Collected Poems (Faber & Faber, London, 1936).

Collected Poems, fifth impression (Faber & Faber, London, 1949).

Collected Poems, tenth impression (Faber & Faber, London, 1969).

Poems and Last Poems, edited by Edna Longley (Collins, London, 1973; Macdonald & Evans, Plymouth, 1978).

The Collected Poems of Edward Thomas, edited by R. George Thomas (The Clarendon Press, Oxford, 1978). Except where otherwise stated all quotations from poems by Thomas — and their titles — are taken from this edition, the text of which differs in some cases from the more familiar version.

b Prose

The Woodland Life (William Blackwood & Sons, London, 1897).

Horae Solitariae (Duckworth, London, 1902).

Oxford (A. & C. Black, London, 1903).

Rose Acre Papers (S. C. Brown Langham, London, 1904).

Beautiful Wales (A. & C. Black, London, 1905).

The Heart of England (J. M. Dent, London, 1906).

Richard Jefferies, His Life and Work (Hutchinson, London, 1909).

The South Country (J. M. Dent, London, 1909).

Rest and Unrest (Duckworth, London, 1910).

Feminine Influence on the Poets (Martin Secker, London, 1910).

Windsor Castle (Blackie & Son, London, 1910).

The Isle of Wight (Blackie & Son, London, 1911).

Light and Twilight (Duckworth, London, 1911).

Maurice Maeterlinck (Methuen, London, 1911).

Celtic Stories (The Clarendon Press, Oxford, 1911).

The Tenth Muse (Martin Secker, London, 1911).

Algernon Charles Swinburne, A Critical Study (Martin Secker, London, 1912).

George Borrow, The Man and his Books (Chapman & Hall, London, 1912).

Lafcadio Hearn (Constable, London, 1912).

Norse Tales (The Clarendon Press, Oxford, 1912).

The Icknield Way (Constable, London, 1913).

The Country (B. T. Batsford, London, 1913).

The Happy-Go-Lucky Morgans (Duckworth, London, 1913).

Walter Pater, A Critical Study (Martin Secker, London, 1913).

In Pursuit of Spring (Thomas Nelson & Sons, London, 1914).

Four-and-Twenty Blackbirds (Duckworth, London, 1915).

The Life of the Duke of Marlborough (Chapman & Hall, London, 1915).

Keats (T. C. & E. C. Jack, London, 1916).

A Literary Pilgrim in England (Methuen, London, 1917).

Cloud Castle and other Papers (Duckworth, London, 1922).

The Last Sheaf (Cape, London, 1928).

The Friend of the Blackbird (The Pear Tree Press, Flansham, Sussex, 1938).

Edward Thomas on the Countryside, selected by Roland Gant (Faber & Faber, London, 1977).

c Autobiography

The Childhood of Edward Thomas (Faber & Faber, London, 1938).

The Diary of Edward Thomas, edited by R. George Thomas *Anglo-Welsh Review*, vol. XX (Autumn 1971); and *The Collected Poems of Edward Thomas*, ed. R. George Thomas (The Clarendon Press, Oxford, 1978), pp. 460-81.

d Editions and anthologies

The Poems of John Dyer (T. Fisher Unwin, London, 1903).

The Bible in Spain by George Borrow (J. M. Dent, London, 1906).

The Pocket Book of Poems and Songs for the Open Air (E. Grant Richards, London, 1907).

British Country Life in Spring and Summer (Hodder & Stoughton, London, 1907).

British Country Life in Autumn and Winter (Hodder & Stoughton, London, 1908).

The Temple and a Priest to the Temple by George Herbert (J. M. Dent, London, 1908).

Some British Birds (Hodder & Stoughton, London, 1908).

British Butterflies and Other Insects (Hodder & Stoughton, London, 1908).

The Plays and Poems of Christopher Marlowe (J. M. Dent, London, 1909).

The Hills and the Vale by Richard Jefferies (Duckworth, London, 1909).

Words and Places by Isaac Taylor (J. M. Dent, London, 1911).

Rural Rides by William Cobbett (J. M. Dent, London, 1912).

The Pocket George Borrow (Chatto & Windus, London, 1912).

The Zincali by George Borrow (J. M. Dent, London, 1914).

This England: An Anthology from her Writers (Oxford University Press, London, 1915).

The Flowers I Love (T. C. & E. C. Jack, London, 1916).

2   Selection of biographical and bibliographical material consulted

Bottomley, Gordon, 'A Note on Edward Thomas', *Welsh Review*, vol. IV, no. 3 (September 1945).

Davies, Anthony, 'Edward Thomas and his Father', *John O'London's*, 28 October 1949.

Eckert, Robert P., *Edward Thomas: A Biography and a Bibliography* (J. M. Dent, London, 1937).

Farjeon, Eleanor, *Edward Thomas: The Last Four Years* (Oxford University Press, London, 1958).

Guthrie, James, *To the Memory of Edward Thomas* (Pear Tree Press, Flansham, Sussex, 1937).

Marsh, Jan, *Edward Thomas: A Poet for His Country* (Paul Elek, London, 1978).

Moore, John, *The Life and Letters of Edward Thomas* (Heinemann, London, 1939).

Nevinson, H. W., 'Fame Too Late', *Life and Letters Today*, March 1940.

Poetry Wales, Edward Thomas centenary issue, vol. 13, no. 4 (Spring 1978).

Thomas, Helen, *As It Was* and *World Without End* (Faber & Faber, London, 1956).

Thomas, Helen, 'Poets' Holiday in the Shadow of War', *The Times*, 3 August 1963.

Thomas, Helen, 'A Memory of W. H. Hudson', *The Times*, 27 August 1965.

Thomas, Helen, *Time & Again* (Carcanet New Press, Manchester, 1978).

Thomas, R. George (ed.), *Letters from Edward Thomas to Gordon Bottomley* (Oxford University Press, London, 1968).

3   Select bibliography of criticism consulted

Ashton, Theresa, 'Edward Thomas: From Prose to Poetry', *Poetry Review*, vol. XXVIII, no. 6 (1937).

Burrow, John, 'Keats and Edward Thomas', *Essays in Criticism*, vol. VII, no. 4 (October 1957).

Bushnell, Athalie, 'Edward Thomas', *Poetry Review*, vol. XXXVIII, no. 4 (1947).

Cooke, William, *Edward Thomas: A Critical Biography* (Faber & Faber, London, 1970).

Coombes, H., 'The Poetry of Edward Thomas', *Essays in Criticism*, vol. III, no. 2 (April 1953).

Coombes, H., *Edward Thomas: A Critical Study* (Chatto & Windus, London, 1956).

Coombes, H., 'Hardy, de la Mare, and Edward Thomas', *Pelican Guide to English Literature*, vol. VII (Penguin Books, Harmondsworth, Middlesex, 1961).

Danby, John F., 'Edward Thomas', *Critical Quarterly*, vol. 1, no. 4 (Winter 1959).

Emslie, MacDonald, 'Spectatorial Attitudes', *Review of English Literature*, vol. V, no. 1 (January 1964).

Freeman, John, 'Edward Thomas', *New Statesman*, vol. X, no. 240 (10 November 1917).

Harding, D. W., 'A Note on Nostalgia', *Scrutiny*, vol. I, no. 1 (May 1932).

Hobsbaum, Philip, 'The Road Not Taken', *Listener*, vol. 66 (13 November 1961).

Keith, W. J., *The Rural Tradition* (The Harvester Press, Hassocks, Sussex, 1975).

Larkin, Philip, 'The War Poet', *Listener*, vol. 70 (10 October, 1963).

Lawrence, Ralph, 'Edward Thomas in Perspective', *English*, vol. XII, no. 71 (Summer 1959).

Lea, F. A., 'On Patriotism and Edward Thomas', *Adelphi*, August 1938.

Leavis, F. R., *New Bearings in English Poetry* (Chatto & Windus, London, 1932).

Leavis, F. R., 'Imagery and Movement', *Scrutiny*, vol. XIII, no. 2 (September 1945).

Lehmann, John, 'Edward Thomas', *The Open Night* (Longman, London, 1952).

Lewis, C. Day, 'The Poetry of Edward Thomas', *Essays by Divers Hands* (Transactions of the Royal Society of Literature), vol. XXVIII (London, 1956).

Longley, Edna, 'Larkin, Edward Thomas and the Tradition', *Phoenix*, nos 11-12 (Autumn and Winter 1973-4).

Longley, Edna, 'Edward Thomas and the "English" Line', *New Review*, vol. 1, no. 11 (February 1975).

Mathias, Roland, 'Edward Thomas', *Anglo-Welsh Review*, vol. X, no. 26 (1960).

Quinn, Marie, 'The Personal Past in the Poetry of Thomas Hardy and Edward Thomas', *Critical Quarterly*, vol. XVI, no. 1 (Spring 1974).

Rajan, B., 'Georgian Poetry: A Retrospect', *Critic*, vol. 1, no. 2 (Autumn 1947).

Scannell, Vernon, 'Content with Discontent', *London Magazine*, January 1962.

Scannell, Vernon, *Edward Thomas*, Writers and their Work, no. 163 (Longman, London, 1962).

Smith, Stan, 'A Language Not To Be Betrayed', *Literature and History*, no. 4 (Autumn 1976).

Thomas, R. George, *Edward Thomas* (University of Wales Press, Cardiff, 1972).

Underhill, Hugh, 'The Poetical Character of Edward Thomas', *Essays in Criticism*, vol. XXIII, no. 3 (July 1973).

Wright, H. G., 'The Sense of the Past in Edward Thomas', *Welsh Outlook*, September 1932.

4 Select bibliography of background studies

Bergonzi, Bernard, *Heroes' Twilight* (Constable, London, 1965).

Bourne, George (pseud. Sturt), *The Bettesworth Book* (Lampley, London, 1901).

Bourne, George, *Change in the Village* (Duckworth, London, 1912).

Cobbett, William, *Cottage Economy* (William Cobbett, London, 1828).

Frost, Robert, *The Poetry of Robert Frost*, ed. Edward Connery Latham (Jonathan Cape, London, 1971).

Frost, Robert, *Selected Letters*, ed. Lawrance Thompson (Cape, London, 1965).

Fussell, Paul, *The Great War and Modern Memory* (Oxford University Press, New York, 1975).

Gardner, Brian (ed.), *Up the Line to Death* (Methuen, London, 1964).

Harding, D. W., *Words into Rhythm* (Cambridge University Press, 1976).

Hardy, Thomas, *The Personal Writings of Thomas Hardy*, ed. Harold Orel (Macmillan, London, 1967).

Hassall, Christopher, *Edward Marsh, Patron of the Arts* (Faber & Faber, London, 1959).

Hassall, Christopher, *Rupert Brooke: A Biography* (Faber & Faber, London, 1964).

Jefferies, Richard, *The Amateur Poacher* (Smith & Elder, London, 1879).

Jefferies, Richard, *Hodge and His Masters* (Smith & Elder, London, 1880).

Jefferies, Richard, *The Story of my Heart* (Longman, Green, London, 1883).

Jefferies, Richard, *The Dewy Morn* (Richard Bentley, London, 1884).

Jefferies, Richard, *After London or Wild England* (Cassell, 1885).

Jefferies, Richard, *Amaryllis at the Fair* (Sampson, Low, Marston, Searle & Rivington, London, 1887).

Johnston, John H., *English Poetry of the First World War* (Princeton University Press, New Jersey, 1964).

Jung, Carl G., *The Integration of the Personality* (Kegan Paul, Trench, Trubner, London, 1940).

Laing, R. D., *The Divided Self* (Penguin Books, Harmondsworth, Middlesex, 1965).

Latham, Edward Connery, *Interviews with Robert Frost* (Cape, London, 1967).

Levine, Israel, *The Unconscious* (Parsons, London, 1923).

Marsh, Edward (ed.), *Georgian Poetry 1911-1922* (The Poetry Bookshop, London, 1912-22).

Murry, John Middleton, *Between Two Worlds* (Cape, London, 1935).

Owen, Wilfred, *Collected Poems*, ed. C. Day Lewis (Chatto & Windus, London, 1966).

Press, John, *A Map of Modern English Verse* (Oxford University Press, London, 1969).

Prince, Morton, *The Dissociation of a Personality* (Longman, Green, London, 1906).

Rank, Otto, *The Double: A Psychoanalytic Study* (University of North Carolina Press, Chapel Hill, 1971).

Rosenberg, Isaac, *Collected Poems*, ed. Gordon Bottomley and Denys Harding (Chatto & Windus, London, 1974).

Ross, Robert H., *The Georgian Revolt* (Faber & Faber, London, 1967).

Sassoon, Siegfried, *Collected Poems* (Faber & Faber, London, 1961).

Sergeant, Elizabeth S., *Robert Frost: The Trial by Existence* (Holt, Rinehart & Winston, New York, 1961).

Silkin, Jon, *Out of Battle* (Oxford University Press, London, 1972).

Stead, C. K., *The New Poetic* (Penguin Books, Harmondsworth, Middlesex, 1967).

Stonesifer, Richard J., *W. H. Davies: A Critical Biography* (Cape, London, 1963).

Thompson, Lawrance, *Robert Frost: The Early Years 1874-1915* (Cape, London, 1967).

Thompson, Lawrance, *Robert Frost: The Years of Triumph 1915-1938* (Cape, London, 1971).

Tymms, Ralph, *Doubles in Literary Psychology* (Bowes & Bowes, Cambridge, 1949).

Williams, Raymond, *The Country and the City* (Paladin Books, London, 1975).

5 Unpublished material

In the Bodleian Library: MS Don d. 28; MS Eng. Lett. d. 281; MS Eng. Lett. d. 282; MS Eng. Lett. c. 280. Letters and papers relating to Judge Robert P. Eckert's collection of Edward Thomas, and to Eckert's published works, 'Edward Thomas, Soldier-Poet of his Race', (*American Book Collector*, vol. IV, no. 1, 1933, pp. 19-21, and no. 2, pp. 66-69), and *Edward Thomas: A Biography and A Bibliography* (J. M. Dent, London, 1937).

In Dartmouth College Library, Hanover, New Hampshire (referred to in notes as DCL): sixty letters from Edward Thomas to Robert Frost, and one letter from Roger Ingpen to Frost.

In Lockwood Memorial Library, State University of New York at Buffalo (referred to in notes as LML): a MS notebook covering the period 16 November - 7 December 1914 marking Thomas's transition from prose to poetry.

In University College Library, Cardiff (referred to in notes as UCC): six scrapbooks used by Thomas to preserve those reviews he thought fit.

INDEX

189